PRAISE FOR *RETAIL MARKETING STRATEGY*

CW00819426

'*Retail Marketing Strategy* is a great handbook for marketing professionals in the industry. It clearly outlines what strategies can be applied by retailers and manufacturers to make their shoppers happy, a concept that is often overlooked in the marketing mix. The passion of the author and his practical experience in retail marketing and shopper insights truly make this an invaluable read.'
Marc Schroeder, SVP, Global Nutrition Group, PepsiCo

'Constant has written a book that will be indispensable to both in-retail professionals at all levels and to their suppliers... There is an admirable wealth of detail from a range of industries and from many continents.'
Andrew Seth, former CEO of Lever Brothers UK and co-author of *The Grocers*

'In this eminently readable book, Berkhout skilfully combines academic research and his own vast experience in retail marketing to provide a wealth of actionable insights for retail marketers. Retail marketers should heed his call to augment intuition with data to make fact-driven decisions.'
Jan-Benedict E M Steenkamp, Massey Distinguished Professor of Marketing, and Marketing Area Chairman, Kenan-Flagler Business School, UNC-Chapel Hill, USA

'Constant Berkhout does a great job dispelling many myths that exist around shopping behaviour that everyone assumes are fact. The book comes to life with many real-world examples from across retailers and categories that can be easily applied to your own business, whether you are a retailer or a manufacturer. It gets your mind thinking about "What could I or my company do differently to influence the shopper and drive better results?"'
Bob Nolan, Senior Vice President of Insights & Analytics, ConAgra Foods

'An accessible must-read for every professional in food and non-food retail, and everybody who wants to gain an in-depth contemporary understanding of shopper behaviour. This book provides all the needed insights to serve customers even better, create more shopper happiness and thus sell more, leading to a better and improved business tomorrow!'
Hans van der Heyden, Vice President, GrandVision

'Shopper marketing and category management are made very accessible with this clear guide that is well underpinned through numerous illustrations and experiments, both from literature as well as from the author's own wide experience.... I particularly enjoyed the suggestion to move from gut feel to fact-based decision making, and from (easy) pilots and experiments to (more advanced) big data analyses.'
Jeroen Van de Broek, Director, Category Development, Maxeda DIY Group

'I agree with the author that "retailers are not particularly known for their love of making decisions based on facts and figures", and I know this book can change that! Constant explains why and how to operate in multiple channels and consider the emotional and experiential needs of consumers (who are not as rational and price-driven as retailers think they are). Important scientific studies and principles are illustrated with excellent examples from Constant's extensive retail experience. This book enables retailers to make data-driven decisions and thus catch up, and even surpass, the current leaders in their field.'
Koen Pauwels, Professor of Marketing at Ozyegin University and Honorary Professor at the University of Groningen

Retail
Marketing
Strategy
Delivering
shopper delight

Constant Berkhout

KoganPage

LONDON PHILADELPHIA NEW DELHI

First published in Great Britain and the United States in 2016 by Kogan Page Limited

2nd Floor, 45 Gee Street	1518 Walnut Street, Suite 1100	4737/23 Ansari Road
London EC1V 3RS	Philadelphia PA 19102	Daryaganj
United Kingdom	USA	New Delhi 110002
www.koganpage.com		India

ISBN   978 0 7494 7691 5
E-ISBN   978 0 7494 7692 2

British Library Cataloguing-in-Publication Data

A CIP record for this book is available from the British Library.

Library of Congress Cataloging-in-Publication Data

Names: Berkhout, Constant.
Title: Retail marketing strategy : delivering shopper delight / Constant Berkhout.
Description: 1st Edition. | Philadelphia, PA : Kogan Page, 2015.
Identifiers: LCCN 2015032588 | ISBN 9780749476915 (paperback) | ISBN 9780749476922 (ebook)
Subjects: LCSH: Retail trade. | Marketing. | Consumer behavior. | BISAC: BUSINESS & ECONOMICS / Consumer Behavior. | BUSINESS & ECONOMICS / Advertising & Promotion. | BUSINESS & ECONOMICS / Industries / Retailing. | BUSINESS & ECONOMICS / Marketing / General.
Classification: LCC HF5429 .B448 2015 | DDC 658.8/7–dc23 LC record available at http://lccn.loc.gov/2015032588

Typeset by Graphicraft Limited, Hong Kong
Print production managed by Jellyfish
Printed and bound by CPI Group (UK) Ltd, Croydon, CR0 4YY

CONTENTS

ABOUT THE AUTHOR

Constant Berkhout is a passionate practitioner of retail marketing and shopper insights. He obtained a Master of Science in Economics Cum Laude with a major in Marketing. His curiosity and career have led him to travel across the world and live in cities including Asheville (North Carolina), Buenos Aires and London.

Constant is the founder and owner of Rijnbrug Advies, a consultancy in the areas of retail marketing and shopper insights based in the Netherlands. With a passion for retail and building on more than 20 years' experience, Rijnbrug Advies finds new ways to grow categories and connect with the shopper. Clients include food retailers, non-food retailers and suppliers (**www.constant-opportunities.com**).

Before setting up his own agency Constant gained broad experience across a large number of categories, functional areas and countries:

- At retailers De Boer Winkelbedrijven and Ahold, Constant got acquainted with the principles of efficient consumer response (ECR) and category management.

- At Kraft Foods he set up the trade marketing practice and worked as customer manager to large supermarket chains.

- At Gillette/Procter & Gamble he led business restructurings in commercial and value-chain departments in several European countries. Later he was given overall responsibility for the marketing at the business-to-business (B2B) division in Europe.

- At PepsiCo he first assumed the responsibility of consumer insights and innovation for Northern Europe. In his last role at PepsiCo he was responsible for shopper insights and marketing in more than 45 countries in Europe. He set up trade marketing in Eastern European countries such as Russia. For Western European markets he increased customer intimacy with customers such as Carrefour, Casino and Tesco. He worked closely with colleagues in North America to apply breakthrough technologies.

Constant is married, and he and his wife have two children together. In his free time he loves reading and travelling, and although he was a passionate handball player in the past, most of his time on the sports field is now spent watching his children play soccer and basketball.

FOREWORD

We have had the pleasure of working with Constant Berkhout in a number of international markets as diverse as China, Indonesia, India and the Middle East. His passion and knowledge in the area of shopper marketing are unrivalled. Driven by the single thought that all actions in the supply chain and product management must be geared to meet the needs of the shopper, Constant has delivered a highly appreciated and impactful category management programme for SPAR International.

The fact-driven approach to achieving improvement in the shopper experience that Constant advocates in this book has been executed at store level with results within our own international store network. Commencing with real shopper insights, including consideration for both the irrational and emotional, Constant lays out the journey for the retail marketer to make choices that allow effective in-store execution and the creation of long-term structure to allow teams to fine-tune an optimum shopper-centric solution.

Globally, in the grocery industry there has been a trend for fast-moving consumer goods suppliers seeking growth to launch multiple line extensions and brand offerings. Supported by above-the-line advertising and below-the-line marketing, the consequence is that the average store shelf is becoming increasingly complicated to navigate and shop. The inefficiencies of this excess supply over demand mean problems and costs in the entire supply chain. At the heart of this problem lies the fact that the most important decision maker has not been properly considered, that being the shopper. As a result, a situation of supplier push exists, and not one of customer pull. By placing our customer at the heart of all our decisions we have the ability to optimize the assortment planning, layout and flow of our stores. As a result of workshops led by Constant, we have had multiple teams re-evaluate key categories, resulting in less duplication in product ranges, improved availability and simplified price points. The interesting aspect is that in all cases shoppers have responded with the perception that there is more choice and that the revised solution is easier to shop.

Constant has worked with us to investigate how we can better understand the shopping behaviour and demand from our shoppers. At SPAR we operate over 12,500 stores in 40 countries in diverse locations, from the Arctic Circle of northern Europe to the Cape of Good Hope in southern Africa, from the Atlantic coast of Ireland to the east coast of China. Such diversity requires adaptability, yet despite the diversity of our geographies, we have found the approach Constant advocates to work worldwide.

I believe you will find the approach outlined in this book a practical step-by-step approach to category management and shopper marketing. Drawing on both academic research and his own extensive experience, Constant has succeeded in demystifying the science of category management by focusing on the art of making shoppers happy.

Tobias Wasmuht

Retail and Marketing Director

SPAR International

ACKNOWLEDGEMENTS

For many years I have been on a journey... collecting case studies, investigating academic articles and structuring my thinking. The result is this book. Fortunately, I have not been alone on this adventure.

My dear wife Carola encouraged me to collect and share my ideas and examples in book form, and improved the clarity of many phrases and concepts. When my son Thomas told friends that his father is an author, the pride in his eyes and voice kept up my spirit. My daughter Isabel typed some of the words you are reading on early mornings after she woke up and tracked me down at the PC.

I want to thank all my (former) colleagues who sharpened my ideas, exchanged best practices, and participated in discussions of how things could be done better for our retail customers and shoppers. And there are people who deserve special words of thanks:

Gé Lommen, chief editor of the magazine *FoodPersonality*. He sharpened the storyline of many of my articles for his magazine. With his deep knowledge of retailing he challenged my ideas in a straightforward manner, whilst always remaining constructive and great fun conversationally.

Jolande de Ridder, marketing professional, dedicated much time to carefully correcting an early manuscript and greatly contributed to making the book easier to read.

Oliver Koll, post-doctoral research fellow at the Innsbruck University School of Management, *and*:

Peter Gouw, director at Vision2B, sourced relevant academic studies for the book from scientific journals and online libraries. Peter has been very supportive, welcoming me to knowledge-sharing sessions on marketing.

Sean Raw, director at RAW Management Solutions, read the manuscript at an early phase and gave great feedback on the structure of the book.

Al Forbes, director at Solvinus, offered to improve my chapter on customer understanding and it has been a privilege to obtain his expert view and constructive thoughts on this.

Jasmin Naim, senior commissioning editor at Kogan Page, believed in the book from the start, and it is thanks to her enthusiasm that this book is now in your hands. She provided clear guidance throughout the project.

Jenny Volich, development editor at Kogan Page, patiently improved the English grammar and syntax, making this book much more fun and enjoyable to read.

With the support of all these people, this book provides you with academic ammunition and practical advice that will help make your shoppers happy and your retail marketing mix more effective. I hope the book will help sharpen your thoughts, inspire you into action and help you to further unlock your capabilities.

Wishing you lots of happiness.

PART ONE
Shopper happiness

Delivering shopper happiness

In the 20th century many retailers operated more or less as a logistical extension to the supplier manufacturing and marketing operations. As long as they maintained stock at an appropriate level, extended their store networks and shipped products efficiently across their markets, they thrived at a fairly comfortable pace. This approach worked to the benefit of large suppliers such as Procter & Gamble and Philips who enjoyed a favourable negotiating position. They produced their brands in substantial volumes and were guaranteed to have their products available in all stores. This was the age of traditional consumer marketing. Suppliers estimated the market size, segmented the consumer groups based on socio-demographics and created demand by communicating the product benefits in large advertising campaigns. The media had not proliferated as much as it has today, so suppliers were fairly sure who was watching television and when. Execution of the marketing plan was described in detail in long-term plans and the 'P' of physical distribution was one of the details taken care of by suppliers.

Of course, things sometimes got tough. At times, consumer demand fell away abruptly and retailers had to cut back costs, for example when the increase in oil prices in the 1970s led to an economic crisis. Moments such as this made it crystal clear as to which retailers had their house in order: those that had invested in the right marketing-mix elements, had embraced logistical efficiency-improvement concepts and had adjusted their organizational set-up in line with the ever-changing environment. This led to a consolidation of retailers still in evidence in both mature and emerging countries. Retail markets such as office supplies, fashion, home decoration and consumer electronics are dominated by a handful of players. The way that these retailers achieved this position was basically by doing two things very well: 1) in-store execution; and 2) organizational development.

In-store execution is about making an efficient transaction between store staff and customers. It spans a whole range of strategic and tactical decisions on the retail marketing mix, from designing the store layout to efficient labour processes for changing price tags.

Organizational development is concerned with finding and applying the best resources for the retail strategy. For example, a big shift in retail activities and focus occurred when retailers made buyers not only responsible for negotiating the lowest price from suppliers, but also for the long-term health of the category. Retailers also need to adjust their model whenever they see that shoppers have moved their spending to other retail channels. As a result, they may be required to open stores in these new retail channels: for example, when a DIY retailer starts operating garden centres to cater to the demand for garden tools from shoppers who expect an inspirational and natural environment.

These two capabilities – in-store execution and organizational development – were critical success factors for retailers in the 20th century. However, in the retail world of today they have become conditions of being in the retail sector. The 21st century has taught retailers that new capabilities are needed. These relate to a better understanding of how shoppers behave and how choices are made at the moment of purchase (Figure 1.1).

Understanding the shopper has become essential. As a reflection of societal trends, shoppers have become more vocal in expressing their own individual wants. They demand services tailored to their needs and are less concerned about adhering to what their parents bought or to what leaders of social institutions (such as the church or trade unions) tell them to consider buying. Moreover, the retail landscape has changed; there are more channels with less-defined boundaries ('channel blurring'). The proliferation of channels has stimulated a decrease in shopper loyalty. At the same time, the wide variety of media that shoppers tune into makes it difficult to reach them through just one channel – and, from a cost perspective, applying consumer

FIGURE 1.1   Perspectives on retail marketing

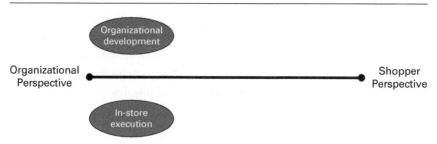

FIGURE 1.2 Evolving perspectives on retail marketing

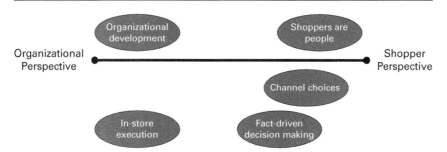

marketing across all media channels is not an option. However, consumer marketers realise that people can be found in at least one place: the store.

Therefore, marketers' attention has shifted from the moment of consumption to the moment of purchase. For suppliers, another reason to move their investment from advertising to in-store marketing is because retailers have become increasingly professionalized, more demanding towards suppliers, and have turned their store names into brands. The consolidation of many retail sectors effectively means that suppliers need to deal with fewer retailers in order to communicate with their shoppers.

In this changing context retailers need to acquire a new set of proficiencies, over and above the operational aspects, in order to shift towards a more shopper-driven perspective in their business (Figure 1.2):

- making decisions in a more fact-driven manner;
- operating within several channels at the same time;
- the skill set to deeply understand shoppers.

Making decisions in a more fact-driven manner

Retailers are not particularly known for their love of making decisions based on facts and figures. They seem to know intuitively that if a competitor reduces prices, then their shoppers also need a price reduction on the same or comparable products. They assume that shoppers compare the products without taking into consideration value-adding elements such as, for example, personal service or the policy of the retailer to only source in a sustainable way. Many retail activities are transactional, repetitive and require short-term focus. Ultimately, as compared with their respective suppliers, retailers often have far lower returns on investments, which gives them a good excuse not to invest in market research.

The amazing paradox in retail is that retailers sit on mountains of data but are not inclined to process the data into meaningful information. I do not want to say that decisions based on intuition are always wrong, on the contrary, but what is wrong is not using available data in order to make a better decision for the retail organization and for the shopper. The department stores, fashion stores and garden centres that buy on the basis of what they feel is the trend are outpaced by retailers that have invented systems that allow them to trial and scale supply of fashionable items. Zara is a great example of how a retailer decides both intuitively and based on facts: the designers at Zara have the authority to order the production of a new range of clothing after observing trends at a fashion show, but production is only scaled up if the sales in the first weeks are good.

Operating in several channels at the same time

The successful retailer of the future will have the capability of operating in several channels at the same time. A grocery chain may choose to operate convenience stores and supermarkets; a fashion store may enable online orders, operate its own stores and set up store-in-store concepts in department stores. The reasons for this are straightforward: the shopper has become less loyal, is more critical and uses digital technology to decide during the shopping journey as to where they can find the best deal.

Channel choice is an outcome of the 'shopping mission', which shows why the shopper is undertaking a purchase. For example, a DIY retailer may differentiate between a house renovation trip, a home security trip and a home decorating trip. Mission segmentation enables retailers to put themselves in the shoes of the shopper and to come up with solutions that the shopper is looking for. It helps retailers to think beyond the products and services they currently offer, to absorb best practices from other channels and even to innovate new shopper solutions.

A skill set to deeply understand shoppers

An essential requirement of success is an eagerness to fully understand shoppers and their needs and to master the instruments to do so. I still meet too many retailers who outwardly advertise how delighted they are to serve shoppers but in their meeting rooms and category management plans the shopper hardly plays a role. That said, the litmus test of shopper focus is whether the shopper feels the intent and touch of service. For example, when I shop at Marqt, a Dutch supermarket that stocks natural and organic products, not one but *all* the staff members I meet take notice of me and greet me warmly. As a shopper this feels better than knowing that they have excellent category management plans. As well as this deep desire to understand and serve shoppers, retailers need to keep introducing new tools that give deeper insight into shopping behaviour, and shoppers' emotions and motives. While retailers might produce outstanding daily sales reports, these are not sufficient to communicate the voice of the shopper.

In conclusion, in order to be successful retailers need to move from an organizational view to a *shopper view* of their business. Every action the retailer takes needs to relate to their shoppers' needs and how their shopper makes decisions. Optimization of in-store execution and organizational development can help retailers to accomplish this. However, note that optimization of the instruments of the retail marketing mix is not an objective in itself.

The emotional shopper

Traditional economic theory assumes that all consumers are rational. The economic models work on the premise that consumers have access to all information, understand it and calculate the benefits of all product characteristics before making a decision. Psychology has shown these assumptions to be wrong. For example, when people have to choose from a shelf of hundreds of vitamin containers in a drugstore, they tend to apply basic rules to simplify their decisions, such as choosing the brand their parents used or a brand that has been in the news lately. These types of choices are not necessarily best for the (long-term) well-being and happiness of the shopper.

Retailers should understand not only the rational side of the shopper but also engage with the shopper's emotions (Figure 1.3). The emotions are the deeper desires, hopes and motives that the retailer can tap into to establish a bond between themselves and the shopper. The retailer relates more easily to the calculating, rational side of the shopper by offering an optimal balance of product quality and price, such as a range of time slots for home delivery and an occasional promotional discount. The retailer may get to know these needs through questionnaires, simple trial and error, or in a

FIGURE 1.3   Perspectives on retail marketing: emotional and calculating shopper

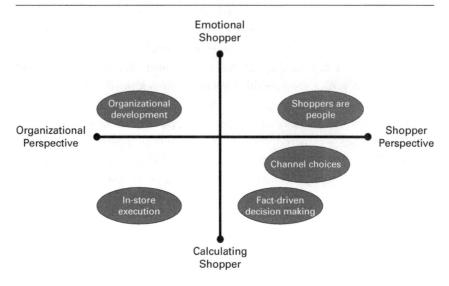

more advanced manner, through big data analysis. However, in order to engage with the shopper's deeper desires, hopes and motives, these types of research need to be enriched with human content; the engagement approaches that are needed to understand these emotions are different. Examples of such approaches are indirect and association-based phrasing at exit interviews (ie when shoppers leave the store) and neuro research. A successful retailer has the desire to transform the financial loyalty of the shopper into a combination of rational and emotional loyalty. There are many factors that influence the success of a retail organization. However, I believe that one is far more important than any other: does the retailer consider the happiness of the shopper in all of his or her decisions? If the retailer is right for the shopper, the shopper will build a relationship and over time will start to trust and bond with the retail brand. The happiness of the retailer's shoppers should be the ultimate goal of marketing professionals. If a retailer works in the interest of shoppers and designs services that they really need, it follows that shoppers will pay for them without hesitation.

Shopper happiness gives meaning to the organization's mission

The mission of my professional life has been to create happy shoppers. To fulfil this mission I have had to find out what makes them happy and which actions organizations could take to accomplish this. The main purpose of this book is to define what shopper happiness looks like and to suggest retail strategies that can help practitioners to achieve this ultimate goal. For example, by considering the shopper when changing the store layout or packaging of products. Retail organizations often define their objectives only in terms of market share, sales, percentage of private label and profit. However, these are only outcomes of retail marketing decisions, reflecting an organizational approach to retail, whereas a shopper perspective is more sustainable and gives true meaning to the mission of the organization.

Let me give an example. Many retail organizations have started to experiment with ambient scents in their stores, a subject that will be explored in depth in Chapter 12. If retailers assume an organizational approach to ambient scents, they focus on the question of how much revenue ambient scents will generate. If shoppers are at the core of decision making, however, retailers want to find out how they can increase the happiness of their shoppers and whether ambient scents can contribute to better moods and influence shoppers to make better decisions. Retailers would then want to know whether the scent helps the shopper not only at the moment of purchase, but also whether the shopper feels comfortable with the retailer's scent policy at a later point, when the shopper is in a more rational and evaluative shopping phase. This book will consider questions such as what effect scents generate in a retail environment, whether shoppers feel better with or without them and whether it is in the interest of the shopper to shop in a scented store. If these questions are answered positively, then ambient scents can be included as an effective instrument in the retail marketing mix. They can help to win the shopper's heart and, as a result, a share of the shopper's wallet. Often I find that retailers focus on the financials and short-term actions. Consequently, they lose sight of what makes shoppers happy. Only by truthfully helping the shopper can practitioners create a fair and sustainable business. Making the shopper happy is what differentiates a successful retailer from weaker counterparts.

Answers to the retail challenges

On my mission to create happy shoppers I have tried to really understand the most difficult issues in retail marketing. Throughout my career, I have engaged with professionals inside and outside the retail discipline, carried out numerous experiments and studied large numbers of academic studies and papers. This approach has helped me to develop concepts and models, and a better comprehension of the following questions:

- How can retailers create an assortment of goods that is large enough to generate a feeling of control but avoids choice stress with shoppers?
- What are the effects of music and ambient scents on shopping behaviour?
- What makes grocery shopping lag behind in online sales versus other retail sectors?
- How can retailers convince shoppers to adopt new shopping habits?
- How can suppliers more effectively sell-in products and ideas to their customer retailers?
- How can suppliers and retailers use their investment in loyalty card data to create success?
- What is the difference between trade marketing and shopper marketing?

This book is the result of a quest of more than 20 years. Each chapter can help the practitioner to take immediate action that increases their mental retail fitness for years to come. This book builds on the solid business experience of professionals in the retail and consumer goods industry in order to further structure their thoughts and to inspire them to implement pragmatic solutions in their daily working environment. In addition, students interested in retail will recognize models from their existing marketing literature and will learn about the practical aspects of retail marketing decisions.

Retail is about thinking and doing

When addressing the retail challenges I started by reaching out to fellow professionals to see what they thought and practised. I experimented, reflected on my trials and reached out to stakeholders to further enhance both their thinking and retail practice. Academic research and validation in practice make me feel confident that this book provides new insights for professionals that will allow them to go further in their work.

Much of what I write about comes from first-hand experience. When leading the shopper marketing arena at PepsiCo Europe I was in the privileged position of working with large international retailers such as Carrefour, Casino and Tesco, obtaining first-hand experience of setting up trade marketing in emerging countries such as Russia, and bringing about innovations such as new store layouts based on big data modelling in developed markets.

As I have spent a significant part of my career in the grocery sector, many best practices in the book come from this area. Nonetheless, I believe there is much in this book that can be applied to the wider retail industry, such as skills for trade marketing managers (ie in the manufacturing industry) when dealing with category managers (ie buyers on the retail side), and technologies such as neuro research. Additionally, there are case studies and knowledge gained from scientific experiments conducted in various retail sectors such as restaurants, banks and sporting goods. The combination of academic studies, field trials and critiques from colleagues and customers has helped me to develop new marketing models that are presented in this book, such as the shopper journey for behavioural insights and the assortment life cycle.

Considerations for the choice of the retail dimensions

This book demonstrates five proficiencies that retailers need for their future success:

- in-store execution;
- organizational development;
- making decisions in a more fact-driven manner;
- operating in several channels at the same time;
- the skill set to deeply understand shoppers.

These proficiencies are illustrated by discussing specific retail topics. My choice for these topics is based on a number of considerations:

- *Bringing an end to myths*
  Myths stop progress and make practitioners go around in circles. One of the most popular beliefs is that most in-store decisions are made on impulse. Academic research has shown this to be incorrect. However, there are parties that have an interest in keeping such myths in play. To progress as a function, retail marketing needs to be clear on what works well and what does not.

- *Shopper insights as new route to innovation*
  Marketing professionals often only view consumption events and contexts as a source of business-generating insights while they disregard the motives, moods, thinking processes and actions during

shopping. Since 2010 behavioural science has made a significant contribution to marketing theories. More than ever before it is clear that buying decisions are context dependent. If innovation is a crucial element to marketing practitioners then gaining insights from shopping context is equally crucial. Recent neuro research techniques help retail marketers to better understand the impact of their actions.

- *Need for actionable insights*
  In the busy lives of marketing professionals it is understandable that they return to the proven models and practices of previous years. Whether faced with a severe price war, or when changing the look and feel of packaging, they feel they need to respond quickly. Indeed, in Western societies fast actions are encouraged. Consultancies and other service industries have become equally action-focused for fear of losing clients. Ideally practitioners would evaluate which marketing instruments worked really well in the past, assess what will work for the present challenge and then move forward. In practice, however, even time for evaluating past experiences is often lacking. Therefore, practitioners need access to tools that are solid, easy to grasp and easy to use, via pragmatic guidance on their application.

- *Stimuli to think long term*
  Most retail businesses are built on high volumes with relatively low profit margins. This is one of the reasons why retailers track daily sales and why so many retailers have become focused on the short term. It is not uncommon for a buyer to spend 80 per cent of their time on short-term decisions such as weekly price adjustments, the introduction of new products and the promotional calendar. Of course, there are exceptions to the rule and even short-term-focused retailers may occasionally deliver innovative practices. Apart from the really large retail organizations, however, most lack business development and strategic departments that collect experiences, set benchmarks or create models and manuals. This book makes the information available to all of them: in an attempt to provide new ways of thinking and make retail practice more agile for everyone.

- *Little connection with the academic world*
  Academic research does not seem to be best friends with retail marketing: it is seen to be too long-winded, too statistics-based and too abstract. Marketing practitioners perhaps often lack the time to absorb relevant academic research, and contact between businesses

and leading academics is not well established. Yet academics have done a great job of, for example, finding out how private label works, whether scent marketing is useful, and how hypermarkets can extend their life cycle. Controlled experiments have provided insight into what works and in which conditions. This book includes relevant scientific research and discusses some of the latest papers on the challenges.

- *A look into the future of retail for marketing students*
  At academic institutions marketing students mostly get to see case studies that deal with large suppliers in business-to-consumer (B2C) marketing. Shopper insight is a relatively new concept for them. Academic institutions have created study programmes for retail marketing, but most of the focus is still elsewhere. In addition, universities discuss marketing models and strategies thoroughly, but spend less time on how to implement them. This is even more important for the retail arena where there are direct interfaces (stores, leaflets, online) with people. It is not that students do not want to hear about the relevance of tools in real life, though access is sometimes limited. They are eager to obtain a taste of where they will work and what it is like as a marketing practitioner.

In conclusion, the five proficiencies are explained by focusing on specific applications and best practices. This book goes further than giving definitions and checklists: there are specific dimensions that illustrate the proficiencies. For example, to explain what depth of expertise retailers need to master when it comes to in-store execution, the following factors come to the fore: development of private label, music, ambient scents and self-scanning. That is not to say that these are the only dimensions within in-store execution. Others could also be attractive such as, for example, store layout and efficient shelf-merchandising principles.

Sharing

Over the years I have written many articles and blogs regarding innovation, cultural differences, retail, shopping behaviour and sales strategies. This has helped me to structure my thoughts, encourage other practitioners to consider and develop their strategies, and refine my ideas and models. Indeed, practitioners may have seen concepts in this book before, as I have previously published on these topics in three business magazines that provide a platform for innovative retail ideas: *FoodPersonality*, *StoreCheck Magazine* and *Innova Magazine*. The continuous evolution of my thinking, the explanation of the latest academic research and the validation by retail practitioners enable me to share with the reader much of what I have learnt about retail marketing. I am happy to share my experiences with practitioners around the world so that shoppers become happier and retail strategies more effective. I share my successes and my failures. My hope is that this book will help practitioners to enhance their knowledge, utilize their capabilities completely and fulfil their ambitions in the retail arena.

Structure of the book

Practitioners could plunge right into a topic and read what is of most interest to them so in this way the book could serve as a manual. However, most will experience the full breadth of what shopper happiness means and which retail techniques are helpful by taking a step-by-step approach. The book first discusses the three proficiencies that provide retailers with a shopper's perspective of their business. These are the most critical areas for success and offer most opportunities for sustainable differentiation. The last two proficiencies in this book are inherently part of the retailer perspective and where retailers already have most experience (Figure 1.4).

FIGURE 1.4   Perspectives on retail marketing and book structure

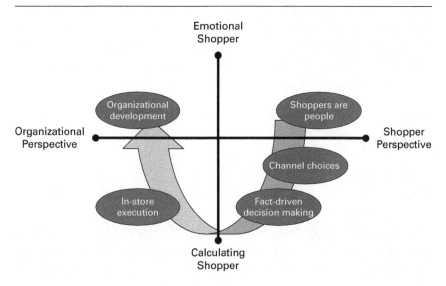

The book is laid out as a journey integrating shopper-driven practices into the operational proficiencies of retail in five steps:

- *Shoppers are people*
  The first set of chapters (Part Two) aims to understand and appreciate the emotional behaviour of the shopper. The book begins by debunking the myth that shoppers make most decisions in-store on impulse at the last moment. Next, I provide an in-depth understanding of the shopper and their behaviour. I focus on the irrational aspects of behaviour and consider approaches to break with shopping routines. Neuro research is a fascinating new technology that generates fresh understanding into what shoppers really think and feel but often do not say.

- *Channel choices*
  Shoppers start with a specific mission in mind: for example, to buy a gift for a birthday or something nice to wear at a party. Next, they evaluate a range of retailers based on different variables such as budget, proximity and choice of brands. Researchers may have defined channel names and sorted retailers into these groups. Indeed, dividing the market into channels is helpful from a managerial point of view, for example when measuring market share, but it is not in itself relevant to shoppers.

  Retailers that focus too much on a certain format may lose the perspective of the shopper. For example, a channel that is under pressure in mature markets is the hypermarket format. In Part Three I explain the original success factors of the hypermarket channel and why shoppers lost interest in favour of the convenience channel, discount stores and online. A significant section of the book discusses the role of online retailers in the grocery sector and what the differences and similarities are between shopping online and in a physical store.

- *Fact-driven decision making*
  Part Four explores how practitioners can tap into loyalty card and big data to better understand shoppers. If loyalty programmes are run mechanically with occasional promotional offers, they make little difference to the lives of shoppers. If, on the other hand, retailers show shoppers that they want to thank them for their purchases and show an eagerness to serve them better, the relationship moves from a solely financial agreement to an emotional relationship. Collecting data and searching for insights are important. Using data for decision making is not an end in itself nor an end to intuitive decisions.

Indeed, when combined they generate more pleasurable and effective retail environments. One of the most difficult decisions in retail is deciding how many products and what type of assortment shoppers like. Shoppers tell retailers that they want choice but they complain when given too much, so this part of the book recommends strategies on how to make shoppers happy with the right assortment.

- *In-store execution*
  Part Five helps retailers to focus on effective retail marketing instruments, aided by straightforward recommendations about whether retailers should invest in in-store music and ambient scents. They feel intuitively very effective, and this belief is supported in popular magazines. In this part of the book retailers are offered a fresh look at the effectiveness of these tools in everyday practice. Retailers, for example in pharmaceuticals, DIY and petrol, consider the grocery sector as outstanding best practice for private label. I also discuss what drives the success of private label and what are the effective instruments for suppliers to keep shoppers happy with their A-brands.

- *Organizational development*
  Part Six deals with the question of how practitioners can implement organizational development knowledge both internally and when working with partners. I begin with a description of how retailers have transformed their organizations from a buying focus to a category management approach. This change resulted in the retail sector becoming more professional and it has generated many strategic tools that are still in use today, such as the category role model.

  Structuring the organization into categories is a great step forward, but the original category management models need to be complemented with shopping missions, basket analysis, shopper research and much more in order to better understand shoppers. Trade marketing and account managers on the supplier side can learn more about the needs of a category manager on the retail side. This helps to improve their approach to service and stimulates collaboration among partners in the value chain. Finally this part of the book describes how organizations can embrace shopper marketing for strategic benefit and to generate innovations based on shopper insights.

My mission is to make shoppers happy. Retailers need advanced strategies in order to create shopper happiness. The book closes with thoughts on how the retail sector can take a new approach to engaging with their shoppers. With that, enjoy the book!

PART TWO
Shoppers are people

The myth of impulse purchasing

02

Category management has drawn increased attention to marketing activities on the store floor. Tastings, product demonstrations and floor stickers are just a few of the arsenal of possibilities available, and the cry of delight from the success stories is that in-store marketing is the most effective marketing investment. Often the investment is justified by the assumption that the shopper makes their decisions only after they arrive at the store. I think it is time for both suppliers and retailers to know shoppers better.

The 70 per cent impulse myth

A percentage that keeps buzzing around in grocery retail is the 70 per cent impulse myth. Shoppers are said to make 70 per cent of all their purchasing decisions on the store floor. The number is based on a study commissioned by POPAI in the United States in 1995.[1] It concluded that 74 per cent of purchases are decided in-store. In 53 per cent of cases, the purchase was completely unplanned before entering the store. Similar results come from a study that POPAI conducted across seven European countries in 1997 and 1998.[2] This showed that the average in-store decision rate is lower at 67 per cent, but with high variations across countries. The study suggested that the most impulse buying occurs in the Netherlands (80 per cent) and the least in Italy (42 per cent).

Often it is implied that shoppers make their in-store decisions in a completely impulsive way. There is a wide array of decisions that are said to be made in-store. Decisions regarding category, brand, size, flavour, segment – such as deciding whether to buy from the pasta category, what brand of butter will land on the breakfast table and whether to buy a 200 ml or a 400 ml bottle of shampoo – as well as a plethora of other options are supposedly wide open and made in the last few seconds in front of the shelf. This myth of the enormous extent of impulse buying is perhaps kept alive by those who benefit from circling store materials. In most countries there are lists of 'top 10 impulse products' in trade magazines. Suppliers use the 70 per cent figure to gain store access for their displays and to sell during promotional events. Buyers love to believe the 70 per cent, because isn't their store the pivot around which everything turns? Shouldn't advertising budget be shifted to store level? The payment for display locations and narrow casting by suppliers are welcome sources of income for retailers. However, the 70 per cent figure has come under attack from research by well-respected agencies:

- Advertising agency Ogilvy & Mather conducted shopper interviews across five retail channels and six product categories in 24 countries around the world. They concluded that in those cases where shoppers planned the category purchase, 28 per cent of the shoppers make the brand decision in-store. Almost 20 per cent choose a category they had no intention of buying before visiting the store.[3]
- Research agency SymphonyIRI suggests that in the United States 44 per cent of decisions are made in-store.[4]
- A 2008 study by Bell, Corsten and Knox shows that 60 per cent of shopping trips contain no impulse-category purchase and that the remaining 40 per cent contain on average only three unplanned products. Some 20 per cent of purchases are unplanned.[5]

Before we examine impulse buying more closely, it is useful to make note of the difference between several types of purchases that can be made by the shopper:

- Unplanned category purchases: the shopper does not intend to buy from the category before entering the store.
- Unplanned brand purchases: the shopper wishes to buy a category, for example tea, but leaves the decision of which brand of tea to buy until the moment they are in the store.
- More-or-less planned purchase: the shopper has decided on all or most characteristics of the purchase, but may leave some decisions to be made in-store. For example, they have decided on tea, and the brand Lipton, but might choose the flavour in-store.

The extent of the shopper's indecision goes up when it comes to the exact shape of the purchase. This is the main playing field for retailers. Still the myth persists that even at a category level the shopper is often undecided. Therefore, I will focus on unplanned category purchases in this chapter, although to a lesser extent my arguments will remain true for the other levels of planning.

Too much stimulation in just two seconds

My main objection to the supposedly high levels of impulse purchasing is that I do not believe the human psyche can cope with such high levels of in-store decision making. In essence, the human being is a creature of habit. Let's describe an 'average' shopping trip. The shopper asks their children what they want to eat and they come up with one thing, which was the same as the previous week: French fries. The shopper has been looking for inspiration on the retailers' websites and advertisements in newspapers. They convince themselves that their favourite supermarket, which happens to be conveniently located close to home, has the most promising promotions. Some nice deals are listed, and so he or she cuts out the promotional coupons in advance of the visit. The shopper does not want to spend their weekend in a grocery store, however, and has plans that afternoon, so subconsciously allocates 30 minutes for completing the shop.

According to TNS research, only 10 per cent of the time in-store is spent on active selection and shopping, while 90 per cent of time is spent on navigating through the store and shelves.[6] The greatest amount of time is spent finding a parking spot, getting hold of a trolley with wheels that actually work, searching through aisles, negotiating with a child over a bag of sweets, tracking down their other child somewhere else in the store, waiting for a few ounces of Italian ham at the deli and queuing for the checkout. So, let's say for product decisions the shopper in our above example has some two minutes left over. If they are on a big shopping trip, and need to buy around 60 items, they have about two seconds per item to choose which product will please the family and suit the budget. This is what a shopper does in two seconds. The shopper does not have the time or willpower to consider the flavour, brand and packaging size for each product. The beer company Old Jamaica Ginger Beer commissioned research into eating habits, and found that 60 per cent of British people eat the same seven meals every week.[7] It even found people who have been eating the same meal on the same day of the week for over 10 years... It concluded: 'This study shows we are really lacking imagination when it comes to experimenting with flavours.'

I have always been impressed by the numbers presented by SymphonyIRI demonstrating that shoppers in Europe buy the same 300 products every year, of which half are on a regular basis. So despite the fact that the average supermarket carries some 15,000 to 20,000 items, and French hypermarkets like Auchan even offer over 100,000 items, shoppers still buy only a selective number. From a shopper perspective the right thing to do seems to be to stick to what has worked in the past. With all the stimuli and messages that a shopper faces every day, they have learned how to cope with them. The shopper applies heuristics to allow them to deal with the pressure. Some 95 per cent of all decisions made by human beings take place in the subconscious. If shoppers were to consider everything, nothing would happen. This is even more true in store environments with many products, an overwhelming amount of information and many social stimuli. The shopper's task is to collect the ingredients for a meal that is both delicious and financially sound. The shopping floor is not the ideal place to take a step back and review all purchasing decisions. Research agency TNS found that 54 per cent of a shopper's purchased items are the same as on the last shopping trip and 24 per cent of the purchases are alternatives from the same brand.[8] Pradeep wrote in his book *The Buying Brain* that human brains are focused on using energy as efficiently as possible.[9] Despite the relatively small size of the human brain it uses up to 20 per cent of a person's energy needs. Endlessly lingering in supermarkets agonizing over purchasing decisions would only make that use percentage higher.

Pitfalls of market research

Perhaps retail practitioners have let their confusion regarding the level of impulse planning stick around too long, because no better research techniques have surfaced. In order to get to the bottom of which type of purchasing decisions are made when, it is not enough to ask shoppers for their intentions before the shopping trip, or afterwards to ask people in hindsight what they have purchased and why. Practitioners have to be careful when asking these questions directly via surveys. Who wants to admit that they are influenced by marketing? Let's assume for a moment that respondents do not feel forced to give socially desirable answers and are not influenced in any other way. Even then, we are forced to hope that the survey respondents truly understand why they make their various purchases, and that they do not rationalize their decisions afterwards.

In *The Buying Brain*, Pradeep poses that the brain of a respondent changes the original data at the moment of response in a questionnaire, especially when it comes to emotions and memories. Our senses take in 11 million pieces of information per second. The majority of this happens subconsciously. If humans really do their best, they process only 40 pieces of information in a conscious manner. A questionnaire is forced to appeal to the conscious level of the brain to retrieve all facts and feelings from the subconscious in a neat way, classify them and translate them into an expression of what people really thought, felt and memorized at that specific moment. When considering the relationship between conscious and subconscious processes, it is clear that this task is almost impossible. Therefore, Pradeep recommends neuro research as a tool to develop advertising, store material and innovations that do stand out, and that are liked and memorized at the same time. To determine the level of impulse in a product purchase, retailers rarely have the opportunity to apply neuro research. Other methods are helpful as well. Rather than just asking for someone's opinion at the checkout, retailers could start relying more on actively demonstrated behaviour obtained from a consumer household panel or store observations. Ideally the latter occurs both at home and during shopping.

Impulse buying

From the above it becomes clear that a shopper has much to gain if they rely on intuition and experiences from past purchases. This is not to say that unplanned purchases are irrelevant – on the contrary. Retailers have to unravel impulse buying and find out which category, which shopping trip and which shopper impulse moments are important. Research from 2009 by Inman, Winer and Ferraro in the United States shows in great detail the circumstances when a shopper is most likely to buy in an unplanned manner.[10] In their data set of 34,000 products, in 61 per cent of cases the category purchase was unplanned before entering the store. They explain that the level of planning depends on the type of category, the profile of the shopper and shopping behaviour. Let's look at these in more detail.

Type of category

Unplanned purchases occur more frequently if there are displays in-store and the category is hedonic and indulgent, such as chocolate, ice cream or salty snacks. Articles with a high purchase frequency have become part of a ritual and have a lower likelihood of becoming an unplanned purchase.

Shopper profile

For larger households it is more difficult to remember what everybody asked for when writing the shopping list. Therefore, the chance of unplanned purchases increases. If a shopper is more familiar with the store, they feel more at ease and more willing to make unplanned purchases. In addition, gender plays a role. Books like Pradeep's *The Buying Brain*, and Brizendine's *The Female Brain* argue that the brains of the different genders work differently and that this influences shopping behaviour.[11] Additionally, contrary to what you may expect, shopping in company with others did not result in significantly more unplanned purchases.

Shopping behaviour

Store visits where the shopper visits all aisles, and the total time in-store increases, tend to include more unplanned purchases. Shopping more frequently and focusing on fewer items per trip will increase the level of planning. Paying with credit cards also increases the chance of unplanned purchases because the pain of payment is transferred to a future date. This corroborates recent findings in behavioural economics that non-cash payments make paying less salient, and therefore debit and credit card payments facilitate more unplanned purchases. Inman, Winer and Ferraro demonstrated that using a shopping list also results in fewer impulse purchases, as would be expected.

Of all the variables researched, displays had the largest effect on impulse purchases. If the shopper sees a display, the chance of an unplanned purchase rises by 39 per cent. In contrast, Bell, Corsten and Knox emphasize that the characteristics of the shopper are more important than the situation in-store. Consider the demographic variables: they found that young adult households with no children and households with above-average incomes show 45 per cent more unplanned category purchasing. Other drivers include the way that shoppers collect information on promotions, and how efficiently they shop. If they like a fast and efficient style, they are 82 per cent less likely to make unplanned purchases. Shoppers who habitually collect information on promotions and prices before shopping make 25 per cent fewer unplanned category purchases. They also found that 24 per cent of shoppers never buy on impulse. Bell, Corsten and Knox think that retailers have to make a strategic choice: do they want to attract shoppers who make more unplanned purchases by nature, or do they want to invest in attracting a broad range of shoppers and let the store environment stimulate impulse sales? The focus and marketing strategy will be different for each. The researchers conclude that a focus on attracting the right shopper target group is more efficient.

Stimulating the level of unplanned purchases is a marketing tactic purely viewed from the perspective of a supplier or retailer. The other side of the study conducted by Bell, Corsten and Knox offers shoppers guidelines on how to make fewer impulse purchases by using some self-control tactics. A shopper should draft a shopping list, seek aisles in a goal-oriented manner, make many and small shopping trips and decide in advance to pay in cash.

Faster is more

I love retailers that inspire me, make the shopping trip lively, and can turn the seduction of shoppers into making unplanned purchases into an art form. However, people should also realize that the commonly quoted figure of 70 per cent of purchases being impulse purchases is a myth. Our brains do not work like this. On the contrary, stimulating the shopping experience into something habitual and efficient would not hurt the retailer. TNS research shows that fast shoppers leave the store with more purchases.[12] In an English supermarket 2 per cent of the products sold are responsible for 25 per cent of revenue. The shopper is greatly pleased when the products they want most are placed prominently at the front of the store. The retailer can further facilitate choice by improving store navigability, on-shelf labels and implementing structured planograms. By applying the knowledge of decision processes that is available in the academic research, retailers can make the shopping experience much smoother for those who buy from their stores.

What can you do to make your shoppers happy?

As shoppers are very habitual, they want to see the categories that they buy most often within easy reach, for example at the entrance to the store.

Shoppers like everything that establishes a link with their previous experiences and purchases, such as online lists of the purchases made at their last visit, a minimum of in-store assortment reviews, and clear navigation and signposting.

Which marketing strategies can retailers apply?

The shopping floor is not the ideal place to communicate anything too complicated to the shopper. Online reviews and magazines distributed before the shopping trip takes place have a higher chance of communicating complex messages.

Though overall impulse is low in-store, shoppers need a reminder for some categories. Certain categories benefit from being allocated to high-impulse locations (for example, end-of-aisle gondolas benefit from a wide range of potential impulse items such as batteries, ice cream and potato snacks).

Notes

1 POPAI (1995) *The 1995 Consumer Buying Habits Study*, The Global Association for Marketing at-Retail, Washington DC

2 POPAI (1997/1998) [accessed 23 July 2015] The POPAI Europe Consumer Buying Habits Study [Online] http://www.popai.com/uploads/downloads/2013/08/ThePOPAIEuropeConsumerConsumerBuyingHabitsStudy_1995.pdf

3 Ogilvy & Mather (2015) [accessed 23 July 2015] Shopper Decisions Made In-Store [Online] http://www.wpp.com/wpp/marketing/consumerinsights/shopper-decisions-made-instore/

4 IRI (2013) [accessed 6 August 2013] IRI MarketPulse Survey Finds Consumers Settling into 'New Normal': Virtually No Decline Found across Wide Variety of Conservative Purchase Behaviors during Past Two Years, *SymphonyIRI* [Online] http://www.iriworldwide.com/NewsEvents/PressReleases/ItemID/1760/View/Details.aspx

5 Bell, D, Corsten, D and Knox, G (2008) The power of unplanned uncertainty, *International Commerce Review*, 8 (1), pp 56–64

6 Gill, R (2013) TNS Retail & Shopper, presentation at TNS Russia conference, Moscow, 21 November

7 Spillet, R (2014) [accessed 23 July 2015] What's for dinner tonight? Lasagne... just like last week: How 60% of people eat the same 7 regular meals every week. *Daily Mail*, 24 July [Online] http://www.dailymail.co.uk/news/article-2703772/What-s-dinner-tonight-Lasagne-just-like-week-How-60-people-seven-regular-meals-everyweek.html

8 Scamell-Katz, S (2010) TNS conference, London, 14 October

9 Pradeep, A (2010) *The Buying Brain: Secrets for selling to the subconscious mind*, John Wiley & Sons, New Jersey

10 Inman, J, Winer, R and Ferraro, R (2009) [accessed 22 July 2015] The interplay between category characteristics, customer characteristics, and customer activities on in-store decision making, *Journal of Marketing* [Online] http://journals.ama.org/doi/abs/10.1509/jmkg.73.5.19

11 Brizendine, L (2008) *The Female Brain*, Bantam Press, London

12 Sorensen, H (2010) TNS conference, London, 14 October

Tapping into irrational shopper behaviour

03

The previous chapter on the myths surrounding impulse shopping made it clear that shoppers like to stick to a routine. The retailer might see opportunities for the shopper to be happier with a new service or product, but the shopper may refuse to change even if the new alternative is in their best interests. In this chapter, more of the emotional elements of shopper decisions will be identified. As mentioned in Chapter 2, proof of the limited extent of impulse purchasing has been established through large academic surveys, such as the 2008 study by Bell, Corsten and Knox. In this chapter I borrow insights from the discipline of psychology to identify more types of emotional behaviour. In Chapter 4, the last chapter in Part Two, I will show how neuro research can allow retailers to understand shoppers better.

Shoppers make irrational choices. This is visible in everyday retail contexts and is no surprise in itself. At Starbucks coffee outlets, for example, customers often do not know what to expect in terms of cup size when they order a 'tall', 'grande' or 'large' and end up selecting the one in the middle ('grande'), regardless of its *actual* size. Shoppers are often prepared to wait longer for their turn at a service counter when they are queuing in a line as compared to a situation where they pull a number and then wait until their number is called. Shoppers, including myself, are so irrational that retailers can even predict the irrationality. And it is this predictable irrationality that makes it interesting for a marketer. In this chapter I elaborate more on irrational choices that the marketer may expect in retail environments and how to tap into these.

What is irrational behaviour?

Before I expand on how this works in retail environments, I will define 'behaving irrationally' and why the attention on this topic has been growing since around 2010. Often behaving irrationally is put on the same level as acting emotionally; however, emotion is just one element of the irrational concept. The simplest starting point is to explain when shoppers perform the opposite: that is, act perfectly rationally. Rational behaviour takes place when:

- Shoppers have access to full information about all aspects, the consequences of a decision and the probability of future events occurring, like when a shopper buys a pack of cigarettes while fully aware of the health risks they may cause.

- Shoppers use only their logical thinking power, so that they fail to take account of emotional aspects: for example, by buying Persil when it is being promoted – and neglecting the fact that they regretted their previous purchase of Persil or that their mother always used Ariel.

- The shopper is perfectly consistent in their choice behaviour. For example, a shopper prefers potato chips version A over version B, and B over version C, always in the same order. In reality, if one product from a range is not present, the order of preference among the remaining items may completely change.

- The shopper's powers of calculation are infinite. This means that retailers would expect shoppers to calculate the price per kilo effortlessly. The shopper only picks up the jam from the shelf after calculating and adding up the value of each of the product characteristics, such as amount of fruit and sugar contents of each variety.

After reading these conditions of rational behaviour it becomes clear that it is impossible to act fully rationally all of the time. The belief in the rationality of human beings has been around for a long time. There is an old Greek legacy that says humans apply a high level of planning and make rational decisions for as long as they can. According to this view, emotions are to be suppressed; however, current scientific research shows that our instincts or emotions actually help us through the day more comfortably.

The insight that people are not as rational as previously thought has already led to important societal changes. A study by Iyengar, Jiang and

Huberman found that US retirement plans with only two choice options obtain more participants than pension plans with a multitude of options.[1] In their research, 59 choice options within a pension plan simply offered too much choice. While economics books often tell us that more choice and more information lead to lower prices and a greater feeling of satisfaction and happiness for shoppers, researchers Cronqvist and Thaler demonstrated that this economic principle does not always apply.[2] In a new retirement system in 2000, Swedes had to select from 456 funds. The Swedes had too much confidence in their own expertise, chose risky funds and then were attracted by familiar Swedish fund names. In addition, they extrapolated recent investment results to future projections, although it is widely acknowledged that past financial results may not be applicable for predictions in the future. In the end, shoppers who made their own choice obtained a lower return on investment than shoppers who used a portfolio of funds that the Swedish government had put together. Ever since the start of the new system behavioural economists have criticized the risk that pension investors have taken, but this has not yet led to big changes. The Swedish government only smoothed down the proposal, for example by setting a maximum threshold when investing in riskier stock.

The challenge of over-choice plays a role in groceries as well. The number of products in an average US supermarket rose by 55 per cent in the 10-year period 2000–2010.[3] Still, shoppers often choose what they have always trusted. Behavioural scientist Soman describes a Chinese restaurant with 185 meals on the menu, of which the top five meals make up 80 per cent of the revenue.[4] From a behavioural economics perspective, too much choice does not work for a number of reasons. The chance of regret if the shopper selects the wrong item increases. When shoppers order a takeaway meal, for example, rather than consider the whole experience they consider one main aspect – such as whether it has fish, chicken or lamb. The consequences of too large an offering are:

- postponement or cancellation;
- conservative choices with low chance of regret;
- buying what your friend chooses;
- selecting something that a celebrity has endorsed;
- selecting those environments that have fewer choice options, such as discounters like Aldi and Lidl.

These consequences are consistent with findings by Barry Schwartz, who asserts that reducing the number of choices leads to increased shopper happiness.[5]

Automatic shopping behaviours and other pitfalls

Although it becomes clear that shoppers do not always make the best choices for themselves, the assumption that people act in a rational and logical manner is at the basis of all important economic models and most marketing plans. Yet thanks to scientific research by psychologists, marketing practitioners now need to take into account new insights. Shoppers process information in a limited way, preferring to take a shortcut to a solution and allowing themselves to be influenced by the environment they happen to be in at a particular moment. The concept of the bounded rationality of the shopper is very relevant to the retail marketing function because the retail environment determines to a large degree how products or brands (often the same) are sold. And this retail environment makes shopping for groceries, with a large offering and colourful communications, a potentially stressful experience. The shopper's options and choices are context-specific, and three major factors influence each product choice. These are: 1) the buying environment (such as a petrol station, a supermarket or with a tablet on the couch); 2) the mood of the shopper; and 3) the other people around the shopper at the time (for example, other shoppers in the store). This clearly presents challenges, and research by psychologists has revealed many irrational pitfalls. Listed below are 14 automatic behaviours and pitfalls that shoppers themselves would acknowledge as irrational if confronted with their own behaviour while sitting on the couch at a quiet moment a week later.

Compromise

As shown by the example of Starbucks at the beginning of this chapter, shoppers faced with small, medium-sized and large cups often choose the medium-sized alternative, regardless of the actual size of the cup. This means that shoppers can be pushed towards buying the version the marketer wants as long as it is the middle option. In a research experiment Simonson describes a petrol station that sells petrol with octane levels of 87, 89 and 91.[6] Following the introduction of a version with an octane level of 94, the sales of the petrol with 91 octane rose. This means that the context of the product determines whether the shopper buys the product, not so much the product itself. This effect occurs mainly whenever it is difficult to determine the quality of the product. Researchers Huber, Payne and Puto point to yet another notable situation that occurs if three products differ in quality in two aspects.[7] Let's assume that cake brand A consists of 10 per cent raisins and

30 per cent nuts. Cake brand B contains 20 per cent raisins and 10 per cent nuts. After adding the third alternative, brand C, which versus brand B scores worse on both aspects with 18 per cent raisins and 8 per cent nuts, more shoppers choose alternative B. In practice, cake brand C assumes the role of bait. (Note: in academic literature the situation that Huber, Payne and Puto discuss is called the asymmetric dominance, or decoy effect. I include this as part of the compromise effect because, like the octane level example, both describe situations in which shoppers mislead themselves on the quality of the products.)

Loss aversion

Everyone understands that winning is great, and as a rule humans try to avoid losing. In Kahneman's famous Nobel-prize-winning research he describes in his prospect theory that the attitude of people differs with regard to the risk of winning or of losing.[8] In other words, people feel more pain when losing than they experience happiness when winning. The positive emotion of a win of €200 equals the emotion felt at the loss of €100. In another research example, Thaler demonstrated the effect when shoppers bundle or split amounts of money in a way that makes them feel most happy.[9] For shoppers it feels better if they take their loss in one blow, for example by paying at one checkout rather than paying time and time again for individual products in shop-in-shop stores. For benefits, the reverse is true: if Amazon delivers the shopper's online order in three deliveries (on time) they feel happier than in the case of one delivery. Thaler also gives the example of a big loss and a small gain.[10] Some supermarkets print the discount the shopper received at the bottom of the checkout receipt. This makes shoppers feel great; however, somewhere at the back of their mind a sense of a loss floats around because of the total receipt amount. In such cases, shoppers feel better if they receive the gain (the discount on the purchase) after a few days or at the next purchase. It is important to realize that this deals with the emotion of the shopper, because postponing the reward to the next shopping trip may result in new behavioural barriers and decisions. A great example of the application of loss aversion comes from Unilever in the Netherlands. As a result of the economic recession in 2008 shoppers had become more open to private labels. This was encouraged by retailers such as Albert Heijn who made the packaging of their own labels similar to the A-brands of Unilever. In response Unilever started advertising campaigns explaining the many good ingredients and benefits that the A-brands offered, and in this way made shoppers aware of what they might lose by switching to private labels.

Framing

The word 'choice' and the type of images used to illustrate choice call on associations that influence the shopper's choice. But shoppers may be given the wrong impression, as has been highlighted by Foodwatch, for example, an organization that strives for honest, safe and healthy food. In 2013 the Dutch branch of Foodwatch publicized the packaging of Kellogg's Frosties bars showing a happy tiger, wheat stalks, a green apple and splashing milk. These are cues for associations like 'healthy' and 'natural' that give shoppers the idea that the snack is suitable for children. However, according to Foodwatch the product contains too much sugar (40 per cent) and unsaturated fat (10 per cent). Foodwatch presents prizes for the most misleading products, so-called Golden Wind Eggs. Winner of the 2014 Golden Wind Egg was Coca-Cola with its sugar-rich Capri-Sun multivitamin drink, also aimed at children.

A special version of framing occurs if retailers break down a large annual expense (for example car insurance) into smaller multiple values to allow for comparison with the daily expense of something else (for example €1.50 for a cup of coffee every day). The amount the shopper pays is the same; however, Gourville showed in 1998 that this 'penny a day' strategy makes you spend faster.[11] Shoppers are inclined to make decisions rather thoughtlessly and the reflective part of the brain does not always check the automated responses. Therefore, product claims with '90 per cent fat free' sound much better than 'contains 10 per cent fat', although they actually say the same thing. Kahneman gives the example of credit card companies that lobbied to have the additional fees on credit card payments framed as 'discounts on cash payments' rather than 'charges on the credit card payment', though again the absolute amount the shopper pays is equal.[12] The effects of framing also become apparent in the advertisements of a former Dutch book club, ECI.[13] In a spontaneous and recalcitrant impulse the ECI team changed its offer from three books for 10 Dutch guilders to two books for 10 Dutch guilders plus one for free. The changed frame led to four times more registrations for the book club.

Limited self-control

If a shopper sees chocolate in a display, they find it difficult to resist, although they know that it is not healthy. In the same way, a psychologist would say that a shopper appreciates more the benefits that they can grab immediately (for example, receiving €10 at this very moment) rather than benefits to come in the future even if they are larger (€12 next week). Put differently, costs that shoppers pay in the future do not feel as heavy as costs shoppers pay now. This effect happens much less if the choice is a long way in the future. For example, if a shopper has to choose between receiving either €10 in 50 weeks or €12 in 51 weeks, more shoppers do want to wait an additional week in this case, even though in both cases the difference is just one week. Shoppers tumble into the pitfall of direct consumption in a variety of ways: for example, when shoppers smell recently baked cookies or see fresh nuts. This effect also materializes when the advertisement visualizes the benefit. For example, lotteries are famous for displaying all the wealth that is within reach after winning: speedboats, large villas, luxury cars. Only after purchasing the lottery ticket do people realize they have only a very small chance of winning. This rational message sinks in later and perhaps then people see the humour in their action, as in Dilbert's words of wisdom: 'Lottery is a tax on people who don't understand statistics.' Finally, shoppers can stop themselves from losing control by drafting shopping lists and by making sure they are not hungry when visiting a supermarket.

Mental accounting

Shoppers divide their incomes and expenditures across all kinds of categories. Examples of divisions include type of income (for example: salary versus money that was a gift) and what they spend their money on (for example: food, children, sports, education). Once shoppers have categorized their money in a certain way, they stick to that categorization even though the circumstances they find themselves in might lead them to act differently. Let's assume the shopper loses their entry ticket to a pop concert that was worth €100. In such a case most shoppers do not buy a new entry ticket. In contrast, if the shopper loses €100 in cash on the way to the pop concert and does not yet have an entry ticket, they will still buy the entry ticket at the box office. In the latter case, the shopper finances the entry ticket from the 'unanticipated circumstances' jar, while in the first case the 'entertainment' jar is now empty for that month. Traditional economists expect money to always be fungible. Money is money, no?

Insights derived from behavioural science can be combined with developments from fields such as neuro research. Leach, of shopper agency TriggerPoint, shows how powerful this combination can be.[14] He found that shoppers keep a mental account in their head, and visualize buying snacks as a withdrawal from that account and buying healthy food as a deposit. This knowledge helped to improve the sales from a display where Mountain Dew soft drink and Doritos chips were offered as a combo named 'Better Together' for $2.22. By combining two snacks, shoppers felt they had to deduct twice from their health food account. Therefore, the message of the offer was changed to a discount on the more hedonistic product, Mountain Dew, while the overall discount remained the same. In combination with a different display that was more tailored to young, competitive shoppers (red colours and a more action-focused text: 'Fuel up, Thirst Down & Drive Away, A Winner') the sales of the display more than doubled.

Transparency of payment

Paying causes shoppers to feel horrible emotions (sometimes unconsciously). The pain of payment increases in correlation with the transparency of the payment method, as in the case of paying by cash. The less transparent the payment method, the less confrontational the payment itself becomes and the shopper is less aware of it. The scale goes from cash to debit cards to credit cards to automatic deductions. Behavioural scientist Soman gives examples of a laundrette and a restaurant that started to accept only prepaid cards instead of cash.[15] In both cases the revenue of the stores went up. In cases of less transparent systems, shoppers behave more impulsively; they forget what they have paid exactly and spend faster.

Perceived progress

Shopping seems to involve unavoidable waiting. Waiting for a parking space, waiting to ask for the specific goods required and, of course, waiting at the checkout. Scientists Zhou and Soman found evidence that shoppers are more satisfied if they know how long they will need to wait.[16] If shoppers have to form a queue they assess this by seeing people pay and leave, and by the fact that the queue shrinks in front of them. If shoppers have to take a number and then wait until their number is called, they are less satisfied. Likewise, in goal-oriented tasks shoppers are more motivated to wait if they receive feedback. Furthermore, another lesson is that what counts is the *perceived* waiting time, not the *actual* waiting time.

Anchoring

Supermarkets use shelf signs to inform shoppers if the price of a particular product in a competing supermarket is higher. It might not be a relevant comparison at all because the competitor may be located several miles away and outside the catchment area. Still, shoppers use the signalled price at the competing supermarket, let's say €5, as a starting point (anchor) to judge whether they like the price of the product that they want to buy, for example €4. They first assess if the anchor is too low or high (in this case the competitor's price is high) and next gradually move from the anchor to assess whether the price on-shelf is right – in this case, compared to the other supermarket, €4 seems to be a good deal. The process of anchoring occurs when a shopper's mental capacity is near its end, perhaps because the children are quarrelling, or they are in a hurry and have other things on their mind. Kahneman gives a good example to show how anchoring works in a supermarket in combination with the urgency effect.[17] Campbell's soup experimented with a shelf sign in a US supermarket. On some days it said 'Limit of 12 per person', while on other days it mentioned 'No limit per person'. In the first case when shoppers were given a limit, they bought seven cans of soup on average, double the quantity bought when no limit was imposed. Another example of the application of anchoring in a supermarket is when shoppers first encounter more expensive products (fresh produce, non-food) and then continue their trip towards dry groceries. The standard store layout of the Dutch supermarket Dirk van den Broek starts with detergents and shampoo, which gives an odd feeling at first as so many other supermarkets start with vegetables and fruit. However, I think this works from an anchoring perspective as shoppers first see only items priced from €3 and upwards, so that anything priced at €2 in the remainder of the shopping journey seems inexpensive by comparison.

Availability

According to Malcolm Gladwell, shoppers in the United States are confronted with some 254 commercial messages per day via television, radio, digital media and magazines.[18] Shoppers do not have the time or energy to process these messages and they may not even be consciously aware they were exposed to them. The availability principle teaches us that people tend to give more attention to those events that are very personal, occurred very recently and were shown via vivid images in the media. This explains why people are overly afraid of shark attacks or car accidents, while far more people die of cancer. In a retail context it means that, in the United States for example, advertisements for batteries and emergency food packages work much better in the weeks after the hurricane season – the purchase has become more relevant because shoppers now see more reason to stock up on these items.

Unrealistic optimism

A bride and a groom, when asked at their wedding, will vigorously declare that they will be together forever. However, the marriage statistics in Western countries are clear: between 40 and 50 per cent of marriages end up in divorce. People have this contagious power to ignore information they do not want to see. They focus on what they want to know about: they see causal patterns when looking back in the past, and when extrapolating into the future they deny the existence of luck and random chance. For me, this at least partly explains why shoppers still buy cigarettes, eat too much fatty food and consume too many sugary drinks. They subconsciously think that other shoppers will experience the bad side effects, but not themselves.

Priming

When subtle stimuli influence a shopper's behaviour it is called priming. These stimuli could be anything: letters, words, images, scents. Researchers Holland, Hendriks and Aarts conducted an experiment that had one group of participants complete a survey in a room smelling of citrus, and another group complete it in an unscented room.[19] The participants were asked to list activities for the remainder of the day: 36 per cent of the people who worked in the citrus-scented room mentioned cleaning, as compared to only 11 per cent in the other group. The researchers explained this by the fact that many cleaning agents have a citrus smell. In another experiment with a citrus-scented room the experimental group and control group received a Dutch cracker as a snack after they had completed a survey. For those who are not familiar with Dutch crackers: they are impossible to eat without crumbling. The result was that the participants who worked in the citrus-scented room cleaned the crumbs from the table significantly more often than the others. The remarkable conclusion from the study is that priming not only influences people's thoughts (an intention to clean later in the afternoon) but also subconsciously impacts their actual behaviour (cleaning the table there and then).

Supermarkets can use the natural scents of categories such as bread, pastries, coffee and fresh nuts to stimulate sales. They may also use visual hints such as photos in the inside of the shopping trolley to prompt a certain behaviour. Berger and Fitzsimons discovered that in the weeks before Halloween shoppers are much more likely to recall brands that are known for their orange packaging than other brands;[20] when asked to list the first things that come to mind in the categories of candy/chocolate at this same period, 54 per cent of shoppers mentioned Reese's (a brand of confectionery that features distinctive orange packaging), while awareness dropped to 30 per cent one week later. A similar thing occurred in soft drinks when a brand with orange packaging – Crush – declined from 47 per cent to 30 per cent one week after Halloween. The researchers explain this by the overwhelming presence of the colour orange at this time of year, through Halloween signs and in-store pumpkins.

Information

At times, mere information alone can influence the shopper. While there are some similarities between information bias and priming, an important difference is that priming includes a wide range of sensual signals whereas information operates purely with textual clues. The information bias feels like good advice or a casual remark, whereas priming is stimuli (text, images, scents) that are more obvious in their intention. Still, there could be a grey area of crossover as to whether a piece of text is priming or offering information bias. A good example of the information bias is the much used phrase online: 'Customers who bought this item also bought...'.

Salganik, Dodds and Watts demonstrated how the information bias works in an experiment where participants received a list of songs by unknown bands.[21] The researchers asked them to make a selection of the songs that they liked, to download them if they wished and then rate them. Some participants made their own decisions and other participants could see the number of downloads of each band in their own subgroup. The study found that people downloaded a significantly higher number of those songs that others had downloaded in their subgroup. In addition, the success of songs was different in each subgroup. Most often the winner was the song that was downloaded first. So people chose what others liked rather than making up their own mind on what would fit their personal tastes best. An information approach could be applied in-store when marketers leave messages on-shelf or on-pack. A packaging textual message like 'no preservatives' may lead to associations of naturalness with the shopper. A shelf talker with the text 'Our Choice' says nothing about ingredients, benefits and the criteria that the supermarket applied, but may sway the shopper's attention to the product long enough to consider buying it.

A great example of the information bias in-store comes from fashion retailer C&A in São Paulo, Brazil. C&A showed a preview of 10 items from its new Mother's Day collection on Facebook. Fans could like their favourite piece of clothing. A clothes hanger showed in real-time the number of likes. Some shoppers might be afraid to wear a piece of clothing that the rest of town wears as well. However, the marketing campaign was successful for C&A. Reportedly the rotation of the items improved in all stores and it helped position C&A as a more trendy and edgy brand.

Social pressure

People probably know from their own experience how social pressure works, but still the results from the study by Asch are pretty revealing.[22] A participant is asked to perform the simple exercise of matching a line on a card to the line of the same length on a screen. If participants are alone, almost no one makes a mistake. The results are very different when five other people, who collaborate in a secret conspiracy with Asch, all make an error as they were instructed. Almost 75 per cent of participants follow the group and point to the wrong line at least once in a total of 12 rounds. If the group makes a clear mistake, the experimental subject concedes and joins in on one out of three cases. This is even more remarkable if one realizes that the group was comprised of strangers whom the experiment's subject would never see again.

Interestingly, brands that help shoppers to resist social pressures are much loved. Think of Dove, inspiring women to be happy with the body they have and who they are. The famous Pepsi Challenge advertising campaign, first used in 1975,[23] encouraged shoppers to find out for themselves what they liked best rather than ordering the default drink that others expected them to choose – Coca-Cola.

Peak–end rule

If people are on holiday for 14 days, I would expect them to be twice as happy with their holiday as someone who was on a similar break but only for seven days. Indeed, the former is better rested, has more opportunities to explore the environment and a better chance of good weather. However, this is not what behavioural scientists find. It seems that the last day of someone's holiday is more determinant for the overall rating. One of the remarkable facts from Kahneman's studies is that people are prepared to suffer more pain as long as the end result is agreeable. From academic studies it appears that people judge the overall experience in hindsight based on the highest or lowest peak (of happiness or pain) and based on the single experience at the end. This is called the peak–end rule. When applying this principle to supermarkets I expect that shoppers judge their satisfaction with a shopping trip by what they experience at the end of the trip (at the checkout, leaving the car park) and/or base the judgement on one really good experience during the shopping trip. This means that although the shopper may have a very long and satisfying shopping experience, still only two moments really count for the final satisfaction score. Supermarkets that wish to apply this principle could, for example, ensure that each shopper has a personal, warm encounter with staff at one of the counters, because personal contacts make the most impression. Retailers should also try to make the checkout procedure as flawless and engaging as possible. The pain of paying needs to be smoothed away by friendly staff, personal attention and great service, because 'all's well that ends well' is a factor in the shopper experience.

In a webinar in 2014, research and innovation agency Brainjuicer showed how insights from behavioural science can help improve the effectiveness of promotions. Brainjuicer showed shoppers several planograms of toilet paper and toothpaste online. For the English toilet-paper brand Cushelle, volume was 8 per cent higher if the brand was promoted with a shelf label 'Max 8 per customer' and a discount of 33 per cent than in the case of a mere discount. The shoppers used the randomly chosen number eight as an anchor for their buying decision. In a similar experiment in Brazil the shelf label 'Max 8 per customer' was more than twice as effective as a 25 per cent price discount. Another behavioural approach that worked well was giving trust to the shopper. If the shelf label of Cushelle mentioned 'recommended by Good Housekeeping Institute', a UK organization that tests products on quality, volume rose by 16 per cent. A third approach was to apply the psychological principle that shoppers feel safer if they are part of a group. The volume of a toothpaste brand went up by 50 per cent in the UK by mentioning on the shelf that '8 out of 10 shoppers would recommend [the brand] to others'. A fourth approach demonstrated the power of the word 'free' in promotions. By adding a free cuddly koala bear to a pack of toilet paper, volume doubled. Not only does such a soft bear suit the category of toilet paper, but on top of that no shopper wants to miss out on such a kind offer.

Why do shoppers fall into irrational pitfalls?

In Kahneman's book *Thinking, Fast and Slow* he explains why shoppers run into so many pitfalls. He separates our thinking process into two parts: system 1 and system 2. System 1 operates automatically and quickly. It generates impressions and emotions without much effort. System 1 works really well in an emergency: if a tiger jumps at a human being, the latter responds quickly. System 1 is also very useful when the shopper repeats routine jobs in an efficient manner. The limitations of this system are that it enjoys answering questions more than asking them, it detests logic and calculations, and is not equipped with an off button.

If system 1 cannot solve something, then system 2 is switched on. System 2 takes care of all strenuous thinking processes. System 2 makes considered choices from a range of options, can handle several topics at the same time, and can tell the shopper's memory not to listen to system 1 – as many of shoppers' irrational pitfalls come from the laziness of system 1. In addition, there are situations where system 2 cannot function well. Think of situations that involve a lot of stress. A supermarket with its huge number of products and information signs is an environment where system 2 quickly becomes exhausted. During very emotional events, system 2 becomes overcrowded and leaves the response to system 1. Another way to look at it in the context of decision processes is to differentiate between intuitive and analytical choices. An intuitive choice comes about without too much effort or apparent consciousness. The intuition follows on from earlier experiences or by comparing patterns. In contrast, when making analytical choices the shopper calculates a total value based on the utilities and evaluation of all partial aspects of a decision.

Nudge: how to apply knowledge of irrational thinking

System 2 reads this chapter and thinks: 'Great, now I can avoid these pitfalls.' And marketers think: 'How can I apply this knowledge about the irrational side of the shopper to sell more of my brand?' Before I answer this question let's take a step back and think through, on a high level, the types of approaches a marketer can use to cause a behavioural change in shoppers. The first approach that comes to mind is advertising: by conveying the right information, marketers attempt to convince the shopper. A second strategy is to give financial incentives: with discounts and subsidies behaviour is stimulated and with help of taxes the consumption of products is reduced. The third alternative is to enforce limitations in the supply. A government, for example, could influence the sales of a product with restrictions and bans. Behavioural scientists Thaler and Sunstein have added a fourth strategy to this with the 'nudging' approach. This is an intervention in the choice system that changes the behaviour of shoppers in a predictable manner without forbidding any options or charging a lot of money.[24] Said differently, the retail marketer should gain an understanding of the context in which the categories and brands are sold.

What is 'to nudge'? The *Oxford Dictionary* gives four meanings:

1 prod (someone) gently with one's elbow in order to attract attention;
2 touch or push (something) gently or gradually;
3 coax or gently encourage (someone) to do something;
4 approach (an age, figure, or level) very closely.

The meaning that Thaler and Sunstein seek to use is: to give someone a small push in the right direction. They designed a nudging strategy because they found that the other strategies did not always work. For example, an advertising campaign where the authorities explain the importance of organ transplantation does not lead to more donors. People understand the message and agree with it; however, the sense of urgency is missing because most people feel alive and kicking. Another reason could be that they lack the personal experience from within their own family to motivate them to register as donors. Financial incentives have their own limitations. A government that raises taxes that lead to higher energy prices may find out to their surprise that energy consumption does not fall. The reasons are that the increased amount is deducted automatically from the user's bank account and the increased amount probably still falls within the range of acceptable payments for energy. This is what I discussed earlier as mental accounting. Attempting to ban products altogether does not work either: laws against drugs have not led to total abstinence. Thaler and Sunstein think that nudging is a more successful approach. It is like giving someone a small push when they are sitting on top of a slide. Nudging is especially helpful in the following situations:

- the shopper enjoys the benefits now and the costs come later (such as cigarettes, snacks);
- the shopper makes an investment of time, energy and/or money now, but enjoys the benefits later (such as a toothbrush);
- it is a complex choice (for example, hair dye);
- the shopper makes the purchase infrequently (such as spices);
- there is no direct feedback on the results (for example, skin care).

It is up to marketers to identify the best intervention or nudge to steer the shopper towards the desired outcome. The selected nudge depends on factors such as the extent to which the shopper is aware of the problem in making the purchase, and if they need more or, on the contrary, less information. Next, the marketer chooses one or more of the relevant instruments of sale; for example the marketing team could apply default choice options or could present information to a shopper as a gain rather than as a loss. Let's assume that a supermarket wishes to reduce the use of plastic bags in order to create a better environment. Of course, the supermarket could remove the bags at the checkout, but that is a limitation: the supermarket takes a choice away from the shopper. The city of Toronto in Canada did it differently: supermarkets in Toronto asked five cents for a plastic bag. This resulted in a more than 50 per cent reduction of plastic bags and a larger awareness of sustainability. A rational shopper would think that five cents is negligibly small in comparison to the total supermarket bill and would not let themselves be influenced by this. However, the fact that a fee is asked is a more important stimulus for behavioural change than the size of the fee. From experiments, the city had concluded that an additional increase of the amount per bag would not lead to a further reduction in demand of the plastic bags, although the classical demand theory would predict so.

Nudging in retail practice

One of the nicest examples of nudging in grocery comes from a machine that takes returnable plastic bottles at Lidl in the Netherlands. Dutch super-markets are obliged by law to charge deposit money on large, plastic bottles. Shoppers receive a deposit note when they return the empty bottle into a machine in the supermarket. At the checkout the deposit note is exchanged for money. This is proof that the discount chain Lidl is bringing science into practice in an excellent manner. In the first place, Lidl, like other Dutch supermarkets, shows through a very large, clear diagram how to feed the bottle into the machine. This is a wise decision, because in a stressful environment like a supermarket shoppers are expected to make mistakes easily. There is a very special button on the machine that allows the shopper to donate the value of the deposit money to a charity, in this case KiKa, a foundation that aims to improve the life expectancy of children suffering from cancer. Because the shopper does not actually receive the deposit money or feel the deposit note in their hands, they do not perceive a loss when pushing the button to donate the money. Reminding shoppers of such a good cause, a charity for children with cancer, makes shoppers feel really guilty if they do not donate. In a more traditional approach Lidl could have tried to convince shoppers to donate by placing leaflets in the stores. Even a tray where shoppers leave their deposit tickets is less effective from a behav-ioural science perspective because this approach makes the shopper hand over the ticket – and that would cause the shopper to experience subconsciously a loss.

In 2011 and 2012 the Dutch University of Wageningen alongside Schuttelaar & Partners carried out several experiments to see if they could find out how to stimulate Dutch shoppers to choose more sustainable and healthy products.[25] In collaboration with the supermarket chain Plus they placed shelf labels and signs at healthy categories. The communication contained the words 'Here I choose consciously' in combination with a logo that is used in the Netherlands to indicate better and healthier choices. Close to unhealthy products, the researchers placed signs reading: 'Choose more often more consciously'. The conclusion from the study was that the provision of information alone is not enough to cause a behavioural change. Another experiment at the retail outlet Kiosk at the Dutch NS national railway stations was more successful. The store placed promotion material with pictures of an apple and a banana with the following text: 'Choose fruit. A lot of train passengers do too!' By pointing out the social norm of eating healthily, the visitors to this Kiosk store bought a healthy snack more often. I think more retailers could benefit from this nudging approach. Although many retailers set themselves the sustainability target of obtaining a higher percentage of sales from healthy products, the number of examples of great nudging are still scarce in grocery retail. Unfortunately, I still see a lot of marketing programmes where supermarket and food service chains eliminate unhealthy products from the assortment and give discount on healthy items. I think nudging works better.

Shopper tool to apply nudges

Behavioural scientists have given the retail marketers rich insights. Sometimes it is difficult to know where to start reaping the benefits. I found it helpful in my consultancy practice to draft a shopper journey that displays the emotions that shoppers have from the moment of planning to the moment of final consumption. This gives an overview of potential touch-points for intervention at the different stages of the shopper journey.

Before starting on the Irrational Shopper Journey (Figure 3.1), the marketer needs to determine for which shopping trip and retail environment he or she is designing the improved experience. The marketer needs to write down:

- The type of category: this should be expressed in terminology that the shopper would use, for example 'a snack to accompany my tea'.

- A description of the shopper: socio-demographics, media usage, type of channels and stores visited, category usage.

- The selected shopping trip: examples are weekend or lunch trips.

- The store (format): describe the channel or specific retail brand visited.

FIGURE 3.1   The Irrational Shopper Journey tool

	planning	shopping	consuming
What do you see the shopper doing?			
What does the shopper feel?	+		
	−		
What behaviour do you want to influence, and how?			

Next the Irrational Shopper Journey tool can be applied. The first step is to describe what behaviour the shopper actually shows: for example, writing a shopping list, finding a parking space, asking for advice at the service desk. The second step is to describe the emotions that the shopper has with each of those actions: for example, confusion, loss aversion, happiness. In Figure 3.1 emotions that are positive (see '+' in Figure 3.1) are on top, with the negative emotions below (the emotions can be connected using a pencil so that a bubbly curve comes into being). The third and last step is to think about how to help the shopper in each of the situations. When the shopper journey is complete, the marketer may realize there might not be enough resources to tackle all obstacles of the shopping trip. In that case it is best to start addressing negative peak emotions, and emotions that occur early on in the shopper journey. By addressing obstacles early in the shopping trip, emotions from the beginning do not influence later events – and maximum impact is achieved.

Public sector takes the lead

It seems that many public authorities are more advanced when applying principles from behavioural science than for-profit companies. The UK government leads the way. The book *Nudge* by the researchers Thaler and Sunstein made such an impression on UK Prime Minister David Cameron that he included it on the reading list of his Cabinet members and created space for a team of behavioural scientists in Downing Street in 2010, the so-called Behavioural Insights Team. In their book Thaler and Sunstein refute the idea that people are rational decision makers who process information without any effort and do not let themselves be swayed by emotions. The authors show that much of the decision process depends on the context. The Behavioural Insights Team advises the UK government on how to get people to make better choices for themselves, and how to make public policy and communication more effective. As part of this, in an experiment among 140,000 laggard taxpayers the British tax authority sent a reminder-to-pay letter referring to the good payment behaviour of the vast majority of their direct neighbours.[26] Immediately, the number of people who paid on time increased. Those who received a letter telling them that 9 out of 10 people in their town had already paid were significantly more likely to pay than those who received the regular reminder. If the British government extends this experiment on a national scale, it could return £160 million worth of tax debts and would free up collector resources that could generate an additional £30 million in tax revenue.

Is nudging shoppers right?

After the publication of *Nudge* in 2008 criticism sprang up regarding Thaler and Sunstein's vision. Indeed, authorities and companies could manipulate people by changing their choice structures. Are shoppers now subjected to political technocrats and incentive-thirsty chief executive officers? It is correct of course that the public authorities and companies try to convince shoppers to think or do something that they feel is right for shoppers. Shoppers should realize that in the case of social topics such as healthy food and taxation, choices are made under the influence of stakeholder organizations and they follow a democratic process. In the commercial arena it is perhaps more difficult to judge when nudging is right or wrong. There is something like nudging for profit. Let's assume the owner of a gym knows that the visit frequency declines significantly a few months after people have paid their annual fee. Will the owner come up with ideas to encourage people to keep on visiting the gym? I think they will, unless they know that the capacity of fitness machines is limited for the number of members and that they will serve current customers better if there are more fitness machines available. In all other cases, the gym owner probably also knows that the cost of acquiring new members is high and they are better off with a stable, loyal group of visitors. However, there are still many questions to be answered. If, as in the example earlier in this chapter, shoppers keep on choosing the medium-sized cup at Starbucks, will the company add larger cups to convince shoppers in turn to buy larger cups of coffee? Are cashiers at Shell petrol stations just being nice to shoppers when they point visitors to a special offer of delicious M&Ms? What about McDonald's – is the reminder of the mayonnaise a gesture of kindness or is this a way to get more money from the shopper? The core idea of nudging is that shoppers make such choices without much effort and are probably not aware of it at the exact moment of purchase. Therefore, Thaler and Sunstein make a plea for all nudging practices to be made public. They argue that if organizations share their nudges with pride, shoppers will have no reason to fear unethical behaviour from them. I agree and I would like to add that shoppers should take the opportunity to increase their insight into their own choice behaviour. Perhaps shoppers will then show more predictable and rational behaviour.

What can you do to make your shoppers happy?

Shoppers happily apply heuristics because this saves time and energy. Retailers may smooth and facilitate the shopping process by leveraging these heuristics through nudges. These nudges are especially relevant if the choices are complex, if the benefits come later, and if the shopper bears the costs of the decision early on in the process.

Which marketing strategies can retailers apply?

Shoppers like to think of themselves as rational decision makers, but most purchasing decisions are very context-dependent. This means that retailers have the opportunity to influence how and what choices are made, both in physical stores and online. At all times marketers should feel that they could publicly, and with pride, share any interventions they may implement. Otherwise, I would doubt whether their intentions are fair and sustainable.

Notes

1 Iyengar, S, Jiang, W and Huberman, G (2003) How Much Choice is Too Much?: Contributions to 401(k) Retirement Plans, Pension Research Council Working Paper [Online] http://system.nevada.edu/Nshe/ ?LinkServID=3F1030DA-E201-CE84-D4690C6A61458841

2 Cronqvist, H and Thaler, R (2004) [accessed 22 July 2015] Design choices in privatized social-security systems: learning from the Swedish experience, *American Economic Review* [Online] http://faculty.chicagobooth.edu/ Richard.Thaler/research/pdf/designchoices.pdf

3 Soman, D (2010) Option overload: dealing with choice complexity, *Rotman Magazine*, Fall, p 42

4 Ibid.

5 Schwartz, B (2004) *The Paradox of Choice: Why more is less*, Harper Perennial, New York

6 Simonson, I (1989) [accessed 22 July 2015] Choice based on reasons: the case of attraction and compromise effects, *Journal of Consumer Research* [Online] http://www.jstor.org/stable/2489315?seq=1#page_scan_tab_contents

7 Huber, J, Payne, J and Puto, C (1982) [accessed 22 July 2015] Adding asymmetrically dominated alternatives: violations of regularity and the similarity hypothesis, *Journal of Consumer Research*, [Online] https:// faculty.fuqua.duke.edu/~jch8/bio/Papers/ Huber%20Payne%20Puto%201982%20JoCR.pdf

8 Kahneman, D (2011) *Thinking, Fast and Slow*, Penguin, London

9 Thaler, R (1999) [accessed 22 July 2015] Mental accounting matters, *Journal of Behavioural Decision Making*, [Online] http://elearning2.uniroma1.it/ pluginfile.php/101759/mod_resource/content/1/Thaler1999.pdf

10 Ibid.

11 Gourville, J (1988) [accessed 22 July 2015] Pennies-a-day: the effect of temporal reframing on transaction evaluation, *Journal of Consumer Research* [Online] http://www.jstor.org/stable/10.1086/209517?seq=1#page_scan_ tab_contents

12 Kahneman, D (2011) *Thinking, Fast and Slow*, Penguin, London

13 Kelder, P (2014) [accessed 1 August 2015] Korting? Morgen geeft de concurrent evenveel of nog meer, *DM, Mediaplein* [Online] http://www.dmmediaplein.nl/marketing/korting-morgen-geeft- concurrent-evenveel-nog-meer/

14 Leach, W (2014) TriggerPoint, presentation at Shopper Insights in Action conference, Chicago.

15 Soman, D (2001) [accessed 22 July 2015] Effects of payment mechanism on spending behaviour: the role of rehearsal and immediacy of payments, *Journal of Consumer Research* [Online] http://www-2.rotman.utoronto.ca/facbios/file/ paymechjcr.pdf

16 Zhou, R and Soman, D (2003) [accessed 22 July 2015] Looking back: exploring the psychology of queuing and the effect of the number of people behind, *Journal of Consumer Research* [Online] http://www.bm.ust.hk/mark/staff/Rongrong2.pdf

17 Kahneman, D (2011) *Thinking, Fast and Slow*, Penguin, London

18 Gladwell, M (2012) *The Tipping Point: How little things can make a big difference*, Abacus, London

19 Holland, R, Hendriks, M and Aarts, H (2005) [accessed 22 July 2015] Smells like clean spirit, nonconscious effects of scent on cognition and behavior, *Psychological Science* [Online] http://goallab.nl/publications/documents/Holland,%20Hendriks,%20Aarts%20%282005%29%20-%20noncsious%20effects%20of%20scent%20on%20behavior.pdf

20 Berger, J and Fitzsimons, G (2008) [accessed 22 July 2015] Dogs on the street, pumas on your feet: how cues in the environment influence product evaluation and choice, *Journal of Marketing Research* [Online] http://jonahberger.com/wp-content/uploads/2013/02/Pumas-Paper.pdf

21 Salganik, M, Dodds, P and Watts, D (2006) [accessed 22 July 2015] Experimental study of inequality and unpredictability in an artificial cultural market, *Science Magazine* [Online] www.princeton.edu/~mjs3/salganik_dodds_watts06_full.pdf

22 Asch, S (1955) [accessed 22 July 2015] Opinions and social pressure, *Scientific American* [Online] http://www.lucs.lu.se/wp-content/uploads/2015/02/Asch-1955-Opinions-and-Social-Pressure.pdf

23 See [Online] https://en.wikipedia.org/wiki/Pepsi_Challenge

24 Thaler, R and Sunstein, C (2009) *Nudge: Improving decisions about health, wealth and happiness*, Penguin, New York

25 Schuttelaar & Partners, (2012) [accessed 22 July 2015] Helpt 'Nudgen' bij een gezonde en duurzame keuze? [Online] http://www.schuttelaar.nl/download/355

26 Cabinet Office Behavioural Insights Team, (2012) [accessed 22 July 2015] Applying behavioural insights to reduce fraud, error and debt [Online] https://www.gov.uk/government/uploads/system/uploads/attachment_data/file/60539/BIT_FraudErrorDebt_accessible.pdf

Understanding the shopper brain through neuro research

04

In Chapter 3 I showed how the discipline of psychology is influencing models and understanding in the marketing discipline. In this chapter I identify how a technology that has been widely applied in the medical world, neuro research, generates new insights into the emotions of shoppers. For too long marketers have relied on what shoppers say about their emotions, rather than probing to learn what the store and the services really mean to shoppers.

Neuro research has been applied in the medical world for many years and entered the marketing discipline in around 2005. With the help of scanning technologies such as functional magnetic resonance imaging (fMRI) and electroencephalography (EEG) retailers can objectively measure which part of their marketing message makes the deepest emotional impact, or which display is best remembered. The EEG technology allows brain readings while shoppers walk around with a cap on their head that holds together tens of sensors. The beauty of neuro research is that the scanning technology measures the signals that the shopper generates even before the shopper expresses them consciously in conversation. Therefore, neuro research addresses many issues in an industry that has relied too much on what shoppers actually say.

Why traditional surveys fail

After years of shopper research involving market researchers asking shoppers in a straightforward manner what they want, neuromarketing experiments now show us what shoppers have really been thinking and feeling. Since around 2005 neuro research has made tremendous developments and has taught practitioners many new things about the shopper. New insights have emerged due to advances in technology and are encouraged by a rising interest from the academic field. Slowly but surely marketing practitioners have come to realize that traditional survey-based shopper research does not deliver the quality of shopper knowledge that retailers need. Surveys have ingrained biases: the moment we ask a respondent to share a certain experience, the respondent changes the original data during their response. Traditional research techniques become outdated. They only speak to the rational part of the brain; they assume that shoppers only make rational choices and hope that shoppers can think about their behaviour in a conscious and discerning manner. Too often it is assumed that shoppers remember all data and observations and communicate these objectively and neutrally to the researcher. Within the market-research world there has been a discussion for tens of years about the relevance of the rational shopper, but marketing guru Lindstrom, in his book *Buyology* (2008), adjusted this image of the rational shopper in the marketing and research functions. It has become evident that shoppers make more than 95 per cent of their decisions subconsciously. Moreover, it is hard to identify the reasons why shoppers bought this product or that, or visited this exact store, using traditional research techniques only.

Benefits of neuro research

Neuro research can understand the shopper brain: it obtains the information without needing the shopper to think about the choices they make in a conscious manner. Of course, brain research is and remains an applicable tool. There are also other research instruments available that overcome some of the disadvantages of straightforward surveys. Think of indirect and association-based phrasing at exit interviews as shoppers leave the store, recognition of facial emotions, eye-tracking, accompanied shopping, shopping-behaviour observations, galvanic skin responses, pilot stores and household audit panels (such as TNS and GfK offer). One by one, it is worth considering adding these techniques to retail sales data that is obtained from companies such as Nielsen or IRI and that tell them how much retailers sell of each product. However, thanks to a number of advantages, neuro research is one up on them. In neuro research there is no manipulation by others, there is no rationalization in hindsight (as in the case of exit interviews and accompanied shopping), and it answers the why-question in a better way (in comparison to just observing shopping behaviour). All this makes a strong case for the importance of neuromarketing research, and the impact of applying the resulting knowledge of the workings of a shopper's brain to the retail marketing instruments.

The various ways in which neuro research can be applied can be demonstrated with a few practical examples. Traindl conducted a study in which price tags on shelves were displayed with a smiley face.[1] Results showed that shoppers perceived the price accompanied by a smiley face as being 7 per cent lower than a price tag without a smiley face. This is explained by the fact that shoppers are unconsciously attracted by pleasure and a feeling of reward, and the image of a smile is capable of creating such an effect. When I read such a study I always wonder how many price wars and disruption in grocery retail can be avoided purely by sticking smiley faces on a shelf. Traindl emphasizes the importance of communicating about product assortments through visuals. These lead to more brain activity. The German clothing discounter NKD, for example, succeeded in influencing the perception of assortment width (ie the number of product assortment types) through its use of visuals: NKD reduced the assortment, which could be perceived negatively by the shopper because they have less choice. However, through the use of certain visuals they could still obtain a favourable image of their assortment width. Neuro research suggested a preference for realistic rather than abstract shapes and found that moving images were not necessary. The result across a number of test stores was that as compared to NKD stores that did not undergo a change, the revenue rose by 17 per cent.

For neuro research retailers need support from neuro scientists who are able to interpret the results in a retail context and have specialized measuring equipment available. There are differences in technology, for example, in an fMRI scanner that people may not move, while EEG sensors on a shopper's head allow them to move around in a store. Neuro scientists will advise retailers which technique is best; for practitioners it is probably sufficient to know that these techniques have been applied in the medical world for tens of years. By searching for the cause of conditions such as autism, Alzheimer's, mania and phobia disorders, medical scientists attempt to determine which part of the brain is responsible for attention, emotions and memory. Brain signals occur in nanoseconds, but despite their speed they can be measured accurately. In this way the whole process of perception, data absorption, information processing, emotion, judgement and action can be tracked. The brain signals reveal something of the shopper before they change their emotion as a result of social pressure, or perhaps even because they want to show off.

Another thing that makes neuro research special is that it not only gives explanations for certain shopping behaviours, but it also helps to give insight into biological differences as a result of gender and age. It provides a broad insight into shopper responses in a specific context. The brains of modern man are the result of their existence in pre-history and their evolution over the past 200,000 years. From this perspective, whatever has happened in the past few hundred or even thousand years has made little difference to the way the shoppers' brains function. As strange as this sounds, the behaviour that people showed 200,000 years ago, so to speak dressed in a bear skin wandering around a cave, can still be used as illustration for shopping behaviour happening today. The application of neuro research knowledge can revolutionize the commercial retail world. It offers better insights into shoppers. For example, shoppers unconsciously stay away from sharp corners – this is as a result of evolution. These corners warn the brain that the body might be in danger of being hurt. In addition, completely smooth surfaces rarely exist in nature and this is a warning signal in itself. From this, I found through neuro research that shoppers have an unconscious aversion to right-angled gondola ends. Shoppers are more drawn into aisles that start with a rounded gondola end and offer a moderate visual variation halfway along the aisle, for example via a protruding piece of merchandising or colour blocks. Neuro research delivers these types of practical suggestions that improve the shopper flow in a store and make the retail experience more attractive.

Gender differences

A big win from neuro research is that retail marketers have an enhanced understanding of why female and male shoppers behave differently in-store and throughout the shopping trip. Evolution has prepared the brains for different tasks and this partly explains why men and women have distinct shopping habits. During the first eight weeks of embryo development there is no difference in the brains of male and female embryos. Under the influence of hormones such as testosterone some brain parts develop more than others in men than in women and vice versa. For example, women have a larger corpus callosum that connects the left and right brains. This results in the well-known head start that women enjoy in the areas of multitasking, adopting a holistic or helicopter perspective, and combining rationality and emotions. The realization that men and women have different habits is very relevant to retail marketing. There are many examples of how insights into gender differences can influence the layout of a store. The arrangement of long, straight lines with logically stapled products is perfectly aligned with the result-driven manner in which some men shop. Female shoppers study their environment more, orientate themselves by focusing on a few points or objects that they use as a beacon, and they enjoy more of the journey towards the end goal. These characteristics are a result of evolution, and it shows that there have always been gender-based differences in the human brain.

Age differences

In addition to gender differences, neuro researcher Pradeep points to the fact that brains change with age.[2] Sometimes the brain changes quickly, like at birth or during menopause. Brains reach their optimal level around the age of 22 and evolve until the age of 60. Therefore, it makes sense for retailers to investigate shopping behaviour in different age groups. For example, shoppers aged 60 and above do not necessarily become more forgetful, but research shows that they have become less capable to resist distractions. This implies that they feel more comfortable in a retail context without moving images and with 'quiet' colours. Communication in magazines and on-shelf banners targeted at people over 60 should, according to the research findings, ideally be very straightforward and have, relatively speaking, a lot of white space.

Applications of neuro research

Most neuro research in the commercial arena focuses on understanding the consumer and consumption occasions: the evaluation of television commercials, product concept testing and the discovery of subconscious associations with the brand. Mainly in the United States awareness has risen that neuro research can also be applied to gain a better understanding of people within a shopping context. Neuro research is useful to apply in a range of ways in retail, and can answer such questions as:

- How can a retailer improve navigation in-store or in front of the shelves?
- What is the optimal shape, colour and material for the store furniture?
- Which displays get most attention?

- Which type of in-store communication is most effective?
- How should promotions be displayed attractively in a leaflet?

Neuro research offers a great understanding of all of these questions. Research into these questions may deliver category- or context-specific recommendations, but there are also a number of universal principles that go straight through all categories, cultures and backgrounds. On one hand, retail marketers can start applying these universal principles in-store, online or in magazines. On the other hand, they need to know which guidelines are only relevant for a certain category or target group. A good example of a universal principle is the attraction value of an image of a child, possibly accompanied by a mother, for parents. Such an image reminds shoppers subconsciously of their desire to protect and care for their own family, and works particularly well in the vicinity of baby products. An image of a face works well in general. From an evolutionary perspective, people automatically look first for someone else's eyes in order to judge whether or not they are safe. The next clue is the shape of the mouth. Therefore, the attention of shoppers is subconsciously drawn to images of people in-store, which can be used as a tool to help shoppers navigate more easily or pay more attention to a certain category. In *The Buying Brain* Pradeep describes the ideal shopping experience based on the neuro research he conducted:

- Shoppers scan a store to find out what has changed and what is new from their previous visit. Signs with images work better than text to avoid overstimulation and allow the information process to run more efficiently.

- From a neurological perspective images in a magazine or online store should be placed on the left and text on the right. The shopper's eyes deliver what they observe on the left to right side of the brain, and the right side of the brain is better equipped to deal with visuals; the left side of the brain is better at numbers and semantics. If the information is provided with the text to the left and the image to the right, the shopper needs to make more effort. It just runs more smoothly the other way around.

- Retail contexts that imitate the consumption moment prompt greater action. This principle could be applied in a store by placing baking products in a display with the look and feel of an oven. Or the shopper hears a can opening when they enter the soft drinks aisle. When promoting breakfast items in a leaflet, retail marketers could use an image of a nicely covered Sunday morning breakfast table accompanied by the many happy faces of the family, rather than focusing too much on the display of the promoted products.

- Entertainment, preferably delivered by a human being rather than a display or some form of technology, makes the mission-driven shopper more relaxed. In addition, it softens the pain of making a purchase.

Practical suggestions from neuro research

I have had the privilege to work alongside neuro scientists since 2007. My passion for retail always made me focus on this question: how can I convert the brain readings into practical retail solutions? Here is a summary of what I have learned:

- Shoppers enter aisles more often if gondola ends are rounded. Shoppers avoid walking down long aisles because it subconsciously makes them afraid they will have no way to escape. Ideally, they would like to be able to leave the aisle after some six or seven metres through a passage in one of the racks. If this takes out too much merchandising space, the shopper is more attracted by aisles with a visual interruption halfway down such as a floor display, protruding shelf element or special lighting feature. This makes it more visually appealing, helping shoppers to relax. Finally, the shopper brains use the gondola ends to navigate through the store. Therefore, they expect that the product assortment presented on the gondola's end should provide a logical clue for the merchandise to be found in the remainder of the aisle.

- Shoppers appreciate support, and like to be shown examples of the differing ways they can use a product as a consumer. A retailer may choose to list an infinite number of promotions in a leaflet, but the shopper's eye will be more drawn to a photo that shows the happy faces of a mother and children baking a cake together. A reference to the required ingredients and special offers next to the image will do. In magazines, food retailers should, for example, try to display pictures of food that is ready to be eaten, rather than showing raw pieces of meat and other unprepared food. Shoppers prefer to anticipate tasting something rather than be reminded of the slaughter of the animal and the effort involved to prepare the meal.

- A related concept is the working of mirror neurons. If shoppers see images of people smiling in the store, the mirror neurons are fired off automatically, and the shoppers are more likely to walk around with a smile themselves. This improves their mood. For example, one application of this concept could involve an image showing someone bringing food or drink to their mouth, so literally on the cusp of actual consumption. This provokes pleasure signals sent to our brain and shoppers already feel good about the product before buying or touching it.

- Shoppers use the eyes of others to judge whether an encounter will be friendly or hostile. Therefore, faces on displays and in magazines can be useful to target shoppers: after looking at the eyes (and mouth) of the displayed face, shoppers will automatically gaze in the direction that the displayed face is looking. Retailers can use these insights to improve the layout of their magazines and stores.

- Subconsciously the shoppers seek real and true experiences. They would rather be in a place that has happy faces, which provoke positive emotions. Images of natural products (fruit, vegetables) also generate positive emotions. The images of food on shelves and walls in-store should be high quality as shoppers will hone in on this and will know intuitively if, for example, the basket holding the vegetables is made of real wood, imitation wood or even plastic. Using wooden racks enhances the impression that the merchandised products are real, authentic and organic. The downside is that shoppers may perceive the product as more expensive if it is in wooden, natural displays rather than in metal racks.

- Shopper brains enjoy touching anything round and soft. Retailers should find out shopper touch while in the store. A new 'touch' moment could generate a new shopping experience. Touch moments during the shopping trip can include:
  - the self-scanning device;
  - the shopping trolley;
  - racks of plastic bags at the fruit department;
  - the recycling machine for plastic bottles;
  - the payment system.

- This perhaps sounds obvious, but retailers should attempt to offer solutions. Positioning a food product as part of a meal, for example, helps the shopper to see how they could solve a problem.

The question arises: are our brains pre-fixed to the point where we are left with no free choices? Is neuro research always accurate? We still have a long way to go when it comes to learning to apply and judge the findings from neuro research. This not only applies to commercial market research, but also for other disciplines such as biology and psychology. There is a hefty debate that sets deterministic neuro scientists against psychologists and psychiatrists. The first group believes that the brains determine everything that people experience. In short, people are their brains and they have no free willpower. The latter group believes that the brain and the spirit are fundamentally different. The spirit is the real you and is shaped by things like life experience and the family environment. Personally, I am not a determinist. I think that brains will continue to adapt to varying circumstances over time. At the same time I acknowledge that there is a large amount of neuro research that proves that the instinctive brain responses are much more equal for shoppers with the same gender and age group than I would have expected based on upbringing, culture and personal values. Therefore, retail marketers are best prepared for developing shopper insights when they combine findings from neuro research and behavioural/psychological research.

What can you do to make your shoppers happy?

By applying the findings of neuro research, retailers can create shopping environments that feel comfortable in a natural, original way.

Neuro research as a new methodology stimulates fact-based decision making in the retail industry, which has previously depended too much on opinions.

The technology of neuro research offers an insight into what shoppers really want even before they express the desire, and includes both functional and emotional aspects of the decision. This therefore allows the retailer to serve the shopper in a better way.

Which marketing strategies can retailers apply?

Many retailers want to appeal to a broad audience, and neuro research allows them to understand deeply ingrained preferences of the human race. These preferences can be converted into concrete solutions. Through neuro research, retailers can learn where their store layout needs improvement or which aspects of their promotional features do not work.

The application of neuro research in the retail industry is still relatively new. Retailers have the opportunity to create a competitive insight into the optimal shopping environment if they embrace the methodology now.

Notes

1 Traindl, A (2006) *Undasch Shop-Concept*, Shop, Aktuell 100

2 Pradeep, A (2010) *The Buying Brain: Secrets for selling to the subconscious mind*, John Wiley & Sons, New Jersey

PART THREE
Channel choices

Channel preference

05

The future of the hypermarket channel

This book started by emphasizing the importance of having a better understanding of the emotions of shoppers. Once these emotions are understood, retailers should engage with shoppers continuously to understand where to drive their organization and where to invest. One of the investment decisions to be made is the type of channel the retailer wants to use to service shoppers. This decision requires a great deal of capital, and therefore has a long-term impact on the retail organization. The hypermarket channel is one instance where some retailers have failed to connect with shoppers after a number of years and noticed too late that shoppers had started to shift their preferences to other channels, such as discount chains, pound stores, convenience stores and digital media. These channels increasingly meet the shopper needs better. In the next chapter I explain why online shopping has become so appealing to shoppers. First, I focus on the reasons why shoppers lost interest in the hypermarket channel, and I offer suggestions for new strategy directions. I illustrate this by focusing on Carrefour, a French retailer with a large international presence that is closely associated with the rise and fall of hypermarkets. It offers important lessons on the necessity of staying in close connection with a large number of shoppers with ever more divergent needs.

Since the Second World War, grocery chains in Western countries have become bigger and bigger. In some countries such as the United States and France the large format dominates the market: they are named super-centres in North America and hypermarkets elsewhere. German shoppers prefer smaller formats such as discount stores and supermarkets and even Walmart has not proved successful there (Walmart entered the country in 1998 and left in 2006 at an estimated cost of $1 billion: one of their biggest ever failures).[1] On the other hand, in emerging markets like Argentina, Brazil and Russia the large format still maintains popularity. As mentioned above, one retailer that has become intertwined with the hypermarket format is Carrefour, one of the largest retail chains in the world of French origin. Carrefour has experienced much trouble since the turn of the 21st century, problems that became very visible in 2008 when the markets they operate in also came under pressure. As much of its revenue comes from the hypermarket channel, the question arises as to whether its decline indicates that the hypermarket channel has reached the end of its life cycle, or if the decline can be attributed to factors specific to Carrefour. Or could it be both? Here, I look for an answer from the perspective of the shopper.

Carrefour at a crossroads

Carrefour derives its name from the location of its first store in Annecy in 1957, which was at a crossroads or *carrefour* in French. A better name could not have been chosen, because the company seems to move from one crossroads to another. The period 2005–15 saw Carrefour achieve stable sales (while the company was in decline in Western Europe it was growing in some South American countries), so it was time for a change. In the words of Margaret Thatcher: 'Standing in the middle of the road is very dangerous: You get knocked down by traffic from both sides.' Until 2000 Carrefour was on an acquisition route; next it started to sell off operations in countries such as Japan. Major change happened when private capitalists invested in 2007 when they thought that Carrefour was at the bottom of its performance.[2] However, accelerated by the financial crisis in 2008 they lost most of their investment and, as a result, there were many changes in leadership. Carrefour appointed Lars Oloffson in 2009 to bring back growth, starting with the hypermarket division. Oloffson launched the plan to revitalize its hypermarket in 2010 under the name Carrefour Planet. A lot of effort went into this attempt but Carrefour as an organization never sailed in calm water. Colony Capital, an American property-investment fund, and Bernard Arnault, private investor and CEO of luxury goods company LVMH, which own together around 15 per cent of Carrefour, applied heavy pressure for better results and better dividend payments. Impactful strategic decisions were made, including the separation of Carrefour's discount division DIA and DIA's listing on the Spanish stock market in 2011 (though the French Dia stores returned to Carrefour in 2014). Other initiatives were less successful. In 2011 Carrefour attempted to merge its Brazilian business with a local competitor, Pão de Açúcar. As of 2015 its idea of spinning off its property division has not yet been executed either: the property division has remained under Carrefour's control so far. In 2012 the shareholders Colony Capital and Groupe Arnault forced the resignation of Lars Oloffson after five consecutive profit warnings, market share loss in its main market (France) and after losing 40 per cent of their original investment. Apart from the significant improvement of the hypermarkets, the number of crossroads has remained high for Carrefour. Crossroads they face as of 2015 include:

- Will Carrefour remain operating globally or will it become a European retailer? Carrefour's current CEO, Georges Plassat, withdrew from countries such as Greece, Colombia, Indonesia and Malaysia, but stayed in Brazil, Argentina and China.

- Will the central organization keep the last word in decisions through, for example, the global purchasing team Carrefour World Trade in Geneva, or will power shift to country organizations? I am not sure which path will be chosen, but currently shoppers experience more local product assortments and store managers enjoy a higher level of decision making at store level.

- Finally, what is the role of the hypermarket in the face of the increasing popularity of small formats and online shopping? I focus on the challenge of hypermarkets here, but it is clear that for Carrefour this cannot be separated from other challenges.

Carrefour, or a hypermarket problem?

In 2010 Carrefour experienced serious declines of its identical hypermarket sales in its top four European markets: France –0.6 per cent, Spain –3.4 per cent, Italy –3.1 per cent and Belgium –6.0 per cent. In the first three markets the problems multiplied and the numbers were even worse in 2011. Only in Belgium, where Carrefour conducted a rigorous restructuring in 2011 and divested stores, was there an uplift in sales. Unfortunately, Belgium is the smallest market of the four and it had become clear that significant changes had to take place. These numbers were alarming for two reasons: 1) Hypermarkets delivered 63 per cent of the total Carrefour revenue; 2) 55 per cent of the hypermarket sales came from just four Western countries: France, Spain, Italy and Belgium.

The problems of Carrefour, and especially the Carrefour hypermarkets, leave the impression that the hypermarket is at the end of its life cycle. Since 2000 the market shares of hypermarkets in Europe have fluctuated around 35 per cent. However, behind this fluctuating 35 per cent there are countries where hypermarkets are on the rise as well as countries where shoppers are moving away from hypermarkets. For example, in Eastern Europe the hypermarket is still a growth factor, as is Carrefour. To say the same thing differently, Carrefour had to address Carrefour-specific issues and problems with the hypermarket in saturated, Western markets.

Reasons for the growth of hypermarkets

Let's investigate the rise of the hypermarket in Europe from the perspective of the shopper. The hypermarket concept comes from the United States, where discount department stores integrated large assortments of food and non-food. Based on new large stores in the United States, the Belgian super-market Grand Bazar opened the first hypermarket in Europe, in Oudergem, in 1961.[3] Two years later the French retailer Carrefour opened its first hypermarket in Sainte-Geneviève-des-Bois, France. However, Carrefour can now claim to have opened the first hypermarket as it acquired the GIB group in 2000. Carrefour converted the former Grand Bazar store to a Carrefour hypermarket. The original Oudergem store measured 9,100 square metres, which was considered gigantic for its time as compared to the French Sainte-Geneviève-des-Bois store, which measured 2,500 square metres.

The grocery market at the time was primarily made up of smaller super-markets and traditional stores with over-the-counter service. The hypermarket broke some of the rules of the game and the shopper welcomed this. The new rules of the game are:

- Assortment – everything you need in one shopping trip:
  - large choice of brands, product variations and formats;
  - not just food, but also non-food;
  - tapping into trends in categories such as clothing and articles for household use.
- Price – always competing, often the lowest:
  - low, fixed prices and attractive promotions;
  - easy comparison of prices (this used to be more difficult);
  - continuous adjustment of prices in response to competition.

- Service – efficient customer focus:
  - longer opening hours;
  - easy parking.

The new hypermarket met some resistance because it snatched sales from traditional, smaller supermarkets. However, the hypermarket fulfilled many functional and emotional needs. On one hand, the shopper could buy everything under one roof and that made shopping better and made life simpler. On the other hand, the new gigantic store created a full day's outing full of surprises. In the 1960s prosperity grew, disposable income rose and shoppers loved spending their increased incomes on durable consumer products in the hypermarket. Apart from this, the hypermarket could thrive because other conditions were met (Figure 5.1). National and local governments liberalized the legislation for labour, zoning plans and zoning areas.

FIGURE 5.1   Growth drivers – hypermarket

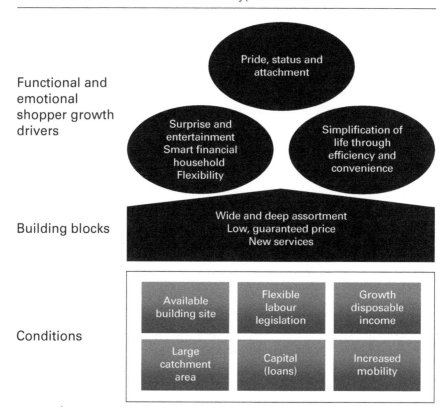

The advantages for hypermarkets disappear

As of 2015 the European hypermarket is more than 55 years old. Meanwhile, society, the competitive field and technology have changed to such an extent that the shopper has now developed completely different needs. Think of urbanization and the ageing of society, which cause shoppers to prefer to have a grocery store in their neighbourhood rather than at the far outskirts of the ever-growing cities. The internet has become a new purchasing channel, especially for the non-food products that are offered in the hypermarket such as clothing, shoes, books, music, domestic appliances. Citizens have become more vocal and demand better service. These are not all new changes, but together they made redundant the pillar stones of the success of the hypermarket of 50 years ago. For some hypermarket brands it was easier to find an answer to this than another.

Assortment

- In the last 15 years shoppers showed hesitation if they wanted a lot of choice and could not actually cope with the large assortment. While at first shoppers thought it efficient to find everything under one roof, it now comes across as overwhelming. Because the hypermarket is ideal for a large shopping trip, the visit frequency is lower, but if the hypermarket does not offer a differentiating category, even this large trip may be cancelled in the busy lives of many shoppers.

- The complete offer of fashion, consumer electronics, home decoration and so on in competing formats both in the centre of towns and on the outskirts has become more differentiating and attractive. Category killers in non-food such as Toys 'R' Us, Mediamarkt and Zara undermine the claim that the hypermarket always offers the widest and deepest assortment.

Price

- Discount chains such as Aldi and Lidl have added new categories both in dry groceries and in fresh produce categories. Lidl has varied the number of products over the years in order to find the right balance between fuller baskets and keeping their promises of low prices, smart shopping and efficiency.

- In addition to the discounters in each of the four large countries where Carrefour operates hypermarkets, successful national and regional players have risen. Colruyt in Belgium, Leclerc in France, Mercadona in Spain and Essalunga in Italy have beaten Carrefour on its price image by pricing the right mix of weekly groceries at the lowest level possible. By purchasing together with other supermarket chains through international buying groups they can still compete with Carrefour, although it is the second largest food retailer after Walmart and Tesco (total revenue in 2014 is about €75 billion).

- Legislation in many countries forbids offering products below cost price. This is unfortunate for hypermarkets as it was their custom to sharpen their price image with loss-leader categories.

- It seems as if hypermarkets cannot escape from the cycle of the wheel of retailing. This old concept from retail says that new players in retail attract shoppers with low prices based on a low-cost strategy, either with a new retail brand or their current one. With the passage of time such new market players attempt to avoid price competition by adding new services and products. In this way they let go of their low-cost strategy. This leads to the rise of new price fighters and the circle is completed (Figure 5.2).

FIGURE 5.2   The retail life cycle

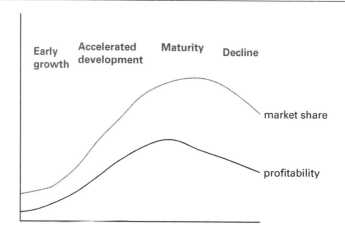

SOURCE: Based on Davidson, Bates, Bass (1976) The retail life cycle, *Harvard Business Review* [Online] http://www.scribd.com/doc/48155351/retail-life-cycle#scribd

Service

- Services and facilities such as parking space and longer opening hours are no longer enough of a cause of differentiation.

- In addition, service is not just delivered through physical and functional aspects that smooth the shopping process. Service also revolves around attention, preferably from store staff. The vocal shopper desires solutions that are tailored to their needs, and this is not met by many long rows of racks where the shopper has to start the treasure hunt without the help of store employees.

Retail life cycle

The concept of a life cycle exists for retail channels, just as it does for products. This term was introduced by Davidson, Bates and Bass in 1976 and offers a good insight into the necessity of a timely, strategic reorientation for retailers.[4] In 2006 Perrigot and Cliquet proved that the French hypermarket channel was saturated, the Spanish hypermarkets were nearing saturation and the Italian hypermarkets were still growing.[5] The hypermarket in Western Europe is in the maturity phase of the retail life cycle because there are many competitors, too many square metres of hypermarket available per household, and new distribution channels popping up. As a result the revenue hardly grows and the profitability is moderate. The life cycle is like a natural, evolutionary process that is impossible to stop, but a company may either slow down or avoid the decline. Davidson, Bates and Bass give a number of suggestions to show how companies can do this, including tapping into new market segments, keeping profits up by working more efficiently, lowering risk by pushing the burdens to suppliers, and copying parts of the model that successful new entrants use. A final recommendation is to ensure that the retailer under pressure is never restricted to only one type of channel.

Strategies to turn hypermarkets around

The revenue of the hypermarket in West European countries has been stagnating since the mid 1990s. The hypermarket no longer meets shoppers' needs when it comes to efficient and pleasurable shopping. The shoppers have proved this – fewer shoppers are visiting hypermarkets, and less frequently as well. Perhaps at first the loss of sales could be balanced by the help of promotions, enlarging stores or acquisitions. Carrefour is famous for its creative bookkeeping, for example by including or excluding petrol sales in the annual reports in whatever way looks most positive. However, the hypermarket will only remain relevant for shoppers if retailers such as Auchan and Carrefour make strategic choices. In an old but still topical article from 1997 McKinsey describes four strategic alternatives for retailers with hypermarkets:[6]

1 *Scaling up*
   Using mergers and acquisitions, the retailer can obtain better margins. The larger scale improves its negotiation position against suppliers and it allows overhead costs to be allocated across more stores and sales.

2 *Stronger retail brand*
   By better branding, the emotional force of attraction and loyalty of the shopper increase. Focus should lie on food and drinks and after that only those non-food items that shoppers purchase frequently. The retailer will attempt to increase the share of private labels to the same level that supermarkets have in the category, in order to stimulate the profitable sales of fresh produce and start in-store concepts of other brands, as has been done by Virgin.

3 *Concept renewal*
   In this strategy the retailer differentiates its offer to appeal to more target groups. Apart from the routine shopping trips where the shopper replenishes their supplies in large quantities, the retailer seeks to prompt other trips. A good example is the 'Easy Break' concept of Carrefour in Brussels to stimulate convenience trips. Easy Break is a concept where shoppers enter an area with drinks, lunch items and snacks through a separate entry and the shopper can either continue for a larger shopping trip or immediately leave though the checkout at the front of the store. As part of this strategy the retailer can leverage its advantage of space by varying the non-food offer at regular intervals using changes of the season, tapping into trend changes, or promoting annual events such as back to school, Mother's Day and Father's Day.
   The retailer may also choose to differentiate the hypermarket brand itself. Auchan provides a good example of this in Russia where it operates with three hypermarket versions: Auchan City for the

inner cities, Radouga (Rainbow) for middle-sized cities and the Auchan brand itself at the edges of large cities. The Auchan store outside Moscow measures some 17,000 square metres, which is much larger than Auchan City of some 4,000 square metres. The size of a Radouga for smaller cities sits between these numbers.

4   *Concept extension*
With this strategy, the hypermarket introduces two of its essential elements – reliability and value for money – to a set of new categories. Often these are services such as insurance, holidays and petrol, which take up an ever larger share of disposable income in Western Europe. The retailer also broadens its concept with alternative channels attached to the hypermarket such as 'drive-throughs' and home shopping.

Carrefour Planet as a solution

Most likely, there is not one clearly superior strategy option for retailers with hypermarkets, and McKinsey's four strategies (as set out in the previous section) can be applied together. Carrefour chose a combination of the last three options for Carrefour Planet. The new strategic direction was set when Carrefour teams in Belgium, France and Spain each worked on a new hypermarket, until CEO Lars Oloffson bundled their efforts together as one of his seven initiatives to turn the Carrefour organization around. The working group reinventing the hypermarket was also known by the name I-6, the sixth initiative. Recognizing the confluence from different countries it is laudable that Carrefour trialled its ideas in pilot stores in three countries at more or less the same time in 2010:

- Waterloo/Mont-Saint-Jean, near Brussels in Belgium;
- Vénissieux and Écully, two suburbs of Lyon in France;
- Alcobendas and El Pinar, cities close to Madrid in Spain.

All pilot stores contributed to the final version of Carrefour Planet. The Carrefour Planet store in Vénissieux formed the foundation and was enriched with elements from the other stores such as the set-up of groceries from El Pinar and the successful book department with reading lights and comfortable chairs from Mont-Saint-Jean. The concept was most crystallized in the sixth Planet store, in Móstoles, a city near Madrid. With the integration of all those experiments Carrefour took account of all national and local differences due to shopper preferences and competition.

Seven initiatives of Carrefour for higher growth and margin

1   Revitalize the Carrefour brand.

2   Improve the price image.

3   Disseminate and adopt best practices.

4   Simplify Carrefour organization and structures.

5   Overhaul the operating model to optimize operating costs and reduce inventories, while improving customer service.

6   Optimizing and reinventing the hypermarket.

7   Reorganization of purchasing processes.

Of course, all seven initiatives interact with each other. Their focus has been on the reinvention of the hypermarket model as the most important approach to restructure the company.

Shortly after the opening I visited the six pilot stores to see how Carrefour brought its idea of the future hypermarket into reality. My first impression was that Carrefour wanted to excel in fresh produce. This will help to increase the visit frequency, improve store atmosphere and offer a higher-than-average margin. High-quality fresh produce was complemented by dry groceries to meet the widest needs, as well as only non-food items that were purchased frequently. The improvement of Carrefour's price image had to come primarily from the dry groceries department. The atmosphere was lacking as the racks were high, with boxes piled on the highest shelf, and there was no marking or signals and no special lighting. Carrefour usually gave price signals by placing its Carrefour Discount brand in a prominent first location in the aisle and by building extended promotional gondola ends. For each of its non-food departments Carrefour selected a different competitive benchmark, and as a result the price experience is distinct. It might not offer the lowest price in the market but it sought to compete with the strongest retailer in each category. So in consumer electronics Carrefour wanted to have lower prices than Mediamarkt and in fashion it wanted to beat Zara. Although the fresh produce department may look fantastic, there is a price tag attached to it. Each country chooses the most beneficial fresh food categories. Further differentiation of Carrefour Planet had to come from seasonality and festival days, for which it created exhibition space, and from special services such as baby and child-care centres. In this manner it exploited its advantage of more space. In order to increase shopper penetration to former levels and to remove the hesitation of coming to a hypermarket at all, Carrefour pulled out all the stops to make the shopping trip more efficient and comfortable. Think of wider aisles, access to the store both at food and non-food departments, self-scanning and the logical placements of permanent displays such as, in Spain, Coca-Cola close to frozen pizza. Navigation in stores was improved with large, round ceiling hangers above 'worlds' of categories and by merchandising products high on shelves in eye-catching colour combinations. For example, brightly coloured towels were piled high so that shoppers could see the textile category from a long way away.

Strengths of Carrefour Planet

In my opinion, the strengths of Carrefour Planet stores are fourfold, as set out below.

Emphasis on fresh produce

The enormous product assortment, the space, the special lighting, the handwritten signs and the many staff members in a Carrefour Planet give the shopper the feeling that they are at a market, like the market hall La Grande Épicerie in Paris. This is not to say that Carrefour offered more fresh products than before. With the introduction of the Planet concept, Carrefour spoke of the things the consumer needed, and sorted categories on the basis of how a shopper recognizes and divides groups of products. Carrefour had discovered this through loyalty card analysis. For example, the fruit and vegetable department was made 33 per cent larger by making aisles wider and by different merchandising. Carrefour also expanded the offered items by 5 per cent to meet consumer needs (for example, offering more types of apples). However, in terms of the number of individual products (stockkeeping units), it lowered its offer by 13 per cent. Fresh products allowed the widest differentiation, and in each country the destination category was tailored to the local market. In Belgium I found that Carrefour was the only service retailer to offer fish in a service department, while in Spain the exhibition of hams and other meat products made my mouth water.

Dry groceries as a discounter

Of course, Carrefour still offered many A-brands at the dry grocery department, but the feeling the shopper got was like being in a discounter: limited lighting, high racks with boxes of stock on top in the French stores, illogical placement of detergents between food categories in Spain. Altogether it delivered the necessary price signal but the downside was that it was sometimes difficult to find products and it was hard to navigate with a shopping trolley. Some grocery categories received special treatment. At the wine department, for example, shoppers got advice from wine experts and could obtain information digitally from monitors. Biological and organic products received much more space than they deserved on the basis of their sales. In Écully these biological products got three times more space than they contributed to the sales of the store, and on top of that the location, prominently placed at the entrance, was great. In later Planet stores the biological category was downsized and moved to a later stage of the shopping trip at the fruit-and-vegetable market square.

Limited non-food

Under the name 'multi-specialist' Carrefour cut the number of non-food categories that were selling too few and delivering little or even no margin. Carrefour reduced space for non-food significantly, for example it allocated 12 per cent less space to fashion and 5 per cent less space to consumer electronics. Categories such as Do-It-Yourself disappeared and my impression was that the space allocation between food and non-food products had been changed from 60 per cent in favour of non-food to 60 per cent in favour of food, so exactly the reverse of the previous split. Carrefour might not have gone far enough with the elimination of space for some categories. In the French Planet stores the fashion space offered no inspiration, no functional items such as mirrors, and the clothing was not considered trendy at the time. What I realized is that Carrefour differentiates from supermarkets by offering non-food items in the same shopping trip but the offer was not enough to differentiate it when compared to specialist brands such as Mediamarkt.

Special services

Of course the Planet stores gave more attention to services such as insurance, travel, home delivery and Carrefour's checkout system of 'fila unica'. This means there is only one line for checkouts and, as soon as there is a checkout available, the first in line may step forward. A couple of services seemed to hit the mark. In France and Spain shoppers could leave their children at a crèche, parents could change nappies and feed babies in a quiet space and some shopping trolleys could carry around both the shopper's groceries and baby. At the entrance of some Planets there was a selling space for snacks and simple meals consumed during a break. This made going through the whole store redundant and was attractive to employees from nearby offices. Another great idea was a bar in the middle of a Spanish Planet store. This gave an excellent reason to take a break during a long shopping trip, to drink Carrefour branded coffee and bring snacks to the shoppers' attention. Only a Wi-Fi connection was missing. However, and unfortunately I come back to weaknesses, some of the services were question marks for me. In Vénissieux shoppers could get a haircut in the middle of the hypermarket while other shoppers were selecting their health and beauty products. I am not sure if that would work for me. I am not only thinking of being in the public view of colleagues and neighbours who shop there too, but also of my shopping trolley containing frozen products. Spanish Planet stores offered bike repair services, but first of all these Planets are only accessible by car and, secondly, I wonder who might bring a bike to be serviced in the middle of the store, wheeling it by the cucumbers and Spanish hams?

Is Planet the answer to the hypermarket challenges?

According to Carrefour the revenue of a Carrefour hypermarket increased by 7 per cent after remodelling to a Carrefour Planet. This is a terrific increase for a channel and retail brand that was in such stormy weather. However, after the first stores opened, the question was asked immediately if Carrefour did not need a higher revenue growth to justify the investments. Full remodelling cost €4.2 million and refreshments cost €1.9 million. In the original plans announced at the start in 2010, Carrefour hoped to fully remodel 245 hypermarkets in Western Europe and refresh 255 stores by early 2013. In total, it was looking to invest about €1.5 billion. Carrefour hoped for an incremental sales growth of 18 per cent over the years 2010 to 2015 in combination with significantly better margins. At the beginning of 2012 Carrefour put the remodelling on hold, and after the departure of Oloffson the Planet brand has disappeared. By the end of 2011 Carrefour had remodelled only 81 of the envisioned 500 stores and spent €400 million (or €4.9 million per hypermarket), above 60 per cent more than it had planned for. Only the

Planet stores in Belgium had been successful; however, the Belgian hyper-markets had deteriorated so badly before the introduction of Planet that probably anything would have worked.

During the restructuring Carrefour attempted to reduce the remodelling costs by standardizing the processes and materials and through contributions from suppliers, but it has not been enough. The shareholders decided to stop Carrefour Planet. Carrefour removed the letters Planet from the roofs of all hypermarket stores. The new CEO Georges Plassat compared the Planet adventure to a trip into outer space from which everyone returned by TGV. He announced that he wanted to keep the name Carrefour only for hyper-markets. The other formats, such as supermarkets and convenience stores, were to use the Carrefour logo instead of the Carrefour name from that moment.

Concluding thoughts

The Planet concept was a great leap forward for Carrefour. It made clear choices in its product assortment, improved its price image, beat competition through its fresh image, rationalized non-food, added new services and took account of regional and local differences. Through the application of loyalty card data it could personalize the shopper experience. I think the Carrefour Planet was a refreshed hypermarket and made the Carrefour brand stronger. However, the Planet concept was not a revolutionary different hypermarket. With the Planet initiative Carrefour has not been able to escape the wheel of retail. To achieve that, Carrefour should meet current and future shopper needs more creatively. Think of Carrefour hypermarkets that become a daily outing. Carrefour may try to lengthen its stay in the maturity phase of hypermarkets with new refreshments and new remodelling; however, lessons from the revolving wheel of retail teach us that newer formats such as convenience stores and online stores have a more promising future in Western Europe.

In conclusion, the hypermarket channel in Western Europe is in its maturity phase. This is different from what happens in emerging countries of the world like China and Russia, where the channel is gaining increasing popularity. The players in the channel in Western Europe could attempt to extend the maturity phase, but this is at incremental cost so they are well advised to develop new distribution channels as well. The response of Carrefour could perfectly reflect this challenge if it decides to invest in hypermarkets in emerging countries and extends its stay in the mature European channel until it finds a suitable solution to meet the needs of the shoppers of the future.

What can you do to make your shoppers happy?

Large formats with industrial merchandising are replaced with small formats that cater to shoppers with fluctuating needs and busy lifestyles in large cities.

Retailers can make shoppers feel comfortable in large formats, for example by breaking up aisles, using more natural materials and offering products most frequently purchased first.

Which marketing strategies can retailers apply?

The retail life cycle shows that low-cost retailers eventually add new products and services. On the positive side this allows them to differentiate themselves, but it also eliminates their competitive advantage. Only one retailer can have the lowest price in the market. Others can avoid the retail life-cycle trap by continuously tapping into new shopper segments and/or using more than one format/channel.

A category manager may find inspiration by selecting the right benchmarks. For example, a category manager for wine may choose a wine bar as a source of inspiration for large stores and a convenience store at an airport as a benchmark for smaller stores.

Notes

1 Macaray, David [accessed 1 August 2015] Why Did Walmart Leave Germany [Online] http://www.huffingtonpost.com/david-macaray/why-did-walmart-leave-ger_b_940542.html
http://www.dw.com/en/worlds-biggest-retailer-wal-mart-closes-up-shop-in-germany/a-2112746

2 See Boston.com [accessed 1 August 2015] Carrefour Profit Rises [Online] http://www.boston.com/business/articles/2007/03/08/carrefour_posts_rise_in_2006_profit/)

3 Grimmeau, J (2013) [accessed 22 July 2015] A forgotten anniversary: the first European hypermarkets open in Brussels in 1961, *Brussels Studies* [Online] http://www.brusselsstudies.be/medias/publications/BruS67EN.pdf

4 Davidson, W, Bates, A and Bass, S (1976) [accessed 22 July 2015] The retail life cycle, *Harvard Business Review* [Online] http://www.scribd.com/doc/48155351/retail-life-cycle#scribd

5 Perrigot, R and Cliquet, G (2006) [accessed 22 July 2015] Hypermarket Format: Any Future or a Real Need to Be Changed? An Empirical Study of the French, Spanish and Italian Markets, International Marketing Trends Conference [Online] http://www.escp-eap.net/conferences/marketing/2006_cp/Materiali/Paper/Fr/Perrigot_Cliquet.pdf

6 Castrillo, J, Forn, R and Mira, R (1997) [accessed 22 July 2015] Hypermarkets may be losing their appeal for European consumers, *McKinsey Quarterly* [Online] https://www.questia.com/library/journal/1G1-20903145/hypermarkets-may-be-losing-their-appeal-for-european

What the shopper wants from online shopping channels

06

Chapter 5 demonstrated that large formats have lost appeal to shoppers because their busy lifestyles make them lose interest in driving long distances to reach a store and then to have to walk lengthy distances inside. This takes too much time and it requires shoppers to plan the trip carefully. Therefore, small formats such as discount and convenience stores see traffic increase. Online shopping is, of course, the other rising star. Retailers need to research which part of the shopping journey shoppers prefer to carry out online versus in-store and invest accordingly. In 2005 there was consensus in the grocery industry that shoppers always wanted to touch fresh products before buying. Already by 2015 the success of online grocery at the likes of Ocado, Tesco and Leclerc has proven this wrong. In this chapter I offer an overview of the opportunities and limitations of online retail from a shopper perspective. While many examples come from the grocery industry, many of the critical success factors are also applicable to other retail sectors.

Online is inevitable

By just looking at the transformation that industries such as books, travel and consumer electronics have experienced, it is clear to everyone in the sector that shopping for groceries will likewise look different in the future. A turning point in the grocery sector is that if a retailer has not invested yet in its online strategy or shopping app, it needs to realize it is falling behind and may be making a fatal choice for the continuity of the brand. The impact of online is not only related to ordering. Internet and smartphones give the shoppers the opportunity to familiarize themselves with the products and services during the early phase of shopping. Therefore, each retail brand should support at least part of the shopping process online.

According to a Nielsen survey of shoppers in 54 countries, 26 per cent of global respondents planned to purchase food and beverage products online in 2012, which was a significant increase compared to 18 per cent of shoppers in 2010.[1] The most frequently mentioned activity was conducting research such as checking prices or reading a review: 49 per cent of respondents said they had purchased a grocery product online in the past month. From those, 9 per cent claim to connect on a daily basis to purchase groceries online. Another Nielsen study finds that 25 per cent of all consumer-packaged-goods (CPG) purchase decisions in the United States are influenced by some internet or mobile activity.[2] This differs per category. For fresh grocery products it is 18 per cent of the decisions, for non-alcoholic beverages it is 34 per cent. Several retailers have started experiments with ordering groceries with the help of QR codes printed on posters, such as Tesco Home Plus in South Korea and Delhaize in train stations in Brussels. Technology providers inform us of the endless possibilities of apps that make the life of the shopper more convenient such as additional product information on your smartphone and navigation on a store map.

However, it feels that the many reports and blogs only predict doom for bricks-and-mortar stores. They make it sound as though online media will take away the sales of traditional supermarkets for the larger part. Yes, internet and social media undoubtedly impact the current state of affairs of the retailer. Mobile ordering meets shopper needs either through a smartphone app or QR code printed on a poster in a public place. This is already visible in the grocery sector: online grocery retailer Ocado in the UK saw 34 per cent of its orders go through smartphones in 2013 and reported that 45 per cent of orders in that year were completed through mobile devices.[3] Aside from these success stories, retailers need to realize that even in the most sophisticated online markets the percentage of online grocery sales is still low. According to IGD, the percentage of online grocery sales in the UK for the year until April 2015 is 5 per cent. Said differently: shoppers allocate 95 per cent of their spend to the traditional supermarkets.[4] Another example is the Dutch market. Many factors seem favourable in relation to the development of online grocery shopping. Many people have high-speed internet access, they are open to technological innovations and many shoppers are time stressed. Reports show that people use online ordering but there seems to be a discrepancy between the penetration figures and the actual amounts of money spent. For example, 10 per cent of Dutch shoppers have experience with online shopping and 6 per cent do so on a regular basis.[5] In terms of shopping trips some 3 per cent of groceries are purchased online.[6] The figures are considerably lower in value terms. Estimates range between a share of 0.7 per cent to 0.81 per cent of online grocery spend.[7] Often the reports are very positive and predictions on the number of users are sky high. For a retail marketer the business model also needs to work financially. This means conducting research into the current shopping journey, identifying shopping tasks that run more smoothly with digital tools, and whether it makes sense from a financial perspective to insert these. In short, a retail marketer should first dig deeper to understand how online shopping supports the shopping process, and then it can adapt its business model.

Popular online product categories include travel, tickets, computer software, games, music and insurance. The internet lends itself well to products that are digital and/or seem to have an infinite assortment size, whereas for instance spectacles, plants, food and drinks are low on the list. Product categories such as computer hardware, household articles and bicycles are increasingly being sold online and the suppliers in these industries are under enormous pressure to change their business model fast. For both supplier and shopper the online channel is interesting for this type of non-daily purchase. First, for the shopper it is financially attractive to browse. However, the risk of a bad purchase and the perception of a missed, exceptional opportunity are greater. The shopper buys such products less often in their life and the lengthy orientation serves to determine which decision criteria are relevant. The shopper takes the opportunity to collect the information online in a conscious manner and the purchasing behaviour is more results driven. For the supplier, online offers a great business model as it saves on storage by keeping everything at a central location. This is even more true for products of high purchasing value and categories that are very sensitive to trends or are impacted by seasonality. In high-speed consumer electronics, sales shift from traditional stores to online as it becomes too costly to distribute all new products to all bricks-and-mortar stores around the country – in the knowledge that they will be replaced by new products within less than a year. Companies such as Samsung and Philips may see their sales shift from high-street stores to almost 100 per cent online within a lifetime.

Why the future is online

Shoppers have come to expect *everything, always, anywhere*. Shoppers expect this in relation to groceries as well and will buy more online. The technical conditions are already there. Think of fast broadband connections for a large audience; the perception that paying online is safe; legislation and guarantees from industry organizations for return policies; fast tablets, smartphones, PCs and complex software to enable logistical processing and invoicing. There is a direct correlation between broadband connection and share of online sales. However, these technical conditions do not explain everything. It is also important to take into consideration the shopper's attitude and motivations to purchase groceries online. I discuss a wide range of these points below.

Convenience of time: 24 hours/seven days per week

Internet offers the opportunity to order groceries 24 hours per day. Shoppers are no longer restricted to the opening hours prescribed by law or offered by the supermarket. In some countries such as Britain and the United States this is not very different to what bricks-and-mortar stores offer. Countries such as Germany and the Netherlands have more restricted opening hours, for example on Sundays. However, in the latter countries there is a trend towards longer opening hours as well, so the relevance of this reason to shop online becomes less important. The benefit of the longer opening hours of the internet then applies to the hours between roughly 9 pm and 8 am, but these are often not the most popular hours for grocery shopping. However, for categories such as travel, books and clothes these might be excellent selling hours.

Convenience of transport

At the start of online grocery shopping, the shoppers focused on ordering products that they would rather not carry such as crates of beer and boxes of washing powder. These are the type of products shoppers do not want to carry up the stairs to their apartment. Carrying is one thing, and also parking has become an issue for shoppers in large cities in Europe. In busy city centres of London and Amsterdam, for example, a shopper could easily find themselves driving around to find a parking space only to discover that they have to carry their groceries on a 15-minute walk from car to house. In the case of online shopping the shopper avoids losing time that they would rather spend on something else as a result of traffic. Yet another motivation for online shopping is the rise of fuel prices, which stimulates shoppers to leave the car at home. Those who order online often pay an ordering fee but in large cities this is compensated by avoiding the parking fee. Citizens in large European cities find yet another, more psychological reason to shift to online: a delivery truck of the online supermarket that blocks the street for a couple of minutes provokes less annoyance with other road users than the car of the shopper themselves.

Convenience of location

Technology such as iPads and smartphones offer the shopper a feeling of freedom and self-determination that is not to be underestimated. They can familiarize themselves anywhere in the virtual world and order from wherever they happen to be. So the shopper could order from Leclerc with their smartphone while shopping with a trolley in Carrefour. This is why Google speaks of the zero moment of truth: the shopper orientates and searches on the computer or tablet before stepping into the store. These decisions formed on websites and social media are, according to Google, more important than impressions built up in-store – or the first moments of truth as Alan George Lafley, CEO of Procter & Gamble, called them.

Price comparison

With a few touches of a button the shopper can compare prices. Just having this possibility gives the shopper a complete sense of control and independence. This benefit has resulted in the development of internet sites with price comparisons such as supers.nl, mysupermarket.co.uk or comparegroceryprices.org. Whether the shopper actually compares between online supermarkets is the next question. Most shoppers do not want to spend too much time on this – and so the comparison should not require too many extra steps. If the comparison site offers the opportunity to order the groceries immediately, or if it offers additional value, for example through nutritional or allergen information, these types of sites might have a better reason for continued existence.

Infinite choice

Category managers like to tell suppliers that the shelves in their stores are not made of elastic – and they are right, of course. In contrast, an online store has an infinite shelf that holds more items than Walmart or Auchan could ever offer. Some bricks-and-mortar stores attempt to create the perception of a large product assortment in order to make the shopper think that its large offering is as attractive as the online offering. Some even give a guarantee. Supermarket chain Jumbo in the Netherlands, for example, positions itself with 'seven certainties', one of which reads that the shopper should expect the largest assortment and, if a product is not available, Jumbo will list it within two weeks. Yet the introduction of a new, specific product will be at the expense of other items, certainly after realizing that the average size of a Jumbo store is 1,200 square metres. In such cases the supermarket may fill the shelves with half of the outer boxes, and run the risk of going out of stock or shoppers having difficulty selecting products from an overcrowded shelf. Local store staff may try to discourage shoppers from exercising the 'for all your groceries' guarantee from the headquarters. Shoppers may typically ask for a product that they enjoy, which may then result in a low rotation for the supermarket but also in high added value and customer loyalty. These types of products seem especially suitable for online sales. For example, think of product assortments that specific immigrant communities want to buy. Often centrally led grocery chains struggle to adjust their efficient logistical process to create a locally relevant assortment. Online retailing is better placed for these products.

Physical limitations

For shoppers with disabilities, for example those in a wheelchair, the internet is of course the solution. They no longer need to worry that someone else has taken the disabled person's parking space, and can stop worrying about how many products they are able to transport from the store to their car at any one time. In addition, many elderly shoppers utilize the internet. In the UK, 8 per cent of those aged between 60 and 64 have difficulty shopping for groceries; this rises to 19 per cent for those aged 80 to 84 and 60 per cent for those aged over 90;[8] 38 per cent of people over 70 in the UK have mobility difficulties. In the UK 86 per cent of those aged 55 and above shop regularly online in the UK, and 36 per cent say they do most of their shopping online.[9] This makes them the most frequent online shoppers. Yet in many countries a large portion of this age group does not have access to the internet. This can be due to lack of interest, because they dislike the cost or the technological challenges. However, if they use the internet they show more or less the same buying behaviour as the younger generations. It is often said that a supermarket is important for the elderly because it offers the social opportunity for a daily chat, a cup of coffee and other social moments. However, if the roads are blocked with snow or if it rains heavily, the possibility of shopping online is a true relief for them. In conclusion, Western society's ageing population offers an extra growth opportunity for online supermarkets.

The internet is a fact of life

For years supermarkets have wondered if the web would be relevant for buying groceries, while the internet has gradually become used more and more widely. Meanwhile, a generation of millennials has never lived without the internet, and a world without it is unthinkable for them. For those shoppers, the internet is one of life's essentials, and online shopping is a natural thing to do. They are now old enough to be starting their own households.

Limited differentiation between current retail brands

Traditionally, very different channels become more similar over time and the borderlines between channels and retail brands become vague. For example, the furniture and home-decoration brand IKEA is successful in food; the discounter Aldi is famous for its sales of PCs and Christmas trees. Within each of the channels the brands have become less differentiating. In the grocery sector full-service brands all want to differentiate their fresh products and attempt to catch the price-focused shopper with value private labels. Meanwhile, discounter Lidl offers a fresher assortment than ever before and slowly extends the number of A-brands in each country where it operates. And are Lidl's customer service and customer friendliness by employees really that far removed from the service that supermarket employees deliver? Personally, I have stopped asking questions about food preparation and less well-known food products in service supermarkets, as the teenage employees look back at me with glazed eyes. Real customer service becomes more hard to come by and, in this way, the step towards the impersonal channel of online shopping becomes easier to take.

Online is not a new industry, but it is a new sales channel that can offer superior benefits. When the differentiation between grocery brands disappears more and more in terms of price, productivity and assortment, the market chances for the strongest brand improve most. In a sales channel where personal contact does not matter or is taken away, it revolves around the degree to which the shopper has confidence in the brand. Every year, research company Interbrand investigates the strength of retail brands.[10] Comfortingly for the traditional grocery chains built on bricks and mortar, they are still the strongest. This should give them a good stronghold against the likes of Amazon. The first grocer on the list of best retail brands in Europe is Carrefour followed by Tesco, Auchan and Aldi. In North America, Amazon and eBay have entered the top list of best retail brands; however, this is still firmly led by Walmart.

No time to waste

This aspect is different from the first in this list (which concerned the possibility of being always able to order). A supermarket trip may result in a lot of time wasted for the shopper. We are creatures of habit that shop for groceries when the remainder of the street is doing this as well. Especially in less liberalized territories, supermarkets are crowded on Fridays and Saturdays. This results in a number of annoyances. If it is busy in-store the shoppers get in each other's way and products become out of stock; checkouts are overcrowded, where shoppers leave their money and their patience. Waiting at a checkout, out-of-stock items and crowded aisles (often caused also by shop employees unloading boxes and filling shelves) are often the top three annoyances of a supermarket trip. The feeling of losing time is the last thing that busy households with two working partners want. It is possible to outsource cleaning of the house, cooking and homework supervision, so why not hand over grocery shopping to someone else? Finally, if products are centrally stored, retailers have better opportunities to reduce the annoying out-of-stock percentages – and online supermarkets *and* shoppers will like this.

Limited buying orientation

The shopper requires a far more limited orientation and service when acquiring food and drinks as opposed to other retail items. Just compare the purchase of a jar of milk with that of a book (Which one should I read? What is popular now?), a TV set (What technology is best? What size should the screen have? What is an acceptable price?) or a travel booking (Where shall I go? How will I get there? What is the total expenditure?). Terms of guarantee, warranties, online reviews, what experts think... None of these really matter when it comes to the purchase of milk, cookies, bananas and other groceries. Of course, supermarkets often have service departments where bread, meat, fish and cheese are sold over the counter; however, other retail brands appear to sell these fresh product groups just as easily in pre-packed trays. In addition, how many shoppers at the supermarket still ask for advice from the person behind the counter?

Why are groceries different online?

Online shopping has received a warm welcome from shoppers. Technology is readily available and ever improving. The large variety of benefits enables supermarkets to create their own unique differentiation in the perception of the shopper, although the online services that the players offer are still very similar. None of the driving factors of online shopping are specific to selling groceries, though they all make sense for groceries. Yet although many of the driving factors make sense, selling groceries online is still very different from selling other products and services online. The fundamental reason why the sales of groceries online are so different from products such as CDs or travel is this: shopping for groceries concerns a range of articles from several categories that are only relevant to purchase in connection to each other. The shopper does not shop online for one jar of peanut butter, but does so for weekly basics, for fresh dinners for a few days, or for a party. The issue becomes even more complex because the shopper sets critical requirements for parts of those groceries regarding hygiene and shelf life such as in the case of fresh, refrigerated and frozen products. Therefore, transport and flexible delivery are highly complex. The shopper only dares to trust high-grade delivery if the supplier has a good reputation. This could work out to be financially attractive but it will be a challenge: compared to fashion and consumer electronics the selling prices per unit of groceries are much lower. When practitioners list these crucial requirements for online sales of groceries it is no wonder that there are so few online supermarkets. From a logistical perspective there are few players capable of delivering this performance. In addition, it requires a strong brand reputation that shoppers trust – enough to buy meat, for example, without wishing to select it themselves in advance. In each country retailers need to measure themselves against these criteria. Typically just a handful of retail brands are loved and indispensable in the eyes of the shopper and it will be difficult to meet the trust factor positively and beyond any doubt. In conclusion, online ordering and home delivery of daily groceries will remain a small segment in most countries.

What is slowing down online grocery sales?

This brings me to some obstacles that are unique to groceries, and to explain why online shopping for groceries has not grown so fast when compared to other product groups such as consumer electronics.

Shoppers want to see, touch, smell, taste

Shoppers pay special attention to anything they eat or apply to their bodies. It is deeply ingrained in human nature to smell something before consuming it, to turn it around and taste it carefully. Today, the shopper surrenders this manner of trying and selecting when purchasing groceries online. This feels like a risk, certainly in the case of fresh products. For online groceries it is more difficult for the supermarket to give signals that emphasize or guarantee the freshness and quality of the products. This is completely different at the butcher's, the meat department of a grocery store, the baker's and the bakery department inside a store. Seeing employees work with the meat, their uniforms, the smell and images from the regions of origin create an artisan atmosphere. Ocado actually turns around this argument: they point the shopper to the fact that they have such fresh products because Ocado operates in a shorter – and in this way fresher – supply chain. It is not clear whether this is based on facts or whether they have found a great way to improve the sales of fresh products online. Online supermarkets not only face the challenge of creating the perception of freshness and quality, of offering tailored advice, and of creating the right ambience, they also have to solve the logistical challenge of delivering cooled and frozen products in good order to the shopper's home.

Stores are close by

Stores are close by for most shoppers in Europe. In the Netherlands the average distance from home to a large supermarket is 900 metres.[11] Of course this is an average: for some cities it is 60 metres, for others it is 12 kilometres. On top of this, growing urbanization around the world makes stores closer for even more people. Because of the small distance to supermarkets and food specialists for daily necessities such as bakery products it is still easy for a lot of people to shop for groceries themselves. Most grocery shopping trips count between four and 10 products, so it is not worth it for the shopper to process this through the internet. Often there is a threshold under which shoppers have to pay for delivery. However, the opportunities for online supermarkets increase if the number of stores in a particular market is low, if the number of retail brands decreases and if the differentiation among the brands (further) declines.

Delivery

The shopper feels that most of the job is done once the products are selected online. However, for the supermarket this is where the job starts. How do they get the order to the shopper's home? All sorts of things have been thought up and trialled. Pilots ranged from a shopper who could pick up their groceries at a petrol station, to recloseable boxes with refrigerated display and freezers in front of people's homes. Home delivery sounds attractive, but in practice most shoppers appear only to accept the delivery of the groceries at more or less the same moment of the day. Supermarket Plus in the Netherlands applies a strict schedule for deliveries, which are only possible during four hours of the day: between 10 am and 12 noon and between 3 and 5 pm. Although this supermarket is fine with delivering to the shopper's workplace the shopper still needs to find a solution for storing their fresh and frozen items at the office. Shoppers in the UK indicate their favourite delivery slot weeks in advance and it becomes less attractive for others to shop online spontaneously. In addition, the UK supermarkets charge higher delivery costs for the most popular days of the week and the most desirable hours. Because home delivery is less convenient than thought in some instances, since 2010 there also has been a surge of pick-up points either at the supermarket or at isolated locations. Following Auchan who set up Chronodrive and Auchan Drive, regional and large players across Europe have started pick-up points where the shopper collects the online selected groceries: Sainsbury's, Tesco, Rewe, Albert Heijn. Despite the strong growth and widespread acceptance of pick-up points it is too early to say if shoppers will really embrace them. Indeed, often they need to step out of the car, load crates into the car and pay. Perhaps shoppers have the perception of saving time but I am not sure if there actually is much time difference between online and traditional ways of shopping.

Limited number of players

The British market is truly unique in the sense that all main players offer online shopping, have user-friendly shopper interfaces and most offer home delivery. They compete heavily on delivery charges and grocery prices. Comparison websites such as mysupermarket.co.uk make it really simple to pick the least expensive supermarket for any of your trips. Not all players make money with online and it often takes years to achieve. In 2014 pure online player Ocado booked its first profit since its existence and reached a mere 0.7 per cent of sales, but Tesco.com is doing well. The number of supermarkets with online services is growing fast in other large European markets as well, such as Germany and France. However, for smaller countries like the Netherlands and Belgium the market structure is developed by just a few players. For new markets like online shopping, the adoption of a completely new product is faster and more favourable if there are several well-known companies that explain the concept, win confidence and stimulate growth through advertising and other marketing investments. The Dutch market offers a good example of how difficult it is to make online grocery into a profitable venture and how important it is to carry the burden of a new market segment on more than one set of shoulders. In the Netherlands for a long time the only established player that offered a full grocery assortment has been Albert Heijn. However, even in this small country they do not offer the service nationwide and, ever since its start when it was named James Telesuper in 1987, it has never made money through online shopping. Innumerable initiatives kicked the bucket, for example Max Food Market, de Boodschappenlijn and Truus.nl or remained regional operations such as Vershuys. Dutch shoppers can order from the German Amazon.com site provided they speak German but it does not really help to let the Dutch online grocery market come to full bloom. Since the start of Albert Heijn's home-delivery service (beginning with orders placed by fax and phone), it took 27 years before a second large grocery store, Jumbo Supermarkten, entered the online grocery market – and this will promote acceptance among shoppers.

Routine

Shoppers are geared towards routine. It takes them a lot of energy to submit a decision each time to a profound evaluation of choice criteria. A re-evaluation of channel choice or primary supermarket brand only happens as a result of important, meaningful life changes such as having children, getting a new job, a divorce, moving home or a strong decline of (expected) income. These life events do not happen too often and certainly not all at the same time. This reduces the chances that the shopper lets go of their grocery shopping routine and all of a sudden sees online shopping as their primary purchasing channel for food and drinks. A reset to online grocery shopping asks for a different routine that first of all needs to be adopted and then to be woven in as a new behaviour pattern.

Price perception

Outside food and groceries, shoppers have the perception that products ordered online (books, travel, hotels and so on) are less expensive than in-store. This is not necessarily the reality, but the perception is there. So far groceries do not carry that perception, especially because of the delivery charges. In addition, since the start of the economic recession in 2008 supermarkets have done their utmost to obtain a price-friendly image. Thanks to their drive, which led them to engage in price wars in countries such as France and the Netherlands, grocery price increases have remained minimal. The supermarkets have taught shoppers to watch their spending. Each transaction fee leads to a conscious or unconscious step back to assess whether the purchase is fulfilling the shopper's needs, and a delivery charge is an example of such a fee. Also, a retailer like Ocado struggles with a negative price image and attempts to solve this through the introduction of their private label, a Smart Pass membership scheme, more promotions and a price guarantee versus Tesco prices ('Cheaper than Tesco or we'll give you a voucher'). Many supermarkets emphasize on their websites that they apply the same prices as in the bricks-and-mortar store, but the real question is whether the shopper thinks they can trust this message and if they are prepared to check this for all groceries online. Some supermarkets such as Jumbo Supermarkten in the Netherlands and Colruyt in Belgium use a type of differentiated pricing whereby the consumer price depends on local competition and shopper profiles. Other supermarket brands have various pricing levels for the same product because their franchisers are free to set their own store pricing. This makes it difficult to promise one price online. In the long run there is a solution for this topic of price perception but it might take some time for the shopper to shake off a certain distrust towards pricing in the online channel.

In the case of groceries it is difficult to create the perception that shoppers are paying less online. By collecting groceries and delivering them, the retailer integrates costs into its system that it outsourced at the time supermarkets came into being: the fundamental business principle was self-service, collection and takeaway by the shopper. In cases where the retailer collects the groceries for the online order not in the stores, it needs to set up a separate logistics system. A separate logistics system aside from the store makes it more difficult to create a favourable price image for the online shopper. In addition, such a separate system may lead to frictions with franchisers that see grocery revenue leak to the online venture of the retailer. Although modern franchise agreements may solve this with revenue sharing in online sales in the catchment area of the franchiser, and fees for returns and other services in-store, it remains a natural area of conflict between the retail headquarters and independent franchisers.

Three business-model questions: picking, routing, delivery

The confidence of investors and the current growth figures show that there must be opportunities for online grocery sales, so where are they? First, the market players need to develop a business model with lower costs. It is still a big jigsaw puzzle for online supermarkets to work this out.

Order picking

Order picking in-store avoids investment in a separate warehouse but it is not efficient to carry this out among regular shoppers and in a standard store layout with products merchandised for visibility and not for efficient picking. In separate warehouses retailers have the option to continuously experiment and adjust the location of products in order to minimize picking time. Franchisers demand their part of the cake if the shopper no longer shops in their store and the retailer delivers from a central warehouse to shoppers in the franchisers' coverage area. There is not one model right for everyone: in the UK Asda uses store picking, Ocado has central warehousing, Tesco uses a hybrid model and Sainsbury's uses mainly store picking. If a supermarket is serving a densely populated area with a high likelihood of finding interested shoppers with a busy lifestyle, it makes sense not to disturb traffic in current stores and to open a central warehouse or 'shadow store' in the catchment area. Performing store picking in current stores might deter shoppers and lead to stock running out unexpectedly. Tesco delivers 80 per cent of its online orders in most densely populated neigh-bourhoods in London from special warehouses, while the remainder are picked up in regular Tesco stores. If the supermarket penetrates new areas and wishes to cover more of the fixed costs of the store, store picking makes sense. Finally, the equation of revenue and costs may evolve over time. In 2000 Sainsbury's was convinced it could do better than Tesco with a dedicated warehouse, but closed the warehouse for online groceries in 2004. Sainsbury's, which has fewer stores in London than Tesco, started operating with order picking in stores and delivering groceries to homes with the help of a fleet of trucks. However, in 2013 Sainsbury's announced plans for a dedicated warehouse.

Route planning

The second crucial element of the business case is route planning. The capability to plan the deliveries carefully with a minimum of cost while still satisfying shopper expectations has a large impact on profits. Albert Heijn has always carefully expanded its coverage across the Netherlands, only going forward in areas when sufficient addresses were en route. Tesco is one of the few supermarkets to work out how to make online grocery sales profitable. In 2013 they made some £127 million from their online business with a fantastic 5.1 per cent profit margin.[12] Pure retail players such as Ocado made a loss in 2013 and great players like Albert Heijn have never succeeded in reaching break-even despite the fact that they have not had a national competitor for online groceries during most of their online sales activities.

Delivery method

The third factor that is crucial for the business model is selecting the right (mix of) deliveries types. One of the most exciting and fast-growing delivery types is a drive-through where supermarket employees place the online order in the shopper's car. It is like a McDonald's drive-through but now the shopper picks up their bread, coffee and cat food. The choice of delivery type is related to the question of where the products are picked up. With the extension of click-and-collect models it becomes less relevant to pick up in a special warehouse as the time and distance between the supermarket and delivery point become smaller. Shoppers at Tesco have already become accustomed to the drive-through. Tesco started this new method of delivery in its Extra store in Baldock in 2010 and then expanded the service to more than 270 stores. The Baldock site experimented with delivery of groceries from a van but now there are delivery points with roofs on the parking space. Delivery from the van returned in 2013 when Tesco opened the possibility to collect groceries at three park-and-ride locations in York. Tesco hopes to expand the grocery delivery locations to schools, libraries and sports centres. Tesco thinks the drive-through is attractive for young working people, and families with young children that have no time to wait for their online order at home. The fast roll-out of the drive-through is certainly stimulated by the fact that a drive-through delivery is free of charge for deliveries above £25 (and costs £4 for orders below) while home delivery charge ranges from £1 to £6.

Delivery types

Too often online ordering is related immediately to home delivery; however, there are more options aside from home delivery and the drive-through. In fact a drive-through is just one of the possible shapes of click-and-collect systems that allow shoppers to buy online and collect the groceries themselves. The other types are pick-up points in-store where the shopper collects the online purchases in a supermarket of their choice, and drive-to points, which are isolated pick-up points or pick-up points that sit within another retail brand. Each delivery type has its own benefits and disadvantages, which are discussed below.

Drive-through

In this alternative the shopper collects the groceries outside the supermarket, mostly at a separate location in the car park. The time slot is pre-booked. Apart from these facilities the retailer invests in making employees available for the collection of products. All in all this is a limited investment. The supermarket still needs to consider that the revenue of the drive-through comes partly at the expense of the sales of the regular store. Typical impulse categories such as chocolate and ice cream are hurt more because of lower traffic in the regular store. However, Asda claims that 30 per cent of its shoppers pay a visit to the store after collecting the groceries at the drive-through because they forgot to order an item online.[13] Staff collect the online order just before the moment of collection by the shopper. The groceries are stored under the right conditions so that the shopper can plan a large shopping trip including fresh and frozen products. The French retailer Auchan pioneered this delivery type and started a pilot in the French city of Leers in 2000. Even in France it took a while before this delivery type became widely available. In 2007 this idea was picked up by Leclerc, and only in recent years have Carrefour and Casino started a big race to recover lost ground in France.

Collection in supermarket

The shopper walks to a service desk in the supermarket. Because this is a delivery method whereby the shopper makes the effort to park the car and walk into the store, many supermarkets apply this model to sell (small) non-food products. This version is also interesting for convenience super-markets because in this way they can extend their non-food assortment in an, in principle, infinite manner. The investment at the point of sale is limited, and because the shopper still visits the store there is a chance of extra impulse sales. Still the picking and logistics are more complex because it often concerns products that are not sold in the store and the collection of orders in the store is not possible. One example is Asda, which uses this type of click and collect for the sale of a wide assortment of non-food, and apart from this it operates with home delivery of groceries. The Dutch retailer Ahold, after the acquisition of non-food online player Bol.com, can optimize its sales per store by letting shoppers pick up non-food orders from Bol.com at the service desks of the Albert Heijn supermarkets in the Netherlands and Belgium.

Online shopping is a fantastic weapon for supermarkets to sell books, consumer electronics, toys, fashion and other non-food merchandise. Tesco shoppers can have their non-food items delivered to their home or to more than 1,800 Tesco stores, which represent over 50 per cent of Tesco's total real estate and include the smaller convenience outlets. For online non-food orders, 70 per cent of Tesco orders are collected by shoppers themselves and the assortment is infinite: more than 200,000 non-food products. In comparison, Sainsbury's offers some 10,000 non-food products.

Drive-to

The drive-to is used when a supermarket builds a network of small warehouses that are open for delivery to shoppers. It is clear that investment in land, buildings and staff is considerable compared to the two types discussed previously. Also, impulse sales are minimal. This type is interesting if a retailer enters a new market area, because the investment is lower compared to a complete new store. In principle, the complete supermarket assortment could be offered, though from a cost perspective concessions to the size of the fresh and frozen assortments are logical. Disadvantages of these concessions are the impact on the sales mix and margin. Both drive-through and drive-to are popular in France because these types of delivery points do not come under the legal restrictions of opening new stores, and because there is so much space available at the current points of sale. A version of the drive-to could be when a supermarket operates in a new market area with a partner, for example a petrol station.

Home delivery

Still the most desired delivery type is to the shopper's home. The shopper makes a reservation for a time slot when the groceries are delivered to their door or even to the shopper's refrigerator. Because the most favourable delivery moments are booked quickly, the shopper uses this type of delivery when they need many supermarket products rather than a single non-food article. In addition, the shopper will evaluate the delivery charge demanded by the supermarket. The storage and combined delivery of refrigerated, frozen and conservable groceries to individual dropping points are extremely complex and expensive and are paying off mainly in densely populated areas. The high investments go together with the fact that home delivery is replacing the current store sales and may affect impulse categories. Supermarkets could, however, use home delivery as a competitive weapon to steal shoppers from other supermarkets. Home delivery is the more traditional delivery method for online orders. For example, Delhaize in Belgium started its Caddy-Home delivery service in 1989, while Delhaize Direct with deliveries in-store began in 2010.

Online as an escape from saturated markets

Boards of supermarkets feel the pressure 'to do something online' but starting an online supermarket is quite a job. Existing supermarkets who already have a reputation for reliable service and good-quality fresh products have a large advantage in the eyes of the shopper. The supermarkets need to choose a clear positioning. This could be functional (for example best price or best convenience) but could also be focused on experience. Shoppers who are open to online sales can be roughly split into two groups. One group likes shopping, is open to new channels and will try them for any category. They seek online supermarkets that offer experience, inspiration and a personal approach. The second group of shoppers are not necessarily fans of online, but they are time-pressured. They can buy what they need online without too much hassle. The latter group pays attention to transparency on pricing and reliability of transaction and delivery.

Starting an online supermarket may not offer the margin-rich escape from saturated markets that supermarkets look for. Efficient home delivery of (refrigerated and frozen) groceries is not compatible with the low prices that shoppers have become accustomed to. Still, online will claim part of the spend on daily groceries and it changes shopper behaviour in a fundamental manner. These are some of the changes I expect:

Personal care migrates to online

Fresh products and frozen foods require seamless logistics in order to work online. Together they make up the majority of supermarket revenue. Sales of frozen products vary by country, but are high in, for example, Germany. So online offers more starting opportunities in other categories. For dry groceries online shopping is fast becoming an alternative to store sales. New market players or non-food players that want to extend their offering with typical supermarket items often start with personal care products: logistics and warehousing costs are lower than for fresh products and they have a higher consumer price than the average dry grocery item. For a bricks-and-mortar player, personal care categories are welcome thanks to the high gross margin. However, focused online players may accept much lower margins and, as a result, take down consumer pricing. New players change the rules of the game for a category manager of a traditional supermarket. When setting prices and developing promotions the category manager needs to take into consideration a new set of competitors. For suppliers, the question is whether they wish to sell their products through the new online market channel. On one hand, they could choose to limit price transparency and work only with existing bricks-and-mortar supermarkets. On the other hand, suppliers may also set up their own website and sell to shoppers directly. This strategy seems to be reserved for large suppliers such as Procter & Gamble and Philips. Indeed, if suppliers cannot convince supermarket customers that they are serving a new target group, letting the total market grow, they risk a channel conflict. From a shopper perspective it may be beneficial if personal care categories move from supermarkets to online, as the many small items often create a confusing on-shelf image, service is non-existent and shopper experience is limited.

The internet impacts the bricks-and-mortar supermarket

Even if the supermarket does not integrate online into its business model, it will still have an impact on the supermarket. Perhaps it may decide to reduce the amount of space for the personal care category, because shoppers prefer to buy these online and suppliers like Procter & Gamble and Danone Baby divert their investments. The category manager also needs to respond to the increased visibility of consumer prices online and the potential for shoppers to check prices with a smartphone in-store. Local farmers may set up a webstore and compete with a specialized assortment of vegetables and/or meat with the fresh products of the supermarket.

Hybrid alternatives

One of the most important obstacles is the delivery in good, hygienic condition at the time the shopper requested. Supermarkets can avoid this by letting the shopper select online, but organize the delivery in a different manner, for example through pick-up points.

Orientation

The supermarket may decide not to invest in the delivery phase and to focus instead on the orientation process of groceries before the shopper enters the store. With recipes and price comparisons the supermarket supplements the role of features and coupons.

Positioning of logistical execution or shopping experience

Much of the focus of online supermarkets is on convenience and competing for shoppers based on delivery costs. However, supermarkets do not only differentiate themselves with logistically driven variables such as the time between order and delivery, the delivery moment and the type of delivery point. Supermarkets can choose to play a more proactive and inspirational role. They could set themselves up as leader for taking away barriers, making home grocery shopping more attractive and more differentiated.

This will boost total online sales. Many options for brand positionings and marketing strategies are available:

- An online supermarket may focus on the efficient processing of large, routine, weekly purchases. As a result, the retailer does everything to avoid delivery stress through flexible delivery times, shorter delivery time slots, and by making it possible to pick up the groceries at more than one address. After the large shopping trip is executed efficiently online, the shopper finds inspiration and new experiences in the bricks-and-mortar store. So the bricks-and-mortar store is redeveloped into a new concept to achieve something that can never be realized fully online: a customer-friendly approach and personalized customer service.

- A supermarket may also develop a strategy to offer exceptional product assortment online. A company can differentiate itself with 'extraordinary food from all places of the world', 'Friday evening with friends' and other similar concepts that offer a concrete suggestion to the shopper. In this way shopping for groceries obtains a new dimension.

- The supermarket can offer the shopper the possibility to visit their own local store in a virtual manner. The simulation enables the supermarket to strengthen the relationship with shoppers and become a centre of the community. The supermarket can add the option to do this with others, with friends and acquaintances from the neighbourhood, add menu and preparation suggestions, and present information on calories and food ingredients.

- There is nothing better than personal contact in the real world. However, online gives supermarkets the possibility to tailor the shopping trip completely around the customer. For example, if the shopper does not have a dog, they do not want to see the dog food category. On the other hand, the shopper is offered promotions for those products they are likely to buy based on previous visits or that fit the lifestyle of the shopper.

- Supermarkets may invest in online strategies in a more opportunistic manner. A supermarket could use this as a careful way to launch new products: the supermarket keeps stock low and if the product sells well, starts extending distribution to all bricks-and-mortar stores. In addition, the supermarket can use online retailing to increase the number of visits and shoppers, with the help of non-food products from outside the supermarket sector.

- Yet another option is to specialize in a certain shopper segment and decide to use online shopping as a separate channel, targeting companies and institutions such as restaurants and nursing homes.

Making online selection inspirational for shoppers

For all these alternatives for online strategies, it is true that the experience of online supermarkets could be improved significantly. Too often the website looks like an online copy of the current supermarket. In this way they do not take account of the way shoppers search and choose their products online. Some retailers even keep the same product hierarchies. Tesco committed the mistake of presenting products and brands in alphabetical order. Think about it: there is no bricks-and-mortar supermarket that merchandises its grocery brands in alphabetical order. Just like in the bricks-and-mortar store, visibility is crucial. If the product/brand that the shopper searches for does not appear on the first page, the chance of a sale decreases drastically. If the shopper seeks a product that starts with a Z, and the retailer lists the products per category in alphabetical order, the shopper loses too much time. Supermarkets can differentiate themselves by making the search for products easy. Delhaize Direct in Belgium makes finding products really simple through many filter options on aspects like price and brand and with the help of a free-text search, while competitors in the Belgian market, Colruyt and Carrefour, have limited search functions. For example, in the fizzy drinks category it is not possible to search online for elements such as sugar content and packaging size.

Much of the retail approach is focused on delivering convenience. Many retailers offer a shopping list based on a list of groceries that the shopper drafted once, or the retailer loads the list of purchases of the previous trip as a basis for suggested products. If the supplier brand is part of the routine, building such shopping lists is great for the brand. Perhaps the brand only needs to find a method to confirm that the shopper made the right choice and to thank the shopper in some way. If the supplier brand is not on the shopping list, it needs to draw the shopper's attention with digital promotion and suggestions. Online is a different channel and therefore suppliers need to research and produce a separate decision tree.

By adding inspiration, excitement and experiences, the borders of online shopping strategies are shaped by the imagination and dreams of the retailer. Let's assume that my local supermarket down the street produces its online version and allows me to shop in a completely virtually rebuilt supermarket. I click on the photo of an employee for advice; when I drop certain products in my shopping trolley I receive a warning for allergens; and when I virtually stand still at the coffee machine I chat with neighbours that happen to be online as well. Today, supermarkets relate the delivery charge too directly with the picking and delivery costs. A very logical and rational thought, but what happens if they connect the shopper with a more inspirational shopping environment? Can supermarkets make online as exciting as Asos.com, where you create outfits by dragging and dropping fashion items? Shoppers get more and more experienced at purchasing online and have ever larger expectations. For an extraordinary trip a shopper is prepared to pay more. In such cases, the share of online shopping will exceed the most optimistic forecasts of the moment.

The addition of new dimensions to the processes of online shopping has to be viewed separately from the fact that the basic principles of how shoppers search and choose their groceries online are investigated too little. For virtual and durable products, the shopper often starts by Googling the product category or brand rather than the retailer. For groceries, the shopping trip is likely to start on the retailer's website, with the exception of a very special item or a price-sensitive product that is found on comparison websites or websites that capture all special offers of the moment. It is the fact that a typical shopping trip for groceries contains more products from very different categories that makes their online sales so fundamentally different to that of, say, books and other durables.

Same marketing principle, different practices

The majority of the retail marketing principles, as we know them from the bricks-and-mortar stores, will remain valid online. Online, the retailer needs to make the same type of decisions on the focus and layers in the product assortment and consumer pricing. A number of retail practices need to be translated. For example, a well-known practice is to give a shopper the physical space and opportunity to rest at the entrance of the store so that they can then continue in a relaxed way with their first product orientation and purchase. A homepage needs to give the same effect. However, the twist is that online the shopper may come in on different pages and the soft landing therefore needs to be executed in more places. An online store has several entrances and an endless number of exits, whereas a bricks-and-mortar store often has only one door that is used for both entrance and exit. This comparison on retail practices can be carried further to the aisle (category landing page) and display (brand page).

Another different practice is that online supermarkets can show the product as many times and in as many combinations as they want. For example, you could list the same soft drink in the categories of non-alcoholic beverages, party mixes and quick meal solutions. The listing on the front end has no impact on the warehousing and logistics. Bricks-and-mortar stores have limited space by definition and they avoid duplication of placement unless the supplier has a really strong business case.

Online retail allows the retail marketing team to experiment and play as often as they like and to measure the results almost immediately. By comparing the behaviour of groups that shop under different marketing scenarios, online supermarkets can learn and optimize much faster than bricks-and-mortar stores. This takes much more time in the physical world; just think of changing the store layout. In other situations when the retailer is testing different price levels this is immediately visible in physical stores to everyone in the marketplace, including competing supermarkets. The point I want to emphasize is that sometimes the similarities between online and bricks and mortar are much bigger than claimed. Reviews and product suggestions seem to originate online; however, these also occur at the service counter, the checkout and at the shelf.

Finally, from a shopper profile perspective, online supermarkets need to take into consideration the differences between the ways in which men and women shop. The principles from the physical store layouts apply online too. When I worked at PepsiCo, neuro research was conducted for most consumer and shopper activities in PepsiCo's own neuro labs. One of the things I learnt is that men have a more results-driven method of purchasing. Female shoppers respond well to more emotional images, and seek clear 'landmarks' to navigate through the store. For these reasons the layouts of typical hypermarkets with long aisles, straight angles and red gondola ends work well for men but not for women. Recent neuro research into the design of online supermarkets is giving similar results. The current online design is often too functional for female shoppers. Women respond differently to moving images, and the use and style of text. Retailers consequently need to take the different gender preferences into greater consideration when designing their online offers.

What makes online retail strategies so interesting and exciting is that online supermarkets can give a different and distinctive shape to each shopper group and change the offering while they shop. In conclusion, the marketing philosophy and principles still hold true, but online the supermarket needs to reconsider marketing practices and choices, and learn new techniques.

Online as incremental sales for traditional groceries

In sectors such as consumer electronics and travel, huge numbers of stores have closed because shoppers began spending their money on online alternatives. The nature of the product (fresh, frozen) and the manner in which it is purchased (in relevant combinations) have ensured that this has not happened to grocery stores. Still, instead of considering online retail as a threat, retailers should embrace online options more openly.

Online retailing leads to incremental sales for the traditional supermarket in a number of ways:

- The supermarket offers new, non-food assortments, and services such as insurance. Though they meet with new competitors such as Amazon, adept solutions such as pick-up points in-store could minimize the investment.

- Online retailing may offer a strategy to enter a new country. Setting up warehouse-style pick-up points may be less expensive than building or acquiring a store network.

- Should a supermarket's key competitors not invest in online options, then the supermarket that does could win the hearts of a shopper segment that is fully converted to online shopping. This is a viable option in small countries that do not make it financially sensible for more players to operate.

- The addition of a new channel makes the shopper more loyal. Tesco claims that shoppers who use all channels spend three times more with Tesco.

- Supermarkets with superior warehousing and logistical capabilities can use these for a low-cost strategy and deter others from the online segment.

- The convenience of searching and, even better, finding inspiration and fun solutions on the front end may help differentiate the supermarket and increase shopper loyalty.

Conclusion

More and more retail sales will occur online. In Western markets the growth was stimulated by fast roll-out of broadband and consumer warranty legislation. More importantly, the online channel caters to various shopping needs, many of which were explored at the beginning of this chapter. Think of the convenience of 24-hour access and easy delivery for the elderly. At the same time, grocery shopping is less well placed for online ordering than are software or insurance policies. For example, shoppers hesitate to have their fresh products delivered without seeing them first. Whether an online sales channel is relevant for a retailer depends on its target shoppers, and the set-up of its physical distribution. The best mix of order picking, route planning and delivery varies by retailer and, therefore, cost structures will be different for each. Many retailers seem to focus on functional motivations for shoppers to use online, such as delivery fees. However, there is a sea of opportunity for retailers to differentiate themselves and to leverage online strategies as a way to sell extra.

Online shopping has its own laws. In the first place, the online supermarket needs to master the algorithms for sales forecast. This concerns aspects such as days of the week, influence of the weather, promotional uplift and affinities among products. In the UK, online sales go up when shoppers return home after their summer holidays and they are not in the mood to go out to shop. The next step is to study and manage the behaviour of clusters of shoppers as well as individual shoppers. Depending on their profiles, retailers can present shoppers with a different web layout, offer different prices and different assortments. When the shopper buys coffee, for example, the retailer can stimulate impulse sales by sending them a special offer for cookies. With a nice term this discipline is named 'shopper analytics' and enjoys an increasing interest from grocery retailers.

In 2011 Walmart bought the company Kosmix for $300 million in order to ramp up its capabilities in shopper analytics. Next, Walmart transformed the organization into a worldwide division for e-commerce strategy: @Walmartlabs. In the following years Walmart acquired more companies (One Riot, Small Society, Grabble and Adchemy) and added hundreds of developers in the area of social analytics and data infrastructure in

Bangalore, India. The investment is aimed at compensating Walmart's stagnant US development. It will make Walmart less dependent on new market entries as a source of growth. Actually, the e-commerce strategy allows it to enter markets without physical stores. Moreover, originally bricks-and-mortar supermarkets utilized an acquisition strategy to speed up their online sales and gain access to the new skills and capacities needed. For example, in 2012 Ahold purchased Bol.com for €350 million, an online store that started in books and later sold many other non-food items. The acquisition seems to suit both parties. Bol.com gets access to Ahold stores that they can leverage as pick-up points for non-food ordered online. Ahold stores do not offer much space for non-food anyway. And, through the acquisition, Ahold strengthens its online expertise. It may also look for synergies with Peapod, its online division in the United States. Many European retailers want to be ready before Amazon enters their countries.

What can you do to make your shoppers happy?

Enabling shoppers to buy online allows them to tap into numerous benefits such as infinite choice and price comparison.

The experience of shopping for groceries online consists of some unwanted side effects such as not being able to touch and smell fresh food, and the complex arrangements for home delivery. Retailers need to find shopper segments that are less concerned about the discomforts, and/or attempt to address each of these barriers.

Shopping for groceries involves purchasing a range of articles from several categories that are only relevant when purchased in connection with each other. Winning online grocery retailers offer extensive assortments, manage state-of-the-art transport and delivery methods for fresh products, and invest in their reputation as solid, quality-oriented retailers.

For some categories and shopping missions, shoppers will more happily switch to online, for example for personal hygiene products and bulky items that are purchased in a highly planned way.

Which marketing strategies can retailers apply?

Retailers may consider a combination of online ordering and pick-up points as an alternative to buying and building a store network when entering a new market (country).

Retailers have started to compete heavily in relation to supply-chain dimensions such as delivery slots and delivery fees. This offers more functional and cost-based motivations to use online shopping. Instead, retailers could differentiate themselves based on dimensions such as target group, ease of selection online and assortment.

Notes

1 Nielsen, (August 2012) [accessed 22 July 2015] How Digital Influences How We Shop Around the World [Online] http://www.nielsen.com/us/en/insights/reports/2012/how-digital-influences-how-we-shop-around-the-world.html

2 Nielsen (2012) [accessed 22 July 2015] Digital Shopping, the Topline on Online [Online] https://www.cangift.org/upload/marketmonitor-september 2012-digital-shopping.pdf

3 Ocado, (2013) [accessed 22 July 2015] Ocado Annual Report 2013 [Online] http://results13.ocadogroup.com/site-essentials/downloads/annual-report-2013

4 IGD (2014) [accessed 22 July 2015] IGD: UK Grocery Retailing [Online] http://www.igd.com/Research/Retail/retail-outlook/3371/UK-Grocery-Retailing/

5 ABN Amro (2012) [accessed 22 July 2015] 2015 boodschappen doen in de toekomst, de supermarket anno 2015 [Online] https://insights.abnamro.nl/app/uploads/2013/06/Boodschappen-doen-in-de-toekomst.pdf

6 Voor Hoofdbedrijfschap Detailhandel en Thuiswinkel.org (2011) [accessed 22 July 2015] Multichannel Monitor 2011 [Online] https://www.thuiswinkel.org/data/uploads/marktonderzoeken/Multichannel_Monitor/Multichannel_Monitor_2011.pdf

7 Roots Beleidsadvies & AnalyZus, Winkelleegstand in 2020. See also ABN Amro (2012) [accessed 22 July 2015] 2015 boodschappen doen in de toekomst, de supermarket anno 2015 [Online] https://insights.abnamro.nl/app/uploads/2013/06/Boodschappen-doen-in-de-toekomst.pdf

8 Age UK (2012) [accessed 22 July 2015] Food shopping in later life, barriers and service solutions, *Age UK* [Online] http://www.ageuk.org.uk/Documents/EN-GB/For-professionals/Conferences/Final_Food_Shopping_Report.pdf?dtrk=true

9 Rigby, C (2012) [accessed 22 July 2015] Older shoppers power online spending: research, *Internet Retailing* [Online] http://internetretailing.net/2012/01/older-shoppers-power-online-spending-research/

10 Interbrand (2014) [accessed 22 July 2015] Best Retail Brands Report [Online] http://www.interbrand.com/assets/uploads/Interbrand-Best-Retail-Brands-2014-3.pdf

11 CBS (2014) [accessed 22 July 2015] Supermarkets within walking distance for most Dutch people, *Statistics Netherlands* [Online] http://www.cbs.nl/en-GB/menu/themas/verkeer-vervoer/publicaties/artikelen/archief/2010/2010-3189-wm.htm

12 Neville, S (2014) [accessed 22 July 2015] Tesco: who says it's hard to make home delivery profits?, *Independent*, 26 February [Online] http://www.independent.co.uk/news/business/news/tesco-who-says-its-hard-to-make-home-delivery-profits-9153185.html

13 Barclays (2012) Aisle Help – Click & Collect, August.

PART FOUR
Fact-driven decision making

Getting your assortment right

07

A retailer's choice of channel demands large investments, and therefore an in-depth understanding of the deeper needs of shoppers is required before such important decisions are made. In Part Two I discussed the emotional needs of shoppers and the role that neuro research and psychology play to better understand these. In Part Four, in addition to these approaches, I recommend that retailers make their decisions in a fact-driven manner and apply techniques that show the more rational needs of shoppers. This chapter illustrates the fact-driven, structured approach to an important question in retail: what is the optimal size for an assortment? Part Four also shows how loyalty card programmes (Chapter 8) and big data analysis (Chapter 9) may contribute to better retailer decisions on what matters to shoppers.

Available space as starting point for product assortment size

A question that remains topical during the annual planning process of a retailer is how many products a category should carry. Both the width and depth of product assortment are crucial elements of differentiation for a grocery retailer. Retailers take a number of factors into consideration when deciding on the assortment size:

- Retail strategy:
  - Mission and positioning of retailer: service-orientated retailers want to please their shoppers. One retailer may choose product assortment as its important instrument to differentiate itself, while others may choose other service elements such as friendly staff.

- Shopper needs: the category manager selects those products that its target shopper needs. Careful environmental analysis, innovation and sourcing policy are key.

● Category strategy:

- Category role: the importance of the category will drive the amount of space that the retailer creates.
- Category objective: even if the category role is of low importance, the category may temporarily serve an important role in fighting competition.
- The assortment of competitors offers a benchmark.

● Available space and online capabilities:

- Available space: the retailer may have a specific strategy for large stores or a good online presence; in practice, retailers have a portfolio of stores that have a certain size and vary widely. This is where ambition meets available space.
- Online capability: offering part of the product assortment online could be a result of shopper needs, or could also be more driven by the lack of space or be part of a broader channel strategy.

● Operations:

- Organizational decision making: buyers have a natural motivation to expand their categories as this may drive category sales, and increase their bonuses and prestige within the organization. Other functions such as logistics are rewarded on the basis of product elimination. The way that decisions are made at the retailer influences the actual product assortment.
- Data systems: first of all, current sales need to be tracked well. How thoroughly a product assortment is analysed also depends on the quality and depth of the data, and the ease of use of software.

The ambitions of the retailer may encounter other obstacles, such as the availability of reliable suppliers. Still, available space across the retailer's current stores is a more important constraint and therefore a starting point for a retailer when it plans current product assortment. The retailer typically starts with a high-level analysis on the amount of space it wishes to reserve for categories. The location in-store is not precise but it drafts 'spots' or 'clouds' of categories in a store map. For the sake of convenience, the visual representation is based on a standard furbishing for the store size that has the highest frequency out of all the retailer's stores. This is used as a benchmark as it represents the ideal. In a more sophisticated manner each department then obtains a proportion of space based on criteria such as the following:

- retailer strategy;
- presence of service counter;
- profit contribution;
- revenue;
- average dimensions of the product.

The last factor may need more explanation. One item of a voluminous product such as toilet paper needs more space than, for example, one tin of salt and the retailer needs to include this in the calculation from space to product assortment size. Retailers that have a wide portfolio of store types and sizes take the 'average store' as anchor and adapt the product assortment for each cluster of stores. The end result is an overview of the amount of space that each category obtains. This is the starting point for category managers to plan the assortment size. Next, retail and category strategies determine the size, width and depth of the assortment. The way these choices are made will be the topic of the remainder of this chapter. What is important from a strategic point of view is to consider online retail strategies early as an option in the assortment decisions. A retailer may need to reduce its assortment in bricks-and-mortar stores but this might be combined with an expansion of the online offering. Nowadays there is a strong surge of click-and-collect points in countries such as France and the UK. Tesco in the UK has become a very good example to illustrate this point. Tesco has cut back on two-thirds of its general merchandise offer in favour of new grocery items. At the same time Tesco expanded its non-food offering to more than 200,000 items online. The shopper has the choice between home delivery or picking up these non-food orders at click-and-collect points at one of the more than 1,800 Tesco stores where this service is available.

Shopper-driven product assortment

An assortment strategy describes not only the size of the assortment per category but also deals with the segmentation, the number of brands, the size of private label and the number of price points. These are all intertwined. To complicate things even more, the optimal size of the category may also depend on the application of shelf materials and whether the retailers present the assortment to the shopper in a structured manner.

As explained above, the available space drives many of the decisions, and one question that comes up is how and when shopper needs are addressed in the assortment process. Put simply, the category manager aligns the assortment to the objectives of the organization and brand strategy. Besides this, in an implicit manner the category manager makes sure that the shopper needs are addressed. The reality is often largely in contrast with what retailer CEOs claim in interviews, stating that the needs and wants of their shoppers are paramount to their product assortment. However, assortment management often lives its own life. Grocery retailers can determine with local market data which product assortment is best in each store they operate, but there are just a handful that exploit this expertise. In the old days the shopkeeper would ask shoppers what they would like to buy and have it ready the next time the shopper visited the store. This sort of personal service guaranteed shopper loyalty. Today, while all the data and systems available should make things simpler, they actually seem to make it more difficult for retailers to meet the local demand and maximize revenue at the same time. The complexity is often huge and remains unaddressed. Perhaps regional and small grocery chains seem best equipped to include local delicacies in the product assortment or source fresh produce from the region. In the ideal scenario grocery retailers select a product assortment per store that is exactly sufficient and addresses the needs of the local catchment area. Larger grocery retailers struggle with taking the shopper as the starting point for their assortment management. The reasons for this vary:

- Most retailers want to be perceived as least expensive or at least as giving value for money. As a result, they place significant efforts in watching competitive prices and managing their own. In addition, prices can change overnight. The price focus overrides all attention for product assortment management, branding and innovation. Price wars are the most extreme situations that cause retailers to forget about assortment. I found that Dutch and French retailers carried out significant assortment cuts and increased the number of private-label lookalikes during the periods in which there was a pure focus on price.

- A practical joke in retail is that the three most important drivers of growth are location, location and location. For many years retailers in Europe relied on expanding the number of stores and enlarging the size of each store to achieve growth. Rather than analysing which product assortment was needed in each new catchment area it was far more efficient to operate with the standard assortment. Larger stores had to be filled, so retailers started overfacing items and adding items without careful analysis as to whether they fulfilled a need, or what the revenue prospects were. New categories were added as well, in order to make the store look attractive. Of course, all this led to higher attention from shoppers and more revenue. The end result is a less-tended product assortment with many ad-hoc processes.

- Some retailers position themselves by offering everything that the shopper asks for. Examples include Auchan in France and Jumbo in the Netherlands. Their own choice of positioning may give them a hard time. When Jumbo acquired some 300 small or medium-sized supermarket stores of the C1000 banner, in its communication it kept the promise of most extensive product assortment, but stores were physically not able to live up to the promise.

- The retailer may struggle to get its product assortment right after acquiring one or more competitors. It may end up with a high variety of store types, service positionings and all kinds of sizes, and it needs to align assortment processes and systems. For the sake of priorities or convenience the retailer might leave matters as they are. A similar issue comes into play if franchisers lack discipline to the retail brand guidelines or make overly creative assortment decisions on their own.

- The natural barrier has been the amount of space both in-store and in warehouses. For some categories, assortment expansion requires the additional investment of coolers, counters, freezers and special shelves, so in these cases category managers have to make an additional trade-off.

- Finally, it is actually quite hard in practice to take the needs of the shopper as a starting point for the product assortment and to comply with the ambitions in the strategic plan. If the strategic plan asks for more soup items, how many are sufficient for the shopper? Are soup vegetables and beef cubes included in the consumer-based definition of soup? Can I adjust the assortment in an efficient manner to the needs of shoppers in a certain region or catchment area? How do I find out that a soup item with extremely low sales needs to be retained in the assortment because its revenue is incremental? Take for example a product such as the light version of Calvé peanut butter. When compared to the regular versions of both A-brand and private labels, its revenue fades into nothing. However, it would be wrong to eliminate this light version because it attracts a group of shoppers who only buy the light version, and if it were removed they would perhaps look out for another store that does carry the item. In this case, category managers may be able to find their way with the help of some of their own consumption experience and intuition, but let's take another example: juice drinks. Tesco in the UK has some 35 different items available. Let's assume that the category manager eliminates the version apple and raspberry and shoppers start buying the version apple and cranberry instead. In that case, apple and raspberry did not offer unique, incremental revenue for the category.

All the obstacles and daily inconveniences mentioned above could be right and justified, but still it is peculiar that grocery retailers find it difficult to create a shopper-driven product assortment. I would have expected that critical and articulate shoppers would leave them no choice. It is a paradox. Retailers see shoppers each day in their stores, but are unsure what the shopper wants and needs. Perhaps the increased scale of retailers is to be blamed. Also, most grocery retailers operate at a low net margin between 1 per cent and 4 per cent in Europe, which makes them less eager to invest in marketing. This brings me to another paradox of grocery retailers. The battle with competition forces supermarkets to respond ever faster. However, decisions on the basis of a gut feeling can no longer withstand the technological changes and the articulate, mobile shopper. Supermarkets have access to the most detailed and reliable data from scanning checkouts and loyalty cards but often they prefer to rely on the feeling that they get in stores. For the design of future stores the CEOs rely on visits to aspiring stores abroad with their advertising agency, but forget to deep-dive into data that consumers give them with their purchases. Tesco in the UK and Kroger in the United States are often acknowledged for turning their data into business successes. Albert Heijn, despite being a highly professional organization, still struggles to make their data work for them. Albert Heijn launched the Airmiles card in 1994 and its own BonusCard loyalty programme in 1997. Both resulted in gigabytes of information on the behaviour of individual Albert Heijn shoppers. For myself, I have been receiving from them coupons with a moderate 25 per cent discount for products that are so generic, such as pasta sauce, that I feel the same mail could be sent to 90 per cent of Dutch shoppers. It is widely recognized that grocery retailers struggle to operate in a more shopper-driven manner and to make decisions based on data.

The two grocery retailer paradoxes – seeing the shopper but not engaging, and having the data but not applying it – have a crucial influence on the way that grocery retailers make product assortment decisions. It is interesting to see how retailers deal with these paradoxes, as it increases the understanding of how they make assortment decisions and identify where they could do better. I found it helpful to segment grocery retailers for their assortment policies on the basis of the following two dimensions:

- aligning to local needs versus maximizing harmonization by offering the same product assortment everywhere as much as possible;
- intuitive assortment decisions versus decisions based on data and insights.

The result is four quadrants that represent phases of a product assortment life cycle (Figure 7.1). Each phase differentiates the manner in which grocery retailers make assortment decisions.

FIGURE 7.1 Assortment life cycle

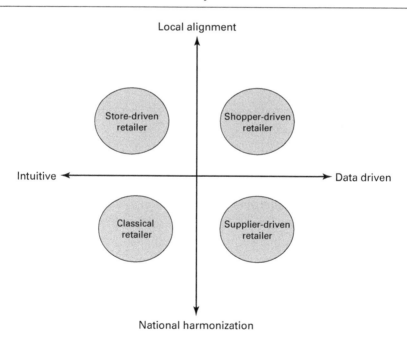

SOURCE: Model by Constant Berkhout

There are four types of grocery organizations. In each phase of the product assortment decisions, the type of data and responsibilities of the buying and marketing departments are different:

[1] The classical retailer keeps the assortment as identical as possible in all stores, based on intuitive decisions.

[2] The store-driven retailer operates with local assortments across stores based on intuitive decisions.

[3] The supplier-driven retailer maintains an assortment that is identical across the country based on data.

[4] The shopper-driven retailer knows how to offer the best assortment in a local store based on data.

There is natural evolution of phases. Organizations transition over the different assortment life-cycle stages. The typical path takes them from classical retailer to store-driven retailer to supplier-driven retailer to shopper-driven retailer. Some grocery retailers have gone through all quadrants. As a result their organizations and assortments may have experienced huge transformations within a couple of decades.

In a moment I describe what each of the phases looks like and the order they often occur in, but first let's look at the most advanced situation: the shopper-driven retailer [4]. This retailer has found a way to address the two retailer paradoxes. It succeeds in converting scanning and loyalty card data into impactful assortment decisions and serves the local needs of shoppers in each store. Characteristics of a shopper-driven retailer are:

- The assortment in each store is aligned 100 per cent with the local needs. The shoppers get the feeling that the assortment is selected completely for them. This is about perception and in reality the assortments of the stores do not need to differ much among each other but it is about making the right difference on item level. A supermarket chain could, for example, keep 85 per cent of its assortment identical in all its supermarkets. In the next step it identifies where it needs to adjust the size to match local needs (for example, ready-made meals and fresh juices) or decides that a category could be taken out, given the individual store data (for example, meat over the service counter, or textiles).

- A differentiating assortment helps to build a strong and unique retail brand. Therefore, the shopper-driven retail brand develops innovations itself and places significant effort in the sourcing of strategic categories. In routine categories it conducts assortment analyses and carries out changes independently and without the help of suppliers.

- Revenue and percentage margin are no longer the deciding factors for introducing or eliminating articles from the assortment, but instead it is the extent to which each article results in new, incremental revenue per store. The shopper is not interested in hearing about the amount of margin, or the contribution to advertising budget of product placement fees that suppliers pay. The revenue of some herbs and other meal ingredients could be extremely low, but if a retailer does not offer these the shopper will not replace them with other products. It is typically these low-revenue products, such as a sea-salt brand mentioned in a popular cooking book, that are under threat of being cut by category managers who start new and fresh in the role. Therefore, some retailers have taken precautionary measures, such as the British grocer Sainsbury's that maintains a list of some 100 products that are low in revenue but highly incremental and should not be eliminated.

An important point I need to make is that knowing the socio-demographics of the target shopper does not guarantee that retailers offer the right assortment. Shoppers with the same age, gender and number of children may end up with completely different items. Under the influence of socio-cultural changes in society, shoppers feel less guided by what their parents or church tell them to do than in the past. I like the following example, in which try to guess which two men I am describing. Both are English and famous. They were born in the same year, 1948, and to my surprise only three weeks apart. Both are members of the Church of England, have been married twice, have children and make a high annual income. Based on this description many would expect they have the same lifestyle and buy more or less the same type of food and clothes. Both Prince Charles and Ozzy Osbourne fit this description. While the first is known for his passion for architecture, organic food and support for environmental causes, Ozzy Osbourne made the news by apparently sucking ants through his nose, his band Black Sabbath and his reality television show *The Osbournes*. Socio-demographics and regional habits are not sufficient.

When drafting the store profile the grocery retailer should consider the actual purchasing behaviour both in terms of the categories bought and shopping process factors, such as time spent and the number of categories purchased. Therefore, a simple grouping of stores based on a region will not work. A convenience store in a high street serves very different needs to a convenience store at the edge of the city, despite being in the same city and the shoppers having the same socio-demographic profile, attitudes and lifestyle values.

An optimal local assortment places heavy emphasis on software, IT infrastructure, activity alignment among departments, and salary and benefits system. The retailer needs to build an enterprise resource planning (ERP) system that automatically delivers recommendations on the assortment per store or store cluster and tracks which changes are needed over time. The marketing and category management departments have mutual objectives expressed with regards to the loyalty of regular customers rather than buying price and percentage margin. The description of the shopper-driven retailer seems idealistic and far away, but it is already happening today. Category managers at the Finnish grocery retailer Kesko, for example, maintain up to 115 assortment plans per category at the same time. Each assortment is aligned with the needs of the local shopper and the size of the store. This is the way it works: the category manager sets assortment and space conditions such as the percentage of private label and the available space. The marketing department can set the rules for the retail banner or enforce category-specific guidelines. Within the set requirements and objectives the Kesko assortment software generates recommendations automatically, which saves the category manager time that he or she can then use to carefully analyse those situations that are more urgent and important. Another good example of a shopper-driven retailer is Kroger in the United States, where category managers are not rewarded on total revenue or total profits but on the objectives set for its most loyal target group. As a consequence, the total revenue of, for example, the beer category may remain stable at Kroger as long as the spend by loyal customers who are beer buyers increases.

Transitioning through phases of assortment life cycle

Often retailers went through several phases before they were able to make product assortment decisions on the basis of fact, and they addressed local shopper needs perfectly. Retailers start as a classical retailer, and evolve to become a shopper-driven retailer.

Often those retailers started life as the owner of just one store that listened to the needs of the shoppers. The assortment is flexible. The store owner buys all products himself or herself, delivers the goods in the quantities the shopper likes and will add new assortment that the shoppers ask for. The most entrepreneurial store owners blessed with foresight start buying and keeping stock for other store owners. They combine retailing and wholesaling into one organization. In the first phase (see bottom-left quadrant in Figure 7.1) a classical retailer [1] adds as many assortments as possible.

The buyer makes all assortment decisions. Larger volumes drive higher discounts so the organization seeks to extend the number of stores which the wholesale operation supplies. Because the network of stores is growing it becomes more important to take the wishes of the local operator into consideration.

Gradually the organization becomes a store-driven retailer [2] (see top-left in Figure 7.1), which carries an assortment that does justice to all needs in the diverse local market regions. Stores may be fully owned or supplied on the basis of a wholesale contract. In this phase the store-driven retailer invests in improving the outbound logistics to the stores. Next the retailer feels the need to counterpoise suppliers. It does so on the one hand by developing its own brands and on the other by building its own marketing programmes directed at shoppers.

The tipping point from store-driven retailer to supplier-driven retailer [3] takes place when the terms and conditions with suppliers make large buying volumes so interesting that the retailer harmonizes its assortment across stores. If the assortments of stores vary, this is most likely due to differences in store size. In the previous phase management spent a lot of time on optimizing wholesale operations and it expanded the store network with the purpose of lowering the wholesale operations costs. A supplier-driven retailer sees warehousing not as an end in itself but as a necessary supply-chain requirement for serving its stores. In this phase, as a retailer there is a lot of focus on operational excellence. Management attempts to consolidate all processes for new product introductions, seasonal changes, category reviews and assortment reductions. The supplier-driven retailer focuses on meeting efficiency objectives so everything that is different from, for example, full pallet loads and quick turnaround times at the warehouse, are unmentionable. Risk of this phase is that the standardization shoots past its target. Decision making slows down and the organization finds itself stuck in a muddy pool. It may even signify the end of the retailer. An example of a retailer that remained in the supplier-driven retailer phase and never reached the final phase is the Dutch grocery Super de Boer. This organization put so much emphasis on process management that it lost sight of the shopper. It was sold to Jumbo Supermarkten, another Dutch chain.

Therefore, in the phase of the supplier-driven retailer there is a crucial role for visionary leadership with excellent marketing skills that steers the retailer away from this trap towards becoming a shopper-driven retailer [4]. Instead of supplier interest the shopper becomes important again. A shopper-driven retailer likes to ensure the attention is on the shopper, so the shopper feels as though they are in a mom-and-pop store. The assortment in each store is 100 per cent tailored to the store, with the help of superb customer service and automated assortment software.

Example: evolution of Schuitema organization

A good example of an organization that went through all phases is Schuitema from the Netherlands. It all started with a single store in the northern town of Groningen. A gentleman by the name of Jacob Fokke Schuitema opened his first grocery store in 1888. The family Schuitema later converted the store operation into a wholesaler with affiliated entrepreneurs. They sought collaboration with other wholesalers for collective buying power and around 1931 they came up with one retail brand label for the stores, Centra. Later, the supermarket label C1000 was developed. In 1988 Ahold bought a majority share in Schuitema in order to stop its competitors gaining market share. Ahold was happy with the investment and market share of Schuitema as such. As a result the Schuitema organization became more inward-oriented and focused on trading relationships with suppliers to support its heavy promotion programmes. Shoppers saw Schuitema stores as places for great deals and they served the role of topping up on purchases made in a primary supermarket. Confidence in the Schuitema organization took a leap when Ahold sold its majority share to a private equity company. This created space for Schuitema to set its own strategy and invest in the organization. One of the pillars was offering local product assortments based on thorough shopper-needs analysis. Schuitema continued professionalizing its space and assortment management until the private equity firm sold the retailer in 2012 to Jumbo Supermarkten, a Dutch family-owned chain.

From this description, it follows that the typical life cycle is from classical retailer to store-driven retailer to supplier-driven retailer to shopper-driven retailer. An interesting observation is that a store-driven retailer meets the needs of the local shopper better than a supplier-driven retailer that is more advanced in the typical life cycle. In the first organization the entrepreneurs of the affiliated outlets feel strong enough in the power relationship to demand that the wholesale or retail organization carry its products with very low but incremental revenue. If the store-driven retailer does not listen, the supermarket manager or entrepreneur will find suppliers that source its store. Such a retailer reminds me of the traditional mom-and-pop stores where the owner knows all its shoppers personally and adjusts its product assortment without much thinking of the needs of the shopper. It also recalls

Albert Heijn, who laid the foundation for what later became the internationally operating retailer Ahold. Albert Heijn opened his first store in 1887 and the 21-year-old entrepreneur had a flexible attitude to product assortment changes to please his shoppers. He removed items such as furniture, which makes sense for a grocery store. However, he also took out items that are now destination groups such as fresh produce, because shoppers obtained these from their own gardens. Instead he introduced coffee, shovels for liquid manure, milk yokes and wooden shoes, clothing and fuel to his grocery store, all of which better fitted the needs of his shoppers.

No matter how intuitive those decisions are, in many ways these stores were more shopper-driven than many retailers of today. Examples of great retailers that do excel in shopper-driven retailing are Kesko in Finland and Tesco in the UK. I have discussed the barriers to investing time on assortment management. The last shift in the life cycle to shopper-driven retailer receives massive resistance in the organization. Management of the warehouses and logistics get nervous when they hear that this shift results in carrying more articles, and in different mixes for each store. Senior leadership needs to persuade supply-chain management that shopper loyalty will deliver more revenue and profits in the long term than efficiency-only measures. With a similar effort the leadership team needs to have the vision to invest in data and research to improve the efficacy of its marketing decisions. Of all Dutch supermarkets Albert Heijn has the most characteristics of a shopper-driven retailer, but it is for the greater part still a supplier-driven assortment organization. Indeed, its brand management thinking stands out. Its brand formats are well positioned: 'AH To Go' for on-the-go convenience, and the larger supermarket format Albert Heijn XL for regional roles with more non-food; and the change of meal deals three times a day in its German 'AH To Go' stores is spot on from a shopper perspective. However, Albert Heijn does not yet use loyalty card data to determine the perfect assortment in each store – even though this data is available to them.

The assortment life cycles give good insight into why bricks-and-mortar stores, and also shopper-driven retailers, have difficulties in competing with online grocery players. Online retailing appeared suddenly out of nowhere, as shown in the top-right quadrant of Figure 7.1 as shopper-driven retail. Players like Ocado and Amazon deliver extreme personalization through a very data-driven approach. It is in their DNA. Finally, for suppliers there is no time to lie back. Suppliers could support their retailers, which operate physical stores, by delivering category planograms tailored to each store or cluster of similar stores. They have more people and time than retailers to analyse the loyalty card data and complement these with category-specific shopper researches. On this basis the retailer could make decisions that are more factually based and more aligned with shopper needs than ever before.

Shoppers like it: more is less

In the previous sections we discussed what a shopper-driven assortment looks like, what a retailer needs to act on and which barriers it will meet along the journey. If you work in the retail sector, you will realize sooner or later that retailers have the unstoppable drive to add product assortment. Where does this come from? Perhaps your like-for-like sales growth is stabilizing and you create space in the hope that the new assortment will add sales. Adding items is essentially also easier, less risky and less data intensive than considering which items to delist. Large multinationals need to report growth to Wall Street and are in constant need for distribution of their latest innovations with higher margins. However, where is the shopper in this?

It seems that shoppers are not particularly uncomfortable with cutting back product assortments. The idea is certainly popular among consultants. Bain & Co published a report in 2007 that concluded that assortment reduction could lead to 40 per cent more revenue and 35 per cent less cost. The following years grocery retailers around the world cut back product assortments. Walmart and Carrefour reduced their assortments by about 15 per cent. Also online retailers can have too much assortment. Researchers Boatwright and Nunes eliminated between 20 per cent and 80 per cent of the assortment across forty-two categories in an experiment at an online US grocery retailer.[1] With an average assortment reduction of 56 per cent the revenue rose by 11 per cent. Practitioners often refer to the evidence delivered in the famous jam study by Iyengar and Lepper.[2] Iyengar often shopped for groceries at Draeger's supermarket in California. This supermarket is literally full of product assortment, the packaged grocery department alone includes more than 50,000 items and it is renowned for its special foods and wines. At the time that Iyengar shopped at Draeger's it carried more than 250 types of mustard. Iyengar was intrigued by the fact that she often left the store empty-handed because the amount of choice overwhelmed her. She decided to make this the topic of her scientific research and in 2000 set up a jam experiment in her local supermarket. The results quickly spread through the world: an extensive assortment of 24 Wilkin & Son jams drew the attention of 60 per cent of the visitors, while at the limited assortment of six flavours only 40 per cent stopped on the shelf. In conclusion, a larger assortment draws more attention. However, when it comes to buying, the numbers are very different. In the case of the extensive assortment, the buying conversion was 10 times as low, so that in the end the limited assortment delivered more shoppers and more revenue. The outcome of the experiment supports the intuition of most practitioners. Society offers people an overwhelming number of choices and supermarkets are no exception to this. Sometimes it is just too complicated to select the best snack to accompany a drink with friends later in the afternoon. As Barry Schwartz simply summarizes in *The Paradox of Choice: Why more is less*: 'Learning to choose is hard. Learning to choose well is harder. And learning to choose well in a world of unlimited possibilities is harder still, perhaps too hard.'[3]

Recent research in the fields of behavioural economics and neuro research has given a better understanding of why product assortments that are too large do not work. If the choice is large, the chance that you make a mistake increases. Having more choice increases the likelihood that the shoppers might feel regret – and this emotion is one of the most neglected emotions in marketing. If the shopper makes a quick choice, they start to worry later on whether they should have invested more time. If the shopper takes a more elaborate approach, seeing more options, learning more about each of them, they may think that some options are equally or even more attractive than the initial impulse. In addition, the shopper could feel ashamed if they arrive at a party with the wrong drink or snack. All of this results in an anxious feeling when faced with a large variety of products. For the sake of convenience and efficiency, humans prefer to rely on their automatic response system and on heuristics. This is most likely to occur in complex environments. A supermarket provides much stimulation as a result of the tens of thousands of products, hundreds of messages and all the new people you see. While the shopper is in the store they also need to remember, for example, where they parked the car and also possibly keep an eye on children or incoming messages on a mobile phone.

A thorough evaluation of products by shoppers is of course possible, but this occurs in the cognitive system, which has much less operating power and is occupied with all these worries and thoughts simultaneously. So instead shoppers rely on a heuristic, either consciously or unconsciously, such as 'I'll buy the product in the middle' or 'I'll buy the brand with the least amount of stock.' In addition, shoppers are often under time pressure so only allow themselves a certain amount of time to complete their purchases. I was confronted with this fact when I looked at the results of a large shopper study I performed at two Morrisons supermarket stores in the UK. Although one supermarket was 30 per cent larger than the other one, shoppers completed their shopping journey in the exact same average time, 28 minutes. In the last phase of the shopping trip the shoppers started walking faster, they skipped complete aisles such as the frozen department that was close to the checkouts and they dipped into just one or two aisles for the absolute necessities. In the larger store, shoppers visited 30 per cent of the surface, compared to 47 per cent in the smaller store. Combining the stress of deadlines because of a busy lifestyle with an overwhelming level of choice, this leads to the idea that supermarkets are possibly the worst place on earth for the human brain to cope with.

Apart from the behavioural arguments there is also a limit to the shopper's vision capabilities. Put simply, the multitude of products stops shoppers from seeing much of what the store offers. Before Iyengar published her experiment in 2000, back when I worked at Albert Heijn, I considered the excessive level of choice of products as a category-specific challenge rather than an issue that might affect all categories. Albert Heijn had discovered the positive consequences of assortment reductions in categories with many small items such as personal care. The challenge of the personal care category for shoppers is that the shelves house many small items with a multitude of bright colours. In the case of a larger choice the shopper needs more time to search and the decision to pick one item becomes more difficult. The category is less frequented so the shopper is less familiar with the planogram. In such a situation it is difficult to find the right shampoo that fixes the precise hair-care problem that the shopper suffers from. In an attempt to solve this, Albert Heijn cut a significant number of items – and shoppers seemed to like the reduction. In a survey shoppers declared themselves to be more pleased with the shelf. To my surprise they also said that the new shelf presentation contained a larger assortment than before. In conclusion, too many choices of products leave the shopper very unhappy. Sometimes having too much choice is demotivating. If the shoppers make a choice, they seek comfort in heuristics that seem perfectly rational at the moment of buying, such as choosing the product that the famous TV star featured on the display tells them to buy – or they stick to what they always have bought before. The shopper becomes more susceptible to social pressures such as store staff or a friend or family member who advises them to pick a certain brand. As a result of too much choice, the shopper may also delay or cancel the purchase. If the shopper becomes more aware of the stress that the large assortment causes, they may come up with proactive shopping strategies such as visiting convenience and discount stores that offer a limited assortment. Indeed, in addition to the economic downturn the feeling of excessive choice is one of the main reasons for the success of dollar stores in the United States, pound stores in the UK, and discounters like Aldi and Lidl in Europe.

Retailer desire for 'more is less'

Retailers have strong incentives to reduce the size of product assortments. First of all, serving the shopper is the very reason for existence of a store, so if shoppers want less of assortment then that is what retailers do. The thought is supported by reports by consultancy agencies that point to the significant financial benefits from assortment reduction such as:

- fewer unique warehouse locations;
- fewer working stocks and working capital;
- less time needed to set up and maintain articles in the internal data system;
- fewer overhead staff needed to manage assortments;
- more negotiation power with suppliers of the remaining items;
- more sales because of visibility of remaining items;
- less running out of stock, and therefore less shopper dissatisfaction and more loyalty.

Product assortment reductions are also subject to fluctuations in the economy. After the banking crises and the ensuing economic recession of 2008 hit consumer confidence and purchasing power, shoppers became more reluctant to spend money and they shifted their budget to lower-priced products. High expenditures such as washing machines were delayed so retailers needed fewer of them and shoppers became comfortable with less choice. With regard to luxury products, shoppers seek less variety anyway: if they feel they deserve a treat, they are fine with fewer options. In times of economic stress shoppers seek comfort by relying on a few, perhaps more conservative, choices. The consultancy agencies may correctly point to the financial benefits of assortment reduction, especially after the good times of unstoppable growth during which category managers enthusiastically added more assortment options with low shopper needs in order to differentiate the retail brand. Finally, a driving factor for cutting assortments in physical stores has been the massive growth of internet sales. Ordering books and travel online, for example, is much more convenient than shopping for these in a hypermarket. Online stores keep stock in central locations or have no stock at all and leave this responsibility to the supplier. Therefore, online stores have the opportunity to sell slow movers in a more cost-efficient manner than physical stores, and the shopper is willing to wait a day or two for the delivery.

Assortment reduction is not easy. Retailers need to know exactly which item they have to discontinue. They should identify, item by item, whether the product serves a unique need. For this, preferably there will be loyalty card data available that shows whether products have low sales but perhaps are purchased by shoppers who are unlikely to buy other items from the assortment. Assortment reduction may go very wrong, as even Walmart, the largest retailer in the world, noticed. In 2009 Walmart rationalized some 15 per cent of its assortment. One year later Walmart found out it had cut too far and too deep, especially in grocery. Though the removed stockkeeping units (SKUs) had low rotation, Walmart found these items were also driving shopping trips. So instead of losing $1 on an item it lost a $70 basket. In 2010 Canada's largest grocery retailer, Loblaw, found out that its assortment reduction of some 10 per cent as part of a larger restructuring process had been too drastic.[4] Half of these products were later returned to the shelves. What is even more worrying is that Loblaw had to depend on the shopper coming back into the store to ask for the products, rather than the store getting warning signals from its information systems. The executive chairman of Loblaw said: 'We knew we'd get probably about half of it wrong, not necessarily across the country, but on an individual store [basis]. Then we'd have to go through the process based on the customer calling us or letting us know what they want, and we'd bring back those 5 per cent of [products] that really matter to that store.' He added that Loblaw was working on a new information system.

An example of where an extensive assortment reduction programme did work comes from Carrefour in France. Carrefour made assortment reduction a fundamental pillar of its new concept of hypermarkets. When hypermarkets opened in Europe in the 1950s, shoppers found it exciting to see such an extensive offer at low prices under one roof. However, this channel has slowly lost its competitive advantage of bargain prices in Western Europe to discount players like Lidl and category killers like Toys 'R' Us. Carrefour also started to doubt whether offering a large assortment to time-deprived shoppers is such a good idea. Most of Carrefour's revenue comes from hypermarkets in Western Europe, precisely where the channel is in most heavy weather. To overcome this challenge in 2010 Carrefour launched a new type of hypermarket store, as already mentioned, named 'Carrefour Planet'. Apart from creating more excitement and more services, a key element of the Carrefour Planet concept was to reduce the number of SKUs by around 15 per cent. What is impressive about this is that despite the reduction in the number of SKUs, Carrefour achieved a better perception of assortment width. They did so by identifying shopper needs for each category with the help of personalized loyalty card data. Nowadays, Carrefour speaks of so-called 'consumer need units'. These are types of needs as the shopper perceives them in the category. For example, Carrefour reduced the number of individual SKUs at the fruit and vegetable department by 13 per cent. However, at the same time it increased the number of consumer need units by 5 per cent and expanded space for this department by 33 per cent.

May I have some more, please?

In this chapter it has become clear that the supermarket trip might be a stressful experience for shoppers. They have little time, many post-trip duties to think about and at the same time they have to steer the shopping cart, with products and perhaps children attached, safely down the aisles. From that perspective, spending too much time deciding which exact tomato ketchup a shopper actually buys seems ridiculous, though the shopper might be researching at home before making their decision. Still, it is not clear what the shopper really wants. If retailers take this to the extreme, is it possible that shoppers are happy with having one option per category? Probably not. If shoppers see a delicious assortment of French cheeses, they are already visualizing the moment they bite into one of them. Scientific experiments show that large assortments are attractive. Rolls *et al* conclude that people eat 23 per cent more yoghurt if they are offered three yoghurts instead of one.[5] Iyengar, who became famous for the limitations of product assortment size as a result of her jam experiment, is less known for her contributions to explaining why large assortments exercise attraction to shoppers. In her book *The Art of Choosing* she points to the intrinsic preference people have for choice, in fact for more choice.[6] Iyengar refers to a study in which babies are sad and angry at the moment at which they can no longer choose the music they want to hear. A large assortment gives people a greater sense of control over the situation. From a biological perspective the sense of control is rewarding: it is associated with better health, a longer life and a greater sense of happiness.

In addition, the need for product assortment and choice is culturally driven. Children in individualistic societies such as the United States and the UK hear from their parents and teachers that they can do everything they want, that they should take control of their lives and should differentiate themselves from others. Over the past century the Western, individualistic culture has won greater influence, for example after the fall of the Iron Curtain in Eastern Europe. Therefore, the importance of choice has increased around the world. Added to this, after the Second World War the increase in prosperity allowed shoppers to buy more. There certainly is a push factor at play here: retailers expand their product assortments in order to differentiate themselves. With a larger assortment the retailer increases the chance to meet the needs of individual shoppers and in this way make them buy more products.

So how do we reconcile these contradictions? We are being simultaneously told that large assortments cause stress for shoppers, but also that those same large assortments feed our biological and cultural desire for greater choice. The paradox is that shoppers love a large assortment but choose less in such situations. This also applies to Iyengar's jam experiment: the large assortment results in much attention but with few purchases. This shopper behaviour can be explained if one realizes that there may be a difference between the *perception* of the assortment size and the *actual* assortment size. The assortment may be large, but the shopper might not perceive it as such. If we make a large assortment easier and quicker to understand, the shopper will experience the sense of choice and control while at the same time being able to choose easily. There are several methods that can be used to achieve this effect, as set out below.

Structure

Researchers Kahn and Wansink delivered a first approach.[7] In an experiment they pretended they were interested in the participants' opinion of TV advertising, but it was really about the snack that people received during the experiment. The snacks were all kinds of trays filled with jelly beans. In total there were four types of trays that differed in the number of offered colours (six or 24) and the level of structure (all colours in one compartment or all colours mixed). Results of the study showed that consumption of jelly beans was more than twice as high in the case of 24 colours if each compartment contained one colour. If all jelly beans were mixed, the consumption was the same regardless of the variety of colours. The remarkable finding is that consumption is highest if the variety is indeed highest, but only if the products are offered in a structured manner. In a similar experiment with six colours of M&Ms whereby the variety (six colours) was held stable and the total assortment sizes differed, the participants also preferred the larger assortment.

Giving structure to product assortments within stores is one of the most important responsibilities of category managers. They can implement structure by carefully examining the shopper decision tree and testing their planograms. On-shelf merchandising may help signal the start of a new segment. With these instruments category managers can reconcile their search for assortment extensions with ease of choice for the shopper.

Asymmetries

In the same paper Kahn and Wansink describe another experiment in which they offered M&Ms during TV commercials. Again they were not interested in the viewing behaviour but in how people selected the treat. This time, apart from varying the number of colours (seven and 10) there were two conditions of symmetry. Here is how the concept is explained: if there are seven or 10 colours and 30 per cent of the M&Ms are brown, there is a lower symmetry than if 10 per cent of the M&Ms are brown. In the case of the asymmetric offer, the number of M&Ms eaten rose from 56 for seven colours to 99 if the mix contained 10 colours. In the case of a symmetric offer there was no difference between giving more or fewer colours. The reason people eat more if the variety of colours increases is that dominant items offer convenience as a starting point in the search process. Retailers can implement this principle by giving a certain product with high recognition value a prominent place as a block on the shelf. For example, the confectionery brands Cadbury and Milka often serve as signals of the category because of their unique and strong colours.

Filtering

The filtering concept involves alternatives from the product assortment being shown to the shopper gradually. This is often applied online. Through several selections (filters) the shoppers pick, for example, a meal sauce of a certain size, price class and flavour through consecutive clicks. In a physical store the shoppers come across this principle in a different manner. For instance, in a jewellery store, staff show selections from the assortment of watches in several batches. Or a wine store may refer a shopper to a different floor or room for more special wine options.

Verbal description if choice is large

Townsend and Kahn demonstrate in a number of experiments that if shoppers were to have the final say, they would want their options displayed with images rather than with words.[8] This is because shoppers process images in a holistic manner that takes less effort, while words are processed in a more considered way, one by one. Still, images do not always work better. Townsend and Kahn asked shoppers to shop online for crackers. In the online store participants were offered assortments of eight or 27 crackers, which were either described in words or showed in images. In the case of a small assortment the presentation method did not matter much, although participants spent more time per cracker when the description was in words. When choosing from a visually presented large assortment the participants spent less time per cracker, but this is understandable as they skipped 10 crackers and looked in a less systematic way. In the case of an assortment of eight crackers, they were likely to remember more if they were displayed visually, while in the case of a large assortment of 27 crackers they were more likely to remember more if they were explained in words. The reason for this is that a visual display of an assortment of 27 crackers not only results in a sense of greater variety but also causes a sense of greater complexity. The two researchers conclude that in cases where there is a small number of varieties, a description with images results in a quick, effortless choice. If there is a large number of varieties, a textual presentation mode works better.

Retailers can easily apply the findings from this research in practice. Think of the menu at a Chinese restaurant. They often have a dazzling number of 200 or more options. The Chinese restaurant will make the decision process for shoppers much easier when displaying the menu in words rather than with photographs printed on the menu. Online players put in an enormous effort to have a photo of each item on the website. This effort could be over the top and is counterproductive if the assortment is large.

Alignability

We expect that if one brand, for example Ariel, adds more versions, its market share will increase automatically. This is not always the case. The addition could also result in more complexity and shoppers choosing another brand. A term that plays a role here is alignment or, said differently, the relationship between products. In an alignable assortment, apart from price the products differ on one dimension, such as pack size. In the case of a non-alignable assortment, products differ on several dimensions. For example, one mayonnaise has a high level of fat; the second one has easy-to-open packaging; the third one is bigger. At such a moment the shopper compares both within a dimension (low and high level of fat) and between dimensions (level of fat and type of packaging). Gourville and Soman showed when researching the choices for a microwave oven that in cases of an alignable assortment, the number of buyers of brand A rises if the assortment of the brand is extended.[9] In this research, alignable means that the preference went up from 53 per cent to 77 per cent with each increase of capacity (and price) while other dimensions did not alter and brand B remained the same in size. In cases of a non-alignable assortment, the choice for brand A rose initially when this was extended with one item (to 63 per cent) but went down in the end until it reached a preference of 40 per cent. In this case, the number alternatives of brand A had been increased to five. Each of these alternatives differed in dimension. From research by Zhang and Fitzsimons we know that the comparison of different dimensions causes much cognitive processing and time.[10] Gourville and Soman conclude that even in the case of a small assortment, but with many different dimensions, it is difficult for a shopper to make a choice.

Information

The manner in which retailers offer information about the products influences the learning process and the satisfaction with the final choice. Huffman and Kahn researched the difference between offering information per product attribute and per product alternative.[11] They conducted their research on couches and hotel visits, but I will use food examples to explain their study. In the case of the product attribute method, the shopper is asked to indicate for each product attribute (for example, type of packaging) which kind (ie glass, tin) they prefer. This results in a long list. An alternative approach is when products are shown randomly, after which the shoppers make a choice. For example, one product is in glass and is tall, a second product contains meat and comes from China. This is comparable with a showroom of cars, whereby the car salesperson points to different car models with different options. With regards to groceries, these types of choices do not prevail in physical supermarket environments but they have become relevant through the online activities of supermarkets, and as a result of them offering non-food products. Huffman and Kahn's conclusion was that shoppers were most satisfied with the shopping process, felt more ready to make a decision and perceived the choice as less complex when products were presented by attribute.

In the same research Huffman and Kahn varied the extent to which the shopper had to actively learn about their own preference. When shoppers were given more information on the attribute or product alternative, half of the respondents were asked which kind (ie glass, tin) within a product attribute (packaging) or product alternative got their preference, and the other half were asked which product attribute or product alternative they recognized. The first approach requires a much larger effort from the shopper, but pays off: the shopper is more satisfied with the decision process and considers the choice to be less complex. By presenting the information in the shape of product characteristics, and by seeking methods to actively engage shoppers, they get to know their preferences better and are more satisfied with the purchase in the end. The final recommendation is that the retailer should not give too much detailed information. The decision process will be too complex and stressful if shoppers have to estimate whether one dimension (for example, packaging) is more important than another (for example, taste).

Retailers can have it all: large product assortment without decision-making stress

With the above suggestions, retailers can help their shoppers to choose from a large assortment in an efficient manner. Of course, each shopper is different and the retailer may have created a divergent and specific environment. Many factors influence an optimal arrangement. For example, the amount of space that a retailer allows for a category influences the sense of variety in a positive way. Van Herpen and Pieters concluded that doubling the assortment within the same products leads to the sense of variety being increased by 42 per cent.[12] The perceived variety is also larger if you give extraordinary fantasy names that you may observe in categories such as paint (Flexa's Balanced Finland) and perfume (Pi by Givenchi), which is in contrast with names like Campbell's Bean with Bacon Soup. Making a decision becomes easier if the shopper's personal expectations on the structure of the supermarket are matched by what they find in the store. The difficulty is that each shopper may see other uses for a product. One shopper sees an apple as a snack, someone else sees it as a dessert and again someone else sees it as a baking ingredient. In addition, it is much easier to navigate a supermarket that the shopper visits regularly each week than one that the shopper visits only for special occasions or a couple of times per year. Research by Kahn and others concludes that products displayed horizontally give a higher perceived variety because (in Roman alphabets) people are used to moving their eyes from left to right, and this allows them to absorb more items.[13] Retailers should realize that there could be a large difference between actual assortment choice and the perception of choice by the shopper. Have clear goals in mind. You might only want to create the perception of a large assortment, while in reality offering little choice. The importance of the difference between perception and reality is already taken into consideration in the price policies of many retailers, where the shopper perception of the least expensive retailer may vary from the actual price difference. The same thinking applies to product assortment. In short, shoppers judge the complexity of an assortment on the basis of *perceived*, and not *actual*, assortment. A successful assortment occurs when shoppers perceive a high variety, while at the same time experiencing minimal feelings of complexity – as this may cause choice stress.

What can you do to make your shoppers happy?

By tailoring to each individual store, shoppers obtain a product assortment that is selected entirely for them so that they can select efficiently everything they need.

If retailers are truly focused on the shopper interests they should introduce only articles that generate incremental revenue per store. Assortment management objectives such as percentage margin are not relevant for shoppers.

Reducing the number of options helps shoppers to make a quicker choice and feel good about themselves. However, taking away choice is not the only means of simplification, and approaches such as better shelf structuring facilitate an easy choice from a wide range.

Shoppers like to have a choice: this is deeply ingrained in us and promoted by the spread of Western culture.

Which marketing strategies can retailers apply?

Consider online options early in product assortment decisions. A retailer may need to simplify the assortment for shoppers in physical stores and create the perception of a wide assortment through its online store.

The use of scanning data and widely available software gives each retailer the chance to determine the best assortment by store.

Retailers only get to know assortment needs well by investigating actual shopping behaviour. Socio-demographics, regional data and lifestyle segments complement the analysis but are not sufficient for assortment decisions by themselves.

The assortment life cycle shows that changing the company culture of decision making from merely intuitive to data-driven helps retailers to compete with new online players that offer a wide assortment and extreme personalization at the same time.

In new, developing categories the shopper has a better chance of understanding new additions if the extension occurs along alignable dimensions. When the category matures and the shopper understands the category better the shopper is capable of choosing from an assortment with many different dimensions.

Notes

1 Boatwright, P and Nunes, J (2001) [accessed 22 July 2015] Reducing assortment: an attribute-based approach, *Journal of Marketing* [Online] https://msbfile03.usc.edu/digitalmeasures/jnunes/intellcont/Reducing%20%20 Assortment-1.pdf

2 Iyengar, S and Lepper, M (2000) [accessed 22 July 2015] When choice is demotivating: can one desire too much of a good thing?, *Journal of Personality and Social Psychology* [Online] http://werbepsychologie-uamr.de/files/ literatur/01_Iyengar_Lepper(2000)_Choice-Overload.pdf

3 Schwartz, B (2004) *The Paradox of Choice: Why more is less*, Harper Perennial, New York

4 The Canadian Press (2010) [accessed 22 July 2015] *Guardian* [Online] http://www.theguardian.pe.ca, 6 May

5 Rolls, B, Rowe, E, Rolls, E, Kindston, B, Megson, A and Gunary, R (1981) [accessed 22 July 2015] Variety in a meal enhances food intake in man, *Physiology and Behaviour*, 26 February [Online] http://www.oxcns.org/ papers/55%20Rolls%20Rowe%20Rolls%20et%20al%201981%20 Variety%20in%20a%20meal%20enhances%20food%20intake%20in%20 man%20.pdf

6 Iyengar, S (2011) *The Art of Choosing: The decisions we make every day of our lives, what they say about us and how we can improve them*, Abacus, London

7 Kahn, B and Wansink, B (2004) [accessed 22 July 2015] The influence of assortment structure on perceived variety and consumption quantities, *Journal of Consumer Research* [Online] http://mindlesseating.org/pdf/downloads/ Variety-JCR_2004.pdf

8 Townsend, C and Kahn, B (2013) [accessed 22 July 2015] The visual preference heuristic: the influence of visual versus verbal depiction on assortment processing, perceived variety, and choice overload, *Journal of Consumer Research* [Online] http://www.jcr-admin.org/files/pressPDFs/101613155527_ Townsend_Article.pdf

9 Gourville, J and Soman, D (2005) [accessed 22 July 2015] Overchoice and assortment type: when and why variety backfires, *Marketing Science* [Online] http://pubsonline.informs.org/doi/abs/10.1287/mksc.1040.0109

10 Zhang, S and Fitzsimons, G (1999) [accessed 22 July 2015] Choice-process satisfaction: the influence of attribute alignability and option limitation, *Organisational Behaviour and Human Decision Processes* [Online] http://www.ncbi.nlm.nih.gov/pubmed/10080913

11 Huffman, C and Kahn, B (1998) [accessed 22 July 2015] Variety for sale: mass customization or mass confusion, *Journal of Retailing* [Online] http://www.ingentaconnect.com/content/els/00224359/1998/00000074/ 00000004/art80105

12 Van Herpen, E and Pieters, R (2002) [accessed 22 July 2015] The variety of an assortment: an extension to the attribute-based approach, *Marketing Science* [Online] http://pubsonline.informs.org/doi/abs/10.1287/mksc.21.3.331.144?journalCode=mksc

13 Kahn, B (2014) Shopper Insights in Action conference, Chicago (referring to Deng, X, Kahn, B, Unnava, R and Lee, H (2013) 'Wide' Variety: The Effects of Horizontal vs Vertical Product Display, Society for Consumer Psychology Summer Conference, Honolulu)

Really making loyalty card programmes work

08

Loyalty card programmes enable retailers to use data to learn what the shopper likes, and to build a communication tool to develop a more personal relationship. The promotional offers often tap into the rational habits of shoppers. However, the better the programmes connect with the shoppers' emotional needs, the more they move from being financial reward programmes to emotional relationships.

The fact that a shopper carries a loyalty card in their wallet is not going to make them more loyal to a supermarket. Nor is it likely that the implementation of a loyalty card alone by a supermarket will cause the retailer to listen to shoppers more effectively. However, when executed well, the benefits of a loyalty card programme are immense. When I worked at PepsiCo Europe my objective was to be among the first suppliers to engage with the loyalty card programmes that retailers such as Tesco, Carrefour and Casino launched across Europe. First of all, it enabled me to speak the language of the retailer more clearly. Second, the resulting data allowed me to make decisions faster and more accurately. I will return to the specific benefits later in this chapter, and also discuss guidelines for engaging suppliers. I start by discussing one of the most successful loyalty card programmes, highlighting the potential that many retailers are still to reach.

What has been learnt from Tesco?

The former CEO of Tesco, Sir Terry Leahy, attributes the success of Tesco between 1990 and 2015 mostly to the Tesco Clubcard and the effective application of data.[1] Leahy points to the fact that the market value of Tesco in 1992 was half the market value of retailers such as Sainsbury's and M&S. By 2011 the value of Tesco had increased sixfold while the other two were still at their market value of 1992. Without major acquisitions and by using shopper data, Tesco had at the time become market leader in the UK. The extent to which the Tesco loyalty card programme contributed to the company's growth is clearly explained in the book *Scoring Points: How Tesco continues to win customer loyalty* by Humby, Hunt and Philips.[2] Humby is co-founder of the research agency dunnhumby, which he started with his wife Edwina Dunn in 1989. In 1994 Tesco entrusted the small but innovative research agency with a set of data and asked what effect the data could have for Tesco. Fortunately, the team found valuable nuggets of insights and, as a result, Tesco continued to invest in their Clubcard trial. From that moment dunnhumby became the key driver of the software development and data exploration of the Clubcard. Tesco took full ownership of the research company in 2010 in recognition of its strategic impact and profitability to Tesco.

The main message from *Scoring Points* is that Tesco did not launch the loyalty card as a simple discount card, but as a valuable token of thanks for the loyalty of the shopper. This does not imply that operational execution, such as mailings with special offer coupons, does not lead to additional revenue. According to the authors of *Scoring Points*, the quarterly mailings have the same effect as four additional Christmas events per year. What grocery retailer wouldn't love that? The personalized mailings are the most visible element of the Tesco Clubcard, but thorough data analysis precedes this. *Scoring Points* explains how Tesco benefits directly from the Clubcard:

- If competitive grocers establish themselves in the neighbourhood of a Tesco store, Tesco follows the revenue of each shopper carefully. Only those Tesco shoppers who start to spend less at Tesco – and are assumed to be visiting the new competitive store – receive a friendly letter and special offer coupons in their letterboxes. Retailers without a loyalty card typically fight off new entrants by publishing huge discounts for everyone in the local papers, which also benefits those who have not reduced their spending at Tesco and remain loyal.

- Through lifestyle segmentation Tesco understands the aspirations of their shoppers better. This leads to new ideas for product development. At first the launch of the premium private label Tesco Finest was a disappointment. However, after analysis of the Clubcard data showed which precise stores the target shopper visited, it was transformed into a success.

- Tesco's database tracks shoppers who, based on their behaviour and buying habits, can be assumed to fall into a particular category of shoppers. If most people in that category habitually visit a certain department (for example, the wine department), but this particular shopper does not, Tesco can try to convince them to begin buying in that department by offering coupons. By encouraging them to trial new products, their loyalty is assured for the long term.

- By launching 'clubs' Tesco attracts new shoppers and encourages spending from existing customers. For example, through its Baby Club it encourages shoppers to switch from the drugstore channel such as the drugstore Boots to its own stores. Surprisingly, Tesco learned that such a club not only changes the buying behaviour within a specific category, but it also leads to a change in the overall shopping behaviour. For example, the Wine Club delivered more purchases of fresh produce.

- The shopping data also formed the basis of several new products and services. For example, the Clubcard provided the insight into shopper trust that led to introducing financial services. Tesco Bank now has some seven million customers. In *Scoring Points* Terry Leahy describes the start of Tesco's online supermarket in 2000: 'We could not have created the dot-com business without the data from the loyalty card.' At the start the Clubcard data helped point Tesco to the catchment areas of those stores where the home delivery service had the most promising potential. This was an even bigger achievement when you realize that the target group that was most interested in and benefited most from home delivery service was not online in the early days. The relationship with the Clubcard was for many customers an encouragement to go online and experiment with online shopping. In the end, three out of 10 online shoppers were new to Tesco.

Nectar card at Sainsbury's

During the presentation of the interim results of Sainsbury's in 2010, the then CEO Justin King expressed his satisfaction with the Nectar card programme. Justin King points to four benefits for the retailer:

- Shoppers start buying products from additional different categories at Sainsbury's. They love to collect points and become more loyal. By the time Christmas arrives the loyalty card is filled with points. In this crucial month for the revenue of supermarkets, Sainsbury's can expect shoppers to redeem their points. So the loyalty card is a way to keep shoppers loyal and contributing to a good revenue in the weeks around Christmas.

- Sainsbury's makes more and more product assortment decisions based on loyalty card data. The supermarket adjusts the assortment and develops innovations based on what it sees happening in the data.

- Instead of discounts for everyone, Sainsbury's sets its promotions on those products that shoppers already buy or are inclined to buy.

- When Sainsbury's opens a new store the supermarket checks, with the help of the card, which shoppers are important and more inclined to buy at Sainsbury's. In the first weeks of opening it communicates directly with those shoppers. At existing stores Sainsbury's knows in time which shoppers decrease spend or which low-frequency shoppers are prepared to visit a larger Sainsbury's store somewhat further away.

Benefits of loyalty card data versus other data

Most suppliers' trade-marketing departments use household panel and retail panel data from companies such as Nielsen, GfK, TNS and IRI to analyse sales and provide recommendations to category managers of supermarkets. These data providers have become established in the way of doing business, and category managers have come to expect suppliers to use the data for explaining sales developments and backing up their proposals. The number of suppliers that leverage data from loyalty card programmes, most likely through programmes of the retailer, is low but growing. Data from loyalty cards offers some of the same functionalities as household and retail panel data, but improves on them in the following ways:

- Analyses are available faster, and are more robust and more accurate. Loyalty card software shows by just pressing on the button whether a new product adds users to the category, and which products the shopper exchanged for this. Often suppliers run into the retailer policy that allows suppliers only to launch a couple of the available varieties of the marketing concept. With the help of loyalty card data, retailers have a good picture just three weeks after the launch as to whether the product is a success, and whether it would be suitable for other varieties to be introduced as well.

- Performance of individual stores can be tracked. On the one hand this enables the measurement of the efficacy of local store efforts such as the usage of a sales force or displays. On the other hand, through the comparison of groups of similar stores (based on shopping behaviour), disappointing performances such as lack of stock and declining distribution rates can be traced and compared to a relevant benchmark.

- By using the loyalty card data the supplier starts to understand its customer, the retailer, better and often adopts its terminology (Table 8.1). Grocery retailers have some different key performance indicators (KPIs) to suppliers, such as number of shoppers and total basket spend. By adopting the retailer KPIs the supplier can strengthen the relationship. In addition, the retailers seize the loyalty card as an opportunity to design their own shopper segmentations. Finally, the launch of a loyalty card system leads to more frequent and higher-quality contacts, because the category manager of the retailer and the supplier want a return on their investment in the card programme as quickly as possible. The French grocery retailer Casino, at the start of its loyalty card programme, held monthly workshops with key suppliers to solve category issues with the help of loyalty card software.

International expansion

Since 2006 the in-depth analysis and true leverage of loyalty card data have increased internationally. Often the retailer called in help from specialized agencies. Carrefour started working with EMNOS in France and Spain.

TABLE 8.1 Loyalty card changes focus of trade marketing function

From	To
Panel research	Shopper insight
Share in total market	Share of shopper wallet
Mass media (TV, newspapers)	Personalized communication
Four-weekly reports	Daily reports
Retail brand policy	Local marketing
National	Several shopper and store segments
What people say	Actual behaviour

Ahold began exploring loyalty card data with EYC in the United States and the Netherlands. Both Tesco and Sainsbury's in the UK have been the true pioneers in this area. For Tesco the impact has been most profound as the card programme enabled it to take over market leadership in the UK and the card has become a crucial element of the company's international expansion. Tesco leverages the loyalty card expertise to all countries where it operates, including Thailand and Eastern Europe. In addition, through its wholly owned loyalty card company dunnhumby, it takes part in joint ventures for loyalty card programmes of other retailers such as Grupo Pam in Italy and Casino in France. It seems strange that Tesco freely offers its expertise in exploring the power of loyalty card data to competitive retailers. However, in many cases Tesco is not active in the relevant country (for example in Italy), or else it provides the expertise to a relatively small competitor such as Casino in France, which is much less threatening to Tesco than Carrefour. Through dunnhumby Tesco offers software products and consultancy services, so it is also a matter of making profits. According to *The Grocer* in 2012 dunnhumby reported sales of £146.8 million and profits of £60.3 million.[3] If we overlay that with Tesco's total annual performance ending 22 February 2014, dunnhumby makes 0.2 per cent of Tesco sales but a fantastic 2.7 per cent of profits. The numbers in themselves are just an indication of the relative importance to Tesco profits. First of all, 2013 and

2014 were not particularly great years for Tesco stores. Further, since 2012 dunnhumby has acquired companies such as Sociomantic Labs that made a revenue of US $100 million selling digital advertising solutions. Still the numbers indicate the strategic relevance in financial terms. Though Tesco is making money by selling data to suppliers and setting up international partnerships, HSBC thinks these funds do not offset Tesco's total investment in the UK Clubcard, which is estimated at £500 million per year.[4] Therefore, it is important that the loyalty card delivers its value in its own right. First, it should be regarded as a strategic instrument to understand shoppers better, operate the stores more effectively and deliver more revenue and higher profits. In *Scoring Points* the authors explain that the data analysis delivered an immediate 4 per cent sales growth in 1995 while at that time only 1.6 per cent was necessary to cover the costs of the programme.

The power shift to retailers

Apart from better decision making and the financial impact, loyalty cards have another advantage for retailers. The loyalty card programmes allow retailers to shift the negotiation power from suppliers to retailers as the latter own and manage the information on the shoppers. The data gives retailers the opportunity to understand shoppers better. Moreover, it is up to retailers as to whether they wish to share the information with suppliers. If retailers are able to better use loyalty and scanning data, they will end the traditional knowledge superiority of suppliers.

A new phase for the market research industry

The exploration of loyalty cards and scanning data is not an easy job. With additional retailers accepting the importance of loyalty cards to success, a whole new industry of service providers such as dunnhumby, EMNOS and Numsight has arisen. Because of the advantages of loyalty card data, these companies will ride the change from retail and household panel data to the new data originating directly from the retailers. This must be a frightening thought for companies such as Nielsen, GfK and IRI. Although a loyalty card does not give direct insight into what the shopper spends with competitors, it does meet a great need. In mature markets in Western Europe it has become more effective to increase the loyalty of existing shoppers than to attract new customers. In my experience 90 per cent of the trade marketing analyses that used to come from traditional panel data are easy to build with loyalty card systems as well. Table 8.2 outlines the benefits that loyalty cards

TABLE 8.2 Comparison of loyalty card with other data for trade marketing analysis

	Application	Advantages	Disadvantages
Retail panel (Nielsen, IRI)	• Overview of historical sales of a category, brand, retail format • Overview of performance indicators: price, distribution, shelf space, (incremental) promotional volume	• Robust sample for continuous tracking • Split by region and retail brand • Explanation of changes in store, eg shelf space	• Often it cannot isolate the cause of a change and gives only indicative cause because of lack of data on the level of individual stores and shoppers • Also comprises purchases made by companies and institutions
Household panel (GfK, TNS)	• Profile of shopper socio-demographic characteristics and shopping behaviour • Origin of (incremental) revenue • Overview of shopping behaviour across channels (including online) and retailers	• Timely update of background data of shopper • Gives insight into spending of the retailer's target shopper at other retail banners ('leakage')	• Sample is often too small for small brands, small grocery chains and categories with low penetration • Participants in panel become atypical over time because of increasing self-consciousness of shopping behaviour • Quality of data dependent on accuracy of scanning at home • Coverage could be low during holidays and for categories with direct consumption (eg snacks)

Continues overleaf

TABLE 8.2   *Continued*

	Application	Advantages	Disadvantages
Loyalty card	• Detailed tracking of shopping behaviour, till levels of individual store, and shopper • Segmentation of shoppers • Price elasticity • Decision tree • Origin of (incremental) revenue	• Robust sample for each single item, also for small brands and categories with low penetration • Evaluation of product introductions and promotions shortly after event • Action plans and experiments on store level • Direct marketing on the basis of real behaviour, not based on (just) socio-demographics • Supplier understands and speaks language of customer (retailer)	• If shoppers of retail brand are atypical, the data cannot be used for conclusions on country level • Background data becomes aged • Unknown what shopper spends at competing groceries • Missed purchases if card is not shown at checkout; for example: quick purchase at convenience store or purchase by firms

deliver that panel data does not. In addition, retailers have found ways to get around some of the disadvantages of card data. For example, Tesco calculates the spend of its shoppers (leakage) from the difference between what an average person eats and how many calories the Tesco shopper buys at Tesco. The ultimate dream of trade marketers is to have access to one portal that combines panel data with loyalty card data. Another helpful aspect is that loyalty card software often offers a view of both the retailer's scanning and loyalty card data (though ideally a trade marketer would like to easily compare this perspective with what happens at other retailers).

Implementation of loyalty card programmes by retailers

Despite the success of retailers such as Tesco in translating their investment in the loyalty card programme into real financial benefits, many retailers seem to ignore the data they get from their loyalty cards. They seem to doubt its effectiveness or shrink back from what it costs to create comprehensive data sets, software and analytics teams. Some retailers have a loyalty card but limit themselves to the operational applications of loyalty card programmes, such as sending out personal special offers. Examples of more strategic types of analytical questions they could be asking are:

- Which articles are most price sensitive?
- What is the ideal price point for each of the products?
- What are the reasons for shopping at a specific store or moment? (Think of weekly restocking, bargain hunting, topping up fresh products such as milk and bread, and searching for tonight's dinner.)

A couple of anecdotes may help to further clarify the difference between operational and strategic applications. A colleague at PepsiCo, who had a partner but no children, once bought a pack of diapers for a cousin and received special offers for diapers for a full year. Another time, I thought that my usual supermarket had carefully selected a jar of Italian pasta sauce as a special offer for me, only to find out the next day in the office that everyone else had received the same offer. For each retailer the road map to implementation is different. Internal capabilities, market challenges and competitive situations lead to different considerations and approaches. Let's look at two examples of retailers who have gone back and forth in their approach to building a loyalty card programme.

Example: Sainsbury's in the UK

Until 2007 Sainsbury hardly used their loyalty card data despite the launch of the Nectar card in 2002. The supermarket primarily used the access that the scheme gave them to the contact details of their shoppers to communicate. Through direct-marketing campaigns, shoppers received personal offers that were not necessarily preceded by insight into what they needed based on analysis of what they bought. Not much happened and suppliers barely collaborated with Sainsbury's to turn the data into insights. This limited output meant that the process was far from smooth in the first years of the programme. First, the supermarket did not set targets for the category management team that made it necessary for them to use the data. As a result they felt hardly involved. Second, 15 per cent of the total shopper data set was used. This could be an efficient approach for learning in the beginning, but the granular insights come from knowing what happens with each customer in each store. In addition, Sainsbury's freed up only limited resources – as only one analyst was available. Instead it relied heavily on a more traditional research agency, TNS.

Traditional research agencies often struggle to develop software to process the large, unstructured data and acquire expertise to turn the data into real benefits for the retailer. In 2007 Sainsbury's ended the relationship with TNS and handed over the data to a company that was called LMG at the time (later renamed Groupe Aeroplan and since 2009 is called AIMIA). This proved to be a successful choice. Within a year Sainsbury's started applying insights from the data intensively, and hundreds of suppliers partnered in the exploration of the data. The collaboration between Sainsbury's and LMG resulted in new ideas such as discount coupons at the checkout and special offers through smartphones.

Example: Albert Heijn in the Netherlands

Albert Heijn has been one of the forerunners in loyalty card programmes in the Netherlands. In 1994, in the same year that Tesco kicked off its own programme, Albert Heijn partnered with Shell and other retailers to set up the Airmiles programme. When I started working at Albert Heijn in 1996 the management of the programme was the responsibility of the communication department. This might be one of the reasons why not much attention was paid to data digging in shopper behaviour and much more was given to setting up campaigns with other partners of the Airmiles programme to collect and spend Airmiles points.

In addition to the Airmiles card, Albert Heijn launched its own loyalty card, named Bonuskaart, in 1998. Still not much data extraction or application of the resulting insights seemed to take place to achieve business results. A strong feeling of self-reliance has always been part of the culture at Albert Heijn, and this culture stopped them from relying on external agencies. So while the amount of collected data grew, it was unclear what purpose it could serve. A couple of events led to a (re)appraisal of the value of data from loyalty cards. After profit warnings in 2002, the growth of Albert Heijn's mother company, Ahold, came to an abrupt end based on more than

50 acquisitions that were executed under the leadership of CEO Cees van der Hoeven. In 2003 Ahold announced that its operating company US FoodService had committed fraud. In addition, it muddled its accounting rules when administrating its ownership in retailers in Scandinavia and South America (the famous 'side letters').

Ahold sold many of its operations abroad, and Ahold and Albert Heijn's team in the Netherlands realized that future growth had to come more from existing shoppers rather than buying retail chains abroad. The second important event took place when shoppers decided to boycott Albert Heijn for one day in 2003 in protest at the compensation of Ahold's newly appointed CEO, Anders Moberg. The loss of some 5 per cent of its weekly revenue warned Albert Heijn that loyal shoppers can voice their opinion in other ways. Its price weapon eventually became less effective after engaging in price wars for many years. In 2003 Albert Heijn initiated a price war in the Netherlands that lasted until 2006. Shoppers benefited from much lower prices and Albert Heijn was pleased with the regained market share. Other consequences included the collapse of retail chain Laurus, the loss of value in the total supply chain, and the deterioration of the collaboration with suppliers. A new price war was announced in 2009 but this made less of an impression on shoppers.

This brief overview of the Ahold history helps to explain why so little thought went into the strategic analysis of loyalty card data. A critical reader could question why Albert Heijn did not apply the knowledge gleaned from the loyalty card in 2003 in order to win back the hearts of the shoppers rather than initiating a price war. Or why it had not picked up on the signals that came from the loyalty card data that showed that by 2003 its shoppers had reduced their spending with Albert Heijn. However, by 2011 Albert Heijn did put more focus on its loyalty card programme. In that year the company decided to look for outside support and conducted several research experiments with specialized research agencies such as EMNOS and EYC. In 2012 it selected EYC, with whom it already worked in the United States, as a loyalty card programme partner. Since then EYC has built a research team to advise Albert Heijn based on the findings in the loyalty card data. The sharing of the data with suppliers rarely happens. Even in recent years the journey has not been easy for Albert Heijn. At the beginning of 2012 Albert Heijn announced that they would start sending personal offers to one million Bonuskaart holders. Nine months later this application faded into the background when it discovered it might not be consistent with privacy legislation in the Netherlands.

From these case studies we can identify a number of potential reasons why retailers do not leverage the benefits from loyalty cards, even if they have a programme in place:

- the partnering (research) agency has limited expertise in loyalty card software and/or insights;
- failure to free up sufficient internal resources;
- lack of data-digging mindset;
- failure to give responsibility for the programme to a retail insights team;
- short-term focus of senior management;
- growth already being delivered in other ways, for example through geographic expansion;
- fear of breaking (privacy) legislation.

Consequences of implementing loyalty card programmes for suppliers

Many retailers have involved suppliers in the analysis, planning and implementation of loyalty card programmes. This surely helps to pay for part of the investment when suppliers order the software and data from the retailer and the research agencies. I would also argue that the commitment of suppliers is indispensable as they often have more expertise when it comes to the category, and they have the resources to dive straight into category challenges. However, suppliers do take risks when they participate in retailer-driven loyalty card programmes. Based on my experience, introducing such programmes in 10 European countries, I see a pattern in the way that the collaboration evolves. Each phase in the relationship – experiment, honeymoon, harvesting, integration – offers risks and opportunities for the collaboration between the retailer and supplier:

1 *Experiment*
   In the first place the retailer needs to prepare the complete back office. That is: they collect and store all individual checkout transactions by shopper. The research agency (for example, dunnhumby or EMNOS) segments the data at household level. This could be based on simple visit metrics such as trip frequency and household size, or the agency could use more complex

segmentations such as lifestyle and actual category and product spend. Together with the consultant the retailers sets up a number of projects that give new insights into some of the challenges that the retailer faces. An example of such a challenge is to find out which households increased their loyalty during an important promotion campaign, and whether their behaviour changed permanently after the campaign ended. Or which households decreased their spending after the competition opened a new store in the same neighbourhood. In addition, the retailer decides which commercial issues for each category level return on a regular basis, and these are addressed in fixed reports in the future software. At the end of the phase, the retailer often invites about three suppliers. In this manner the retailer can see if the software works in various different environments. For example, when Casino in France started working with dunnhumby software there was a considerable time gap between the formulation of the analytic question in the software and the delivery of the report through the internet. The invited suppliers are often pleased to be part of the happy few, because they receive the data on a one-off basis for free and they obtain the opportunity to solve a category issue with help of a fresh new method. The start-up phase requires category analysts and customer managers to devote lots of time to the analysis of the data and project meetings, but this also enables them to strengthen the relationship with the retailer. The experimental phase takes some three years for the retailer, and only six months for the supplier. Some retailers such as Carrefour prefer to analyse the data thoroughly before making it available to suppliers. Another factor is training for the category managers. If retailers have always applied a conflict model in their negotiations with suppliers, then the step towards sharing data requires a dramatic change in the working style of category managers. At first, category managers need to negotiate using facts instead of leveraging their power. The retailer's senior management needs to make sure they spend enough time on training.

2 *Honeymoon*

So far the retailer has borne all costs of the system and the consultancy, and thinks that the time has come to push these costs to suppliers. The retailer calls for new suppliers to join the programme and often the first handful of partners of the experimental phase remain committed. Sales directors on the supply side hurry to sign up because they realize that the programme offers a chance to improve the reputation of the company's trade marketing function. However, the retailer will only register the suppliers after they have agreed to pay for the software, data and consultancy programme. The research agency appeases the supplier with a discount for the first year. Often the retailer forms a joint venture with the research agency and each takes 50 per cent of the profit.

In hindsight I realize that I made huge mistakes 20 years ago. These decisions/actions were right at the time as I worked with the then latest information and technology. However, with the research and technologies available in 2015 I could have done so much better in 1995. When I experienced the power of loyalty card software first hand, I realized how many category issues it can address and how many wrong decisions I have probably made in the past, thanks to older technologies. During the honeymoon phase the retailer and supplier are both undertaking analyses that can be translated into the stores relatively easily. An example is a decision tree analysis that typically leads to some 5–8 per cent more category revenue, even in saturated markets.

3 *Harvesting*

Because both retailer and supplier see a significant uplift in sales and profits the honeymoon phase usually transitions smoothly into the next phase. Now suppliers sign up for more categories and more complex types of reports that fall outside the basic contract. New suppliers sign agreements with the retailer for data sharing so that the revenue stream from supplier partnerships increases. The trade marketing departments at suppliers are often under time pressure and for them it is a case of making tough choices. The specific loyalty card software demands time that then cannot be spent on other customers or data sources. Budget for the programme becomes an issue as well. During the experimental phase, often the European head offices subsidize country agreements. Surprisingly often during the honeymoon phase, brand marketing teams will raise the issue of budget: they see short-term opportunities such as hurrying along the adoption of a newly launched product. However, neither European head offices nor brand marketers wish to carry the burden on a continuous basis and kick the ball to trade marketing and sales teams. At the same time, the boards of the retailers impose targets on category managers telling them how much income they need to generate from the loyalty card programme through the suppliers they deal with for their categories. Therefore, some category managers only accept reports and analyses that are built with the help of the loyalty card data and refuse to discuss reports built from other data, no matter how valuable and meaningful the reports might be. In this way they make loyalty card data a requirement of doing business with the category manager. The improvement of software has had a profound impact on the depth and quality of the conversations between the retailer and supplier. Many topics now have a chance to be explored, from generic analyses such as shopping behaviour by region, to evidence that the latest innovation increased revenue and added customers to the category.

4 *Integration*

In the integration phase the game between retailer and supplier becomes more relaxed. The category manager realizes that several data sources are required in order to understand the category and the shopper. One example is consumer household data that shows how the shopper spreads their expenditure on a certain category across all retailers. For this, the supplier has to structure its analytics and customer team better. It makes informed choices about how many and which people are freed up for the analysis of loyalty card data and finds a permanent source for the required budget. The type of analytical questions changes. The emphasis shifts from category and sales challenges to marketing and individual store analyses. For example, the marketing department prepares a national campaign by initially pre-testing a new product in four pilot stores of the retailer. Or the marketing team compares the effects of different media types such as outdoor, radio, regional TV and in-store media with the help of the loyalty card data. When I worked at Gillette in the UK in 2004 I admired the level of professionalization of sales forces that maintained relationships with stores. The Gillette sales force had access to reports on shopper behaviour by store, and discussed them with the general manager. The reports included store revenue and shopper KPIs such as number of customers, type of customer, number of visits and total spend. This is remarkably different from the common practice, which is to focus sales forces on merchandise, information collection and sales outcomes of promotional displays. Finally, some suppliers end the loyalty card collaboration with the retailer, or renegotiate the contract. Therefore, the research agency introduces new services such as selling store-based advertising in order to keep increasing their income stream.

Risks

The supplier runs a number of risks with the purchase and integration of loyalty card systems. At the start the retailer and research agency offer attractive concessions on price; for example in the first year there is a 15 per cent discount or free availability of a second category. These benefits fall away until eventually discounts; are reduced and improvements in the consultancy offering are only available at additional cost for the supplier – for example, data on store level, splits by sub-banner and additional 'standard' reports.

The second risk is that the purchase of loyalty card data, as opposed to data from Nielsen, IRI, GfK and TNS, is not without obligations: the retailer counts on the annual income stream from the loyalty card programmes. In France I learned that category managers place great pressure on customer managers, wanting them to sign new card contracts and threatening to lower the number of promotional events or reduce the assortment if they do not.

A third risk is the complete transparency of analyses to the retailer. Because all queries for analyses run over the internet and have the resulting reports stored in central locations, retailers can see exactly which analyses the supplier conducts and what the results are. This once again emphasizes the importance of keeping the role of trade marketing as objective and independent as possible.

Finally, a very specific type of risk. Dunnhumby is fully owned by Tesco but also acts as a research agency in several countries with retailers such as Casino in France, Kroger in the United States and Gruppo PAM in Italy. If a supplier shares information about its marketing or customer strategy with dunnhumby, this information is indirectly available to Tesco. Is this what a supplier wants? This issue was especially relevant for suppliers in the United States when Tesco operated as a retailer with its Fresh&Easy banner from 2006 until it withdrew from the United States in 2013. I am not sure if competition legislation has an answer to this. A retailer that hires the services of another retailer has the freedom of choice; however, the supplier that works with the research agency to improve the relationship with one retailer is indirectly tied to another retailer.

In order to avoid the above risks, I have some suggestions that will allow retailers and suppliers to collaborate in loyalty card programmes:

- Focus on the mid to long term and do not dive into loyalty card data in an impulsive fashion. Estimate the future revenues and investments per year. A supplier can enlarge the investment, for example in terms of the number of categories or step-by-step services in order to have something to fall back on if the return on investment is lower than hoped.

- Make the investment transparent. Suppliers should allocate the account-related costs in the customer profit-and-loss statement and shift the costs of those activities to marketing, as they contribute to brand building on a national level.

- Supplier and retailer should both establish at the beginning of each year which topics they want to address and investigate further with loyalty card data. Decision makers from a variety of roles from both sides should come together in a workshop facilitated by the research agency.

- Encourage the application of data and transference of best practices across departments in both the retailer and supplier. Results from the loyalty card analysis are not purely a victory on behalf of the sales department. It is better to involve the supplier marketing department early on so that the application of the data occurs as broadly and deeply as possible.

- International suppliers can call on their overseas colleagues to benchmark the price that the research agency requires and the types of services it offers.

- Evaluate the analysis and collaboration process on a regular basis with both the retailer and the research agency.

- Walk before you run. Perhaps for some organizations the four phases are somewhat too structured. In that case, just remember that you do not have to do everything at the same time.

- Do not make the loyalty card programme too small or too big:

  - Too small? I found that senior managers at retailers are very ambitious in what loyalty cards can achieve, but that category managers continued with business as usual by making decisions based on intuition and experience. They flatly ignored the loyalty card programme: a missed opportunity.

  - Too big? Other retailers changed their dealings with the suppliers completely after launching the loyalty card programme: everything had to be and would be analysed with the help of loyalty card data. Another missed opportunity.

CASE STUDY   Coop Norway

At the Shopper Insights conference in Amsterdam in 2012 Geir Jostein Dyngeseth of Coop Norway and David Ciancio of dunnhumby presented their practical outcomes from the loyalty card data. Coop used to attempt to pull shoppers into their stores with three promotions on the front page of the weekly feature, mostly showing dry groceries. This had little effect on loyal shoppers. Coop expanded the number of offers to eight and included more fresh produce. As a result, 68 per cent more shoppers bought the products on promotion and the total value of the shopping trip rose by 8 per cent. Coop also used the loyalty card to optimize its planograms. The loyalty card data showed that Norwegians buy potato chips based on type of flavour and care less about the brand. A new planogram with flavour blocks resulted in 6.5 per cent more shoppers, 23 per cent more items per trip and an incremental revenue of 4 per cent for the category.

What can you do to make your shoppers happy?

Loyalty cards help retailers to get to know shoppers better and tailor their product offerings, promotions, services and experiences to each individual shopper.

Loyalty programmes should feel special and trustworthy, without any concerns about privacy. Shoppers enjoy rewards and like being thanked for their loyalty.

Shoppers should only receive personalized, relevant promotions and suggestions for new product assortment and services.

Which marketing strategies can retailers apply?

Taking ownership of scanning and loyalty card data gives retailers more control in the value chain. Giving suppliers access to data should be evaluated as part of a strategic supplier management plan.

The data, the software and the capability of extracting insights could become a business of its own. The retailer could design paid services for suppliers and non-competing retailers. This knowledge of its shoppers may lead to additional businesses, such as banking and travel, which could be operated with or without partners.

Loyalty cards allow retailers to understand shopper motives more thoroughly and efficiently, so that they can respond more quickly and avoid engaging in price wars.

Loyalty card programmes are most attractive in mature markets where retailers find it difficult to win new customers, for example by store expansion.

Insights from the loyalty card programme help retailers to accelerate their innovation strategy and outperform competition.

Notes

1 Leahy, T (2014) Shopper Insights in Action conference, July, Chicago
2 Humby, C, Hunt, T and Philips, T (2007) *Scoring Points: How Tesco continues to win customer loyalty*, Kogan Page, London
3 Zuke, E (2012) [accessed 22 July 2015] Expanding dunnhumby sees profits and sales up, *The Grocer*, 14 December [Online] http://www.thegrocer.co.uk/home/topics/technology-and-supply-chain/expanding-dunnhumby-sees-profits-and-sales-up/235039.article
4 Ruddick, G (2014) [accessed 22 July 2015] Clubcard built the Tesco of today, but it could be time to ditch it, *The Telegraph*, 16 January [Online] http://www.telegraph.co.uk/finance/newsbysector/retailandconsumer/10577685/Clubcard-built-the-Tesco-of-today-but-it-could-be-time-to-ditch-it.html

Making big data digestible

09

Chapter 7 showed that making retail decisions, such as the size of your product assortment, is worth doing in a substantiated, research-driven manner. Tools for retail data analysis are continually becoming more advanced. In Chapter 8 I provided an overview of best practices followed by retailers such as Tesco to better connect with shopper needs through loyalty card programmes. In this chapter I look into one of the most advanced approaches: big data analysis.

At the start of my career, research company Nielsen provided me with printed market reports. Although the reports only showed basic indicators such as numeric distribution and unit sales with a reporting frequency of two months, I thought it was a lot of data. The same reports are now available on a weekly basis, integrated with many more dimensions and the electronic format allows users to slice and report the data as they wish. The amount of data available to decision makers has grown exponentially: apart from scanning data they use loyalty cards, consumer panels, industry reports, store data, ad hoc research and social media. There is no doubt about it: the reports on my table in the mid 1990s were peanuts compared to big data 20 years later.

What is big data?

Morrisons was using it when it tracked shopping carts for its store layout optimization; Procter & Gamble (P&G) was using it when it set up Vocalpoint, a domestic management website. They carried out experiments to better understand the shopper, which resulted in large amounts of data. Yet even larger amounts of data now flow from online: interactions on social media such as Facebook and Twitter, Google searches and online shopping. The term big data is used for:

- Data that comes in large amounts. It is not relevant to describe what large is and how many terabytes you are talking about, because big data increases every minute. For example:
  - In 2007 six hours of video material were uploaded every minute on YouTube. In 2012 it was 60 hours; now this number is over 100 hours per minute.[1]
  - Twitter processes one billion tweets per week.
  - Walmart handles 200 million transactions per week.[2]

- Data that is unstructured. Organizations collect data from many sources and in many forms, including video, audio, numbers and reports. Unstructured data is not completely new as such: in the past there was also unstructured data, but retailers were not able to analyse it. What is new is that the shapes and sources of data grow in numbers. We can now start to analyse the 80 per cent of data that organizations hold in unstructured formats.

- Data that comes in fast, immediately and at different intervals. Gone are the times when we waited for a monthly meeting to discuss the sales numbers or to look into the bimonthly audit tables from Nielsen. Sales reports can be delivered in real time. Insights from loyalty card analysis are completed within a few hours or days.

- Data that is complex. The data includes so many variables that it is impossible to see relationships among them without profound statistical analysis. It has become difficult for organizations to judge who needs which part of data.

So, big data is so large, so complex and unstructured that normal database management systems cannot store or analyse it. Shoppers may receive too much information; managers struggle as well. When the printer Johannes Gutenberg lived in the 15th century, for example, people could claim to be able to read all books that had ever been printed in their own language. Nowadays the amount of information is too large. Research by Neuman, Park and Panek shows that US citizens are offered 884 times more media content than minutes they have available for consumption.[3] Retailers need to develop systems and processes to convert these large amounts of unstructured data into insights of shopping behaviour:

- In 2003, a team of Accenture researchers showed what it could do with large sets of transaction data of a US retailer.[4] They built a model they could use to forecast which products each shopper would buy during a shopping trip. An application of such information is that the shopper's smartphone or hand-scanner shows at the beginning of the trip a list of groceries the shopper is likely to need. During the shopping trip the shopper only receives suggestions if the product sits in the aisle that they visit. The study shows that supermarkets can increase revenue by 11 per cent by reminding shoppers of products that they would have otherwise forgotten. Getting to the bottom of the data and finding the deeper-lying causal relationships are essential to understand the shopper. (As a side note, one of the researchers, Rayid Ghani, was later hired by Barack Obama as chief scientist to shape the project Dream Catcher – data-digging into the dreams that people had shared told Obama's campaign team which arguments they had to use in each neighbourhood and in swing states. Big data was a major factor in Barack Obama's re-election as president of the United States in 2012.)

- Electronics retailer BestBuy changed its stores after data analysis showed that 7 per cent of its shoppers brought in 43 per cent of the revenue.

- Walmart is always careful to have sufficient stock of batteries and torches when the hurricane season starts. Deeper analysis showed that shoppers buy a certain set of other products, such as cereal bars, that are easy and nutritious when the hurricane prevents shoppers from visiting a store for some length of time.

Drivers of big data in retail

A good plan starts with information. It has become less expensive to obtain and store information, and new technology allows retailers to use the information in a quicker and more user-friendly fashion. Enterprise resource planning (ERP) systems connect data from different functional areas, such as marketing and logistics. Better business intelligence software unlocks the insights. The retail sector is in an excellent position to benefit from the big data trend. The logistical channel is equipped with sensors that generate a continuous stream of data on incoming and outgoing products. A grocery retailer receives many customers per day resulting in many more details on the transaction, such as type of product, moment of shopping and method of payment. Some retailers, such as mail order companies, have always had a deep interest in knowing everything about their shoppers. They have become one of the first to see the benefits of big data along with the banking sector, credit card companies, telecom operators and insurance companies. The internet and social networks such as Facebook and Twitter have caused a revolution by making information about shoppers widely available to companies. They enable shoppers to change from passive buyers into vocal activists. This requires retailers not just to offer information or track behaviour but to respond as well. Shoppers review and discuss all companies and brands on blogs and other digital platforms, regardless of whether they sell cosmetics, cleaning products, fresh food and so on. With the help of smartphones, shoppers can tell the retailer what they think of the store and its assortment. Retailers and suppliers can read on Twitter just what shoppers think of their advertising campaigns, and can use this to adjust them. It is not just their regular business activities and ongoing marketing programmes that form the big data: retailers can set up experiments that make data come in every second. Here are two examples:

- In two Morrisons stores in the UK, shopping trolleys were tracked with the help of radio-frequency identification (RFID). This delivered a lot of information such as search times, shopping paths and conversation rates. By comparing stores and conducting small experiments Morrisons could optimize its store layout. For example, moving a category might create a longer shopping path, or mean less time is needed to find a particular product in the category, or that more categories end up in the shopping trolley.

- At the Shopper Insights in Action conference in 2012, Metro Romania showed how it continuously adjusted the location of categories based on video recordings. For example, it discovered that it is more important to place related categories together (for example powdered milk with coffee) as a traffic builder than to give categories prominent visibility at the beginning or end of an aisle. From the experiments Metro concluded that the highest total sales are generated when it places leading brands such as Coca-Cola at foot level on promotional gondola ends.

Although suppliers have fewer opportunities for direct interactions with all end consumers, and receive masses of data, they may seek their own ways to generate big data programmes. For example, P&G set up the website Vocalpoint. With suggestions about travelling with children, cooking and money, P&G stimulates discussions among more than 500,000 users. This gives P&G new perspectives on its target group and especially its most loyal fans. At the site P&G investigates how it can improve the messages of its advertising campaigns. Next it offers its readers samples, discount coupons and quizzes. P&G measures the effects of its campaigns by looking at how widely the product news was shared, and through the redemption rates of discount coupons for the next purchase.

Opening new ways to make the shopper happier

Big data can be applied in so many ways that companies may underestimate its speed and impact. Technology enables retailers to influence purchase decisions at any moment of the transaction. When I visited my local gardening centre I was positively surprised when an employee informed me, after a quick glance at a hand terminal, about the remaining stock and order time of parasols. The US gaming store Gamestop has checkout software that shows the most recent transactions when shoppers pay. This enables employees to remind the shopper of videos or games for family members. Pricing is usually the key concern of retailers and is one of the main factors that can quickly make the shopper experience less positive. For example, blogs are full of shoppers who complain about travel websites that offer the same plane ticket for a higher price the second time the journey is searched for online. It is difficult for shoppers to notice when an online retailer like Amazon.com applies personalized pricing. Bricks-and-mortar stores such as Kroger can do so with the help of personalized coupons but it will be difficult to accept, for example, if grocers charged shoppers more during busy hours of the week.

Big data offers opportunities to get to know the shopper better and optimize the product offering. In fact, it is possible to convert the collected information into a product itself. When shoppers place reviews on the retailer site, they add to the service experience of other shoppers. The new technology and big data let shoppers co-create: individual shoppers participate in the developing and production phases, and decide together what a product should look like. Car manufacturer BMW asked shoppers to help build the car of the future at BMW's online co-creation lab. Retailers could similarly ask for help developing new services.

With all its possible applications and benefits big data requires a strong marketing vision and a strategic approach to market research and information technology (IT). However, the required investments are significant and will be more difficult in times of financial crisis and moderate economic climate. Fortunately, several studies show that big data leads to better decision making and higher returns on investment:

- In 2011 Brynjolfsson, Hitt and Kim demonstrated that companies that use data and business analytics are 5–6 per cent more productive and have a higher market value.[5] They introduced the term 'data-driven decision making' (DDD) to describe the technique of applying data to create new products, and for decision making throughout the organization.

- According to an estimate by McKinsey in 2011 the collection and application of big data result in an annual productivity increase of from 0.5 to 1 per cent.[6]

- The value of the investment in IT and data analysis software is also evident when a company succeeds in transforming data into a service for other organizations. Think of Tesco leveraging its ownership of dunnhumby to sell shopper data, analytical methodologies and other consultancy services.

According to a survey by McKinsey in 2012, for 23 per cent of companies in the United States big data is one of their top three priorities.[7] Yet even if the trade marketing or research department has support from top management and has been allocated the necessary budget, it is difficult to know where to start digging into the data. The early adopters of big data show that retailers and trade marketers get to grips with big data by using a step-by-step approach and lots of experiments:

- Capital One is a credit card company that is not one of the most well-known to shoppers, but it is often seen as the founding father of experiments with big data.[8] Capital One has segmented its shoppers and offers each segment a different view of the website, each with its own prices. Imagine that the regular grocery down the street asked for the same bottle of beer at 4,000 different prices. Still, that is what Capital One achieves in the financial services market.

- Amazon followed in the tracks of Capital One. It continually plays with the design of the website and offers information to selected shoppers. Next Amazon compares their behaviour with that of shoppers who are seeing the 'old' website. Amazon compares what people buy and how they buy, for example at the moment of purchase. In this manner they conduct some 200 experiments per day. Often Amazon knows after a couple of hours what works best for them. Experimentation has become second nature to Amazon.

- Anderson and Simester shared a success story from the US grocery sector in the *Harvard Business Review*.[9] The supermarket segmented its stores in six clusters and started playing with the pricing of promotions. It learnt that it could increase its profitability by 10 per cent if it matched national brand promotions with moderate discounts on private-label products as compared to not discounting the items at all. In order to protect sales of its profitable private label the grocer decided to match a 'Buy one, get one for 50% off' promotion on a national brand with the same offer on the private label, and compared the outcome to a 'Buy one, get one for 50% off' promotion on a national brand matched with a straight discount on the private label.

Experimentation as second nature in fast-moving consumer goods

Most people would agree that big data is important when it comes to gaining a better understanding of the shopper. However, if the organization has a lower budget and fewer data experts than P&G, Morrisons, Amazon, Tesco or Walmart, big data might seem too much of a challenge. I think that starting with experiments is the way forward. However, there are freelance consulting services available; one is Kaggle.com, and organizations should not be afraid to take advantage of them. Data scientists are eager to collaborate in exchange for prizes and a declaration of honour. The more successful solutions these data scientists provide, the higher their ranking among their colleagues from around the world.

In addition to starting with lots of experiments, I think we can be more creative in the ways in which retailers and trade marketers collect information. For self-service restaurants there are soft drinks dispensers that pass on information about buying behaviour over the internet in real time. First of all, this allows the retailer to decide whether the technical defect requires a service visit from a technician. The data also provides insights into flavour preferences, time of consumption and other shopping elements. Another great source for shopping behaviour comes from customer responses, complaints and returns. An organization uses the information, of course, to solve the issue. However, the data can be a great driver for innovations if it is aggregated, integrated in the data management system, analysed and made accessible to the brand team.

Privacy challenges

The question of privacy plays an important role when discussing big data, especially when companies use that data for internal analyses of individual shopping behaviour without the shopper's knowledge, or if the shopper does not realize they have left a digital footprint. As a shopper and as a professional I have sometimes felt that companies come very close to – and occasionally blatantly cross – the borders of acceptable behaviour. Here are some examples of big data practices that are on or just over the borderline:

- The US hypermarket Target was involved in a privacy scandal in 2012. A father complained to Target that they had sent his teenage daughter promotional offers for pregnancy products.[10] He expressed his outrage to Target about this unsuitable promotion, but a few days later his daughter confessed to him that she was actually pregnant. What had happened and how did Target know even before her family? Target can predict the arrival of a baby based on the purchase of some 25 products such as nutritional supplements, unscented lotion and a bag that is common in itself but often used to carry diapers. Target uses the information to make personalized promotional offers via letter or e-mail. The objective is to win the shopper's loyalty before the birth, and months before competing stores come into action. Target assigns an individual code to each of its shoppers and links this not just to all product purchases but also to information about income, online search behaviour and whatever other data it may buy about the shopper. Unfortunately, on this occasion Target did not consider (or did not know) the age of the mother when sending out its offers.

- In the publishing sector many companies compete to bring their e-readers to the attention of shoppers. Online retailer Amazon competes in this race with its own e-book reader, the Kindle. The Kindle registers and transmits how readers read a book. Amazon receives information on whereabouts people stop reading a book, which page they start on, which passages are highlighted, and how long it takes them to read. According to Amazon's website, the most frequently highlighted sentence from the popular book *The Hunger Games: catching fire*, by Suzanne Collins, is the sentence 'Because sometimes things happen to people and they're not equipped to deal with them.' With this type of information Amazon can determine the real success of a book and improve previews and reviews on the

Amazon site. A more scary thought is that Amazon can link the information about how and what shoppers read to their online purchasing behaviour.

- The pharmacological and insurance industries are preparing themselves for a digital revolution. Because of the introduction of electronic medical files, more sensors and monitoring equipment, and more online health discussions, the amount of data available on the health status of individual citizens is unprecedented. These are used to detect diseases at an earlier stage and to improve treatments. However, the increased data analysis also means that US insurers demand higher payments from those who smoke than those who do not. Similarly, the insurers found out that women visit a physician more often and take more medicines. If insurers buy data about online visits to blogs about serious diseases, they can use this as an additional risk factor when setting the insurance premiums.

Big, clean and open data

A lack of data is no longer a good excuse for organizations not to get into action. There is more data than ever before and it is often very detailed. One excuse is allowed: it is better to work with a small, 'clean' data set than a large, flawed data set. If organizations wish to maintain the speed of their retail and trade marketing decisions and see immediate results I suggest setting up a continuous stream of marketing experiments. This enables them to look forward, rather than back to endless reports full of numbers, tables and figures. This requires a company culture where learning is important and mistakes are allowed. Senior managers need to ask themselves if their past experiences are as good as the knowledge that can come from the continuous experiments and deep data analyses possible today. Retail marketing is becoming more of a science, and big data allows marketing practitioners to hold themselves more accountable for their 'artwork'. The next data revolution will be 'open data', whereby organizations give access to each other's large data sets.

What can you do to make your shoppers happy?

Internet forums, loyalty card systems and other technology and software allow retailers to obtain a better perspective into the needs of shoppers. It is not just listening to the shopper, it is building a dialogue with them.

Big data helps to solve one of the biggest problems: running out of stock. Through sensors and the codification of products, retailers can track stock and inform shoppers when the product is available and whether they can have it delivered from another store.

Which marketing strategies can retailers apply?

Sometimes an experimental approach is a better fit to retail marketing – this usually occurs when an organization has embraced the opportunities that technology offers and discovered that competition comes from unexpected sources. The experiments need to be planned and measured so that the short-term focus of many retailers does not jeopardize the learning curve.

Investments in big data cannot be made without privacy guidelines that are clear and transparent for all shoppers.

Notes

1 YouTube (2015) [accessed 22 July 2015] About YouTube [Online] https://www.youtube.com/yt/about/

2 Walmart (2012) [accessed 22 July 2015] Walmart U.S. Reports Best Ever Black Friday Events, 23 November [Online] http://news.walmart.com/news-archive/2012/11/23/walmart-us-reports-best-ever-black-friday-events

3 Russell Neuman, W, Park, Y and Panek, E (2012) [accessed 22 July 2015] Tracking the flow of information into the home: an empirical assessment of the digital revolution in the United States, 1960–2005, *International Journal of Communication* [Online] http://ijoc.org/index.php/ijoc/article/viewFile/1369/745

4 Cumby, C, Fano, A, Ghani, R and Krema, M (2003) [accessed 22 July 2015] Predicting Customer Shopping Lists from Point of Sale Purchase Data, *ACM* [Online] http://rayidghani.com/publications/kdd2004.pdf

5 Brynjolfsson, E, Hitt, L and Kim, H (2011) [accessed 22 July 2015] Strength in Numbers: How Does Data-Driven Decision-making Affect Firm Performance? [Online] http://ebusiness.mit.edu/research/papers/2011.12_Brynjolfsson_Hitt_Kim_Strength%20in%20Numbers_302.pdf

6 Brown, B, Chui, M and Manyika, J (2011) [accessed 22 July 2015] Are you ready for the era of 'big data'?, *McKinsey Quarterly*, October [Online] http://www.t-systems.com/solutions/download-mckinsey-quarterly-/1148544_1/blobBinary/Study-McKinsey-Big-data.pdf

7 McKinsey (2012) [accessed 22 July 2015] Minding Your Digital Business: Mckinsey Global Survey Results, *McKinsey & Company*, May [Online] http://www.mckinsey.com/insights/business_technology/minding_your_digital_business_mckinsey_global_survey_results

8 Clemons, E and Thatcher, M (1998) [accessed 22 July 2015] Capital One: Exploiting an Information-Based Strategy, *System Sciences* [Online] http://ieeexplore.ieee.org/xpl/login.jsp?tp=&arnumber=654788&url=http%3A%2F%2Fieeexplore.ieee.org%2Fiel4%2F5217%2F14260%2F00654788

9 Anderson, E and Simester, D (2011) [accessed 22 July 2015] A step-by-step guide to smart business experiments, *Harvard Business Review*, March [Online] https://hbr.org/2011/03/a-step-by-step-guide-to-smart-business-experiments

10 Duhigg, C (2012) *The Power of Habit: Why we do what we do and how to change*, Random House Books, London

PART FIVE
In-store execution

The unstoppable growth of private labels and opportunities for A-brands

By adopting a shopper-centric perspective, retailers will find it easier to decide whether a certain retail marketing mix tool is worthwhile investing in. The chapters so far in this book have explored the emotional needs of the shopper, how preferences on where to shop may shift over time, and how data analysis and fact-based decisions help retailers to make better decisions on things that matter to shoppers. An in-depth understanding of the shoppers' needs combined with a structured approach to decision making can help retailers to choose which retail marketing instrument will yield the highest return on investment. As retail margins are often low, close attention to detail is needed. Retail is detail! For example, the perfume worn by the cashier may make your investment in ambient scents a waste of time. However, sometimes retailers become bogged down in details. They may forget why they started looking at investing in a retail marketing instrument in the first place. It means starting a project with the shopper in mind. Next, the retail organization benefits from a stringent eye for detail and flawless execution when decisions are made regarding retail marketing instruments. Throughout this chapter I discuss a number of possible instruments that retailers may choose to adopt. The first from the retail marketing mix is *own brand management*.

Almost all retailers have their own brands. They are also referred to as store brands and private labels. These brands are managed and available either at one single retailer, or otherwise within the stores of a group of collaborating retailers (such as a buying group). Private labels come in various qualities and their brands are positioned in a range of ways, but increasingly they are meant to compete with A-brands. A-brands have an excellent reputation for quality and are well-known and widely advertised. Their producers seek broad distribution across retailers. At the expense of supplier brands, private labels keep growing almost everywhere in the world. However, take warning from the experience of the supermarket chain Mercadona in Spain, who expanded private labels, eliminating A-brands from the shelf, and thereby lost shopper loyalty. So behind the façade of rising market shares being a symbol of success, retailers often struggle with price, quality perception, the upper limits of private label share, and fluctuating shopper responses. This therefore offers opportunities for an A-brand supplier to support the retailer.

Recessions accelerate private labels

Private labels have close to a 14 per cent share in the grocery sector around the world, if fresh products like meat and vegetables are excluded.[1] The shares differ widely per region of the world. Private labels are very strong in Western Europe with a share of 36 per cent, followed by the United States (19 per cent), Eastern Europe (6 per cent) and only some 1 per cent in Latin America. Some countries reach a far higher level. In the UK and Switzerland, half of the market revenue comes from private labels. The question arises as to whether there is an upper limit or a ceiling to the impact of private labels in these countries, and what other countries can expect from the growth of their own private labels. A study by Lamey *et al* does not offer an optimistic forecast for A-brands: private labels are expected to grow in Western markets annually by more than 2 per cent.[2] This is as a result of structural factors such as continuous quality improvement and extended distribution levels. During times of economic regression the growth rate rises to 7–8 per cent. In conclusion, private labels will keep growing and each recession acts as an accelerator that causes the share of private labels to restabilize at a higher level than before the economic slump.

Possibly the first private label products were the coffee and tobacco that grocers in Western Europe packaged in the precise quantities that shoppers desired. A-brands did not play a role at all. During the industrial revolution manufacturers wanted to convince shoppers that their mass-produced goods were as reliable as locally produced alternatives. So they started labelling their products with brand names. Brands such as Quaker Oats and Campbell Soup were among the first. Although A-brands had been around for some time they became loved and genuinely wanted when welfare began to improve after the Second World War. Only in the 1960s did private labels became a real policy instrument. The first retailer to use them was the French hypermarket Carrefour, who introduced so-called 'white labels' – products without branding in simple packaging that displayed only the product name. These inexpensive products were an option for price-conscious shoppers. In this case, inexpensive also meant poor quality. This bad reputation has stuck to private labels for many years. Private labels became a strategic weapon when retailers linked their own names to the products. Connecting their own names to the products meant they wanted the products to be really good. So retailers started programmes to improve the quality of private labels. This does not mean that each retailer saw private labelling as a serious marketing instrument. When I worked as market researcher at De Boer Supermarkten in 1995 I remember being confronted with the launch of private-label frozen pizzas. I asked the category manager how she selected the type of flavours and the colours of the packaging. She told me her usual system: take the top three flavours that the market leader Albert Heijn had picked. Indeed, when I worked at Albert Heijn a few years later I found out that they carefully tested each private label with shopper panels to ensure products lived up to the same quality expectations shoppers had for leading A-brands. Finally, the growth of private labels was also pushed along by the rise of discounters such as Aldi and Lidl with their own fancy names, especially during the 1970s. Despite all the additional efforts and costs for packaging, product development and brand management, retailers thought it was worth the effort and this attitude towards private labelling has remained ever since.

Motives for private labels

In order to understand why private labels grow in a structural manner I detail below what retailers hope to achieve through them.

Shopper loyalty

The primary reason for using private labels has shifted to building shopper loyalty. For retailers, A-brands are commodities they cannot do without in their product assortments. However, a private label helps to build an image, an identity, and if everything works out well, private labels become a reason for shoppers to choose exactly that store. For this reason private labelling is more common in countries such as France and the UK than in emerging countries such as Poland and Russia. Retailers in Western Europe attempt to increase the share of wallet they get from their existing shoppers, while in emerging markets retailers can grow by expanding the number of stores or luring shoppers away from competitors. Retailer discount labels are set up to prevent leakage from shoppers to discounters. Examples are AH Basic from Albert Heijn, Everyday Value from Tesco, Great Value from Walmart, and Tous les Jours from Casino. They are also used to communicate price competitiveness online and in weekly magazine ads, because the retailer hopes that shoppers, once in the store, will forget the value labels and buy products with a higher margin. At the other end of the spectrum are premium brands such as AH Excellent from Albert Heijn and Finest from Tesco, which compete with brands from speciality stores.

Channel power

Another motivation for private labels is the opportunity for greater leverage against the suppliers of A-brands. If the shelf space remains the same, the launch of a private label results in A-brands having to fight to keep their location and shelf space. The retailer charges a price for this by demanding higher payments and bigger margins for features and displays. In other words, the retailer uses private labels not only for obtaining a higher relative margin of the category directly, but also as a means to put pressure on suppliers who want to keep their products on the shelf.

Profitability

A third important reason to launch a private label is to increase the profitability of a category. Although I work with retailers where private labels have the same relative margin as A-brands, generally speaking the 'standard' private label that competes directly with an A-brand has a higher margin for the retailer than the A-brands themselves. The reasons for the higher margin are clear. The retailer often does not invest in advertising or innovation to stimulate demand. Introduction costs (displays, feature fees, listing fees etc) are omitted.

The motivations for retailers to establish private labels make a lot of sense: they lead to higher shopper loyalty, more power in the supply channel and increased profitability. However, this is not to say that private labels succeed in any situation:

- In categories such as cheese and paper kitchen towels, for example, the share of private label is high, but in deodorants and razor blades it is not.

- In Germany the share of private labels at discounter chains is high, but the share of private label at service supermarkets is not.

- Parents of a newborn do not want to run any risks, and will initially buy A-brand diapers and baby food. However, after a few months this changes.

- Competitor actions should be taken into consideration. In 2009, Mercadona in Spain removed 25 per cent of A-brands while at the same time other retailers such as Lidl increased the share of A-brands in many countries.

In conclusion, there are many differences between countries, categories, shoppers and retailers. From a supplier perspective these differences can be leveraged to ensure that private labels do not saturate categories. Indeed, if a supplier does not adapt their stance on the A-brands battlefield, they usually get hit first.

The A-brand answers to private labels

So what is it that A-brand suppliers can bring in against private-label arrangements?

Turning point revenue/loyalty

A study by Kumar and Steenkamp shows that there are limits to shopper loyalty.[3] When a retailer extends the share of a private label, shopper loyalty initially grows. A good experience with private labelling in one category leads to a trial purchase of a private label in another category. Eventually, this converts into brand value for the retailer. However, there is a turning point where the shopper is more interested in hunting for savings than appreciating the private label itself. As a result, the total value of the category decreases, as the now regularly purchased private label products have lower prices than the A-brands purchased previously. In the end, the shopper also targets the private labels of other retailers. The shopper now enters the store of a retailer they used to love only when there are fantastic promotions on offer. Kumar and Steenkamp calculated the turning points for several grocery retailers. For Albert Heijn, the turning point lies at an average of 37 per cent of private labels in dry groceries. Of course, this average still allows for differences per category. Let's say the retailer improves shopper loyalty with an extension of private label in meat sauces, but it also causes leakage in, for example, the coffee category. When the share of private labels is continuously extended the shopper will miss essential products. The rigorous reduction of assortment and expansion of private labels by Mercadona in 2008 caused it to be more clearly positioned as a retail brand, but it also resulted in less loyalty. Shoppers could no longer find everything they wanted to buy. Even Walmart, one of the most advanced retailers in the world, made a mistake when it rationalized 1,000 products in the United States. Shoppers looked for missing products at competing retailers and Walmart had to relaunch 300 of the original 1,000 items.

The reverse of channel power

The extension of private labels can lead to more power for the retailer, but it does not necessarily result in more category revenue. By comparing stores with quantities of private labels, retailers can learn whether private labels lead to a stabilization or even a decrease of the category revenue. The category manager may not notice such changes if they only watch the total revenue from private labels. Or even worse, some retailers judge their category managers on the total number of private-label products that they launched on the market, without considering revenue at all. The saturation point for private labels is dependent on the category and the retailer, but the maximum for grocery retailing is usually around 40 per cent for dry groceries. If the private label replaces an existing, higher-priced A-brand, the category manager should estimate price elasticity in advance: the rotation of the lower-priced private label should be above the volume of the A-brand in order to compensate the value loss as a result of the price difference.

The objective of increased channel power is very relevant in emerging countries such as Poland and Russia. In France, for example, the level is already high. The argument of channel power is not relevant to all categories, and each supplier should decide for themselves whether the top three retailers in their country actually improved their share in the categories relevant to the supplier. In addition, the situation of each supplier within the category might be different. Sometimes the leading A-brand succeeds in keeping its share intact when the retailer expands its private label, and at other times a supplier without strong A-brands will yield to the private-label entrants.

Limited profitability

Another argument that retailers use for the expansion of private labels is profitability. This term needs a more precise explanation. Retailers can look at both percentage margin, as Albert Heijn and Tesco do, and at absolute cash margin, which many French retailers use and refer to as *'masse de marge'*. I think the French have adopted the right approach for a number of reasons:

1 A direct comparison between supplier brands and private labels on the basis of relative margin is impossible, because it does not consider off-invoice discounts and payments for features and merchandising.

2 In addition, retailers pay their staff not with percentages but with cash.

3 Finally, a high relative margin could signal a diminishing role for private labels and working counter-strategies. While researching for a US retailer, Ailawadi and Harlam compared shopper groups that bought varying amounts of private labels.[4] Their study showed that shoppers whose groceries trips consist of more than 35 per cent of private labels delivered the highest relative margin to the retailer, but also brought in the lowest absolute margin and lowest total spend. However, shoppers with a limited purchase level of private labels (10 to 20 per cent of their groceries) delivered the highest cash profit and left the most money in the retailer's cash register. If suppliers wish to stop further roll-outs of private labels with a certain retailer, they should investigate whether the same arguments of profitability apply to their categories.

Discussions between the retailer and the A-brand supplier

If a supplier is not selling private-label products itself, it is often hard to discuss the role of private labels with a retailer. Not every retailer is open to discussing the role of its private labels, or they may strictly regulate the terms of the discussion, or have the discussion only with a limited number of suppliers. At the beginning of the recession in 2008 retailers felt compelled to offer more space to private labels, more than was in fact justified on the basis of revenue or rotation. The first sales numbers were encouraging. However, many private labels simply sold more because they were allocated more space and received a disproportionate amount of media share. At Tesco's launch of its Discount Brands in 2008, the company went to extreme lengths to create a mental space in the shopper's head: outdoor ads were posted announcing that Tesco was to become Britain's biggest discounter;

complete aisles were 'painted' yellow; and all new discount products with fancy names, such as Trattoria Verdi for anti-pasta, were showcased at the front of the store. Tesco even let go of the Tesco name in order to compete directly with Aldi and Lidl, who also used private labels carrying fancy names. Unfortunately, the strategy did not work out. Discounters like Aldi have kept growing and many of the discount products have long disappeared from the shelves.

What suppliers can do

I am convinced that all suppliers can hold a productive discussion on private labels with a retailer as long as it is based on facts. Suppliers can build up their story based on what they see in store, or by diving into data sources such as the loyalty card information or retail panel feedback. Furthermore, international suppliers have the potential to exchange best practices among countries. Finally, the academic world offers an array of research that may not always be topical but is nonetheless solid and offers comprehensive perspectives.

In the outer ring of Figure 10.1 you find the objectives that retailers strive for with private labels: more shopper loyalty, power and profitability. Each

FIGURE 10.1   Pitfalls for private label

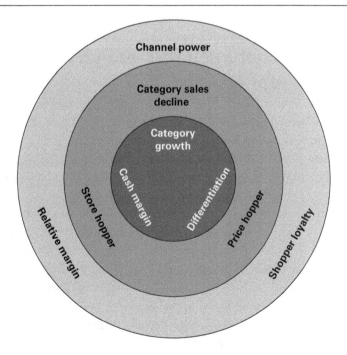

of these objectives has its limitations and even pitfalls, and these are displayed in the second ring:

- Retailers who find it most important to show they are in the lead are often lacking in foresight, and may ultimately find their total category revenue falling. They make the mistake of ignoring the direct investments from suppliers into innovation to enable future category growth.

- Retailers that push private labels too heavily make their shoppers more price aware and price conscious – and they become price hoppers. Ultimately, price becomes a critical decision factor for even the most loyal shoppers, and eventually they will shop more at other price-focused competitors, or else only buy during promotions.

- Retailers that always give preferential treatment to private labels and consistently offer them the best location on the shelf will find their shoppers searching for A-brands. They will switch stores and again become store hoppers.

The centre of the circle in Figure 10.1 shows the deepest desires of retailers: differentiation, category growth and cash margin. When retailers realize that shopper loyalty comes into being by offering something unique, a much wider spectrum of solutions opens up for them. Retailers cannot differentiate themselves only with private labels, but they can combine this with a pleasant shopping experience or an assortment of organic products. For suppliers that see their market share crushed by private labels, this provides the opportunity to steer the discussion in a new direction. Suppliers could help differentiate retailers in different ways. They could support the retailer's positioning through promotions or assortments that are specifically tailored to the retailer. To help category managers make sound decisions, suppliers can analyse and identify the level at which the revenue share of private labels caused the overall category revenue to go down. This is a gigantic job for the trade marketing department because each recommendation should be made by the retailer (brand) and should be specific to every category.

I believe that private label will continue to grow unstoppably around the globe. However, this is not to say that A-brand suppliers have lost the opportunity to grow:

- First, retailers themselves made a gaffe. When retailers such as Metro and Tesco started their private labels in Eastern Europe, they first launched their 'value' private labels. This sounds reasonable when you take into consideration the large numbers of shoppers with low incomes within those territories. However, shoppers in countries such as Poland and Romania thought the quality was disappointing and relied again on the trusted A-brands. The poor-quality image has stayed with Tesco for many years after they developed the standard private-label range.

- In addition, a supplier could opt to side with the winner and produce private labels itself. Because of the incremental production volume, the supplier uses its production capacity more effectively and the category manager is likely to reward the supplier with some extras for their A-brands, such as a 'free' feature or display. The supplier should also look into the consequences of its decision on the longer term. The price that the retailer pays should cover the total and not just the variable costs of the product. This requires the supplier to make a thorough and correct allocation of costs. The supplier should not be surprised to find the retailer increasing pressure after some time to supply at lower costs on a continual basis. And why would a supplier blame a category manager for doing what they are paid to do? For pure private-label suppliers this has become a major cause for concern. In many markets, neither private-label suppliers nor retailers make money on value private labels. The private-label supplier only produces the value labels in order to win the contract for the standard private-label range. Standard private labels are, however, not the ultimate solution as this market does not look promising either. For a retailer, the margins are fine but the private-label supplier needs to fight for its contract via internet auctions that only consider price against fixed quality requirements. Family-owned private-label companies come off badly, and private equity firms have started to acquire them to build large private-label houses that can withstand the pressure from retail chains. Europe has seen a rise in private-label production powerhouse companies such as United Coffee and Continental Bakeries. I think that in time they will become the true competitors of multinationals such as Unilever, Procter & Gamble and PepsiCo. Finally, from the perspective of the shopper, it is doubtful whether an A-brand supplier should produce both A-brands and private labels. A shopper who knows – or even just assumes – that a supplier produces a private label next to an A-brand starts to have doubts about the quality of the A-brand and is no longer prepared to pay the extra amount of money for that A-brand.

- Finally, the chances of survival for small private-label companies improve if they offer retailers a differentiated product at a premium price. Think of the biological products or regional products that Carrefour offers under the label 'Reflets de France', and Leclerc markets under the name 'Nos Régions ont du Talent'.

For me the advance of private labels does not mean that A-brands are written off. If anything has become clear from the past, it is that A-brands should increase rather than decrease their advertising and innovation investments during times of pressure from private labels. Often the number one A-brand can maintain its market share. Figure 10.2 shows that there are many opportunities for sales and marketing teams to let the A-brands and private labels coexist in balance. The figure shows that suppliers can choose from the following models to achieve coexistence with private labels:

- Do your homework: analyse private labels and their effects on the category and the A-brands. If necessary, suppliers should take action, but do not discuss this openly with retailers.
- Tactical influence: with some analysis, but mainly with profound determination, the supplier demonstrates the strength and role of its A-brand products and shares its comparison in a fair, transparent manner with the retailer.
- Customer focus: the supplier supports those retailers that back their brands and de-invests actively from retailers that do not come up with the right counter-performances.
- Strategic marketing: an integrated effort from the supplier's marketing and sales teams to reduce the share of private labels by increasing its innovating and advertising efforts and with the help of tactical moves, such as the introduction of lower-priced B-brands.

Figure 10.2 shows that suppliers can vary the extent to which they involve the retailer in their approach. They also differ as to whether they find a solution for the shorter or longer term. As such, very often a combination of the approaches is best. There is not just one strategy that stops the growth of private labels in the supplier category, because the situation differs so much across country, category, shopper segment and retailer. Suppliers should resign themselves to the fact that retailers want to increase the share of private labels in a structured manner. However, that should not stop them from identifying the opportunities per category and per retailer.

FIGURE 10.2 Response models from supplier perspective

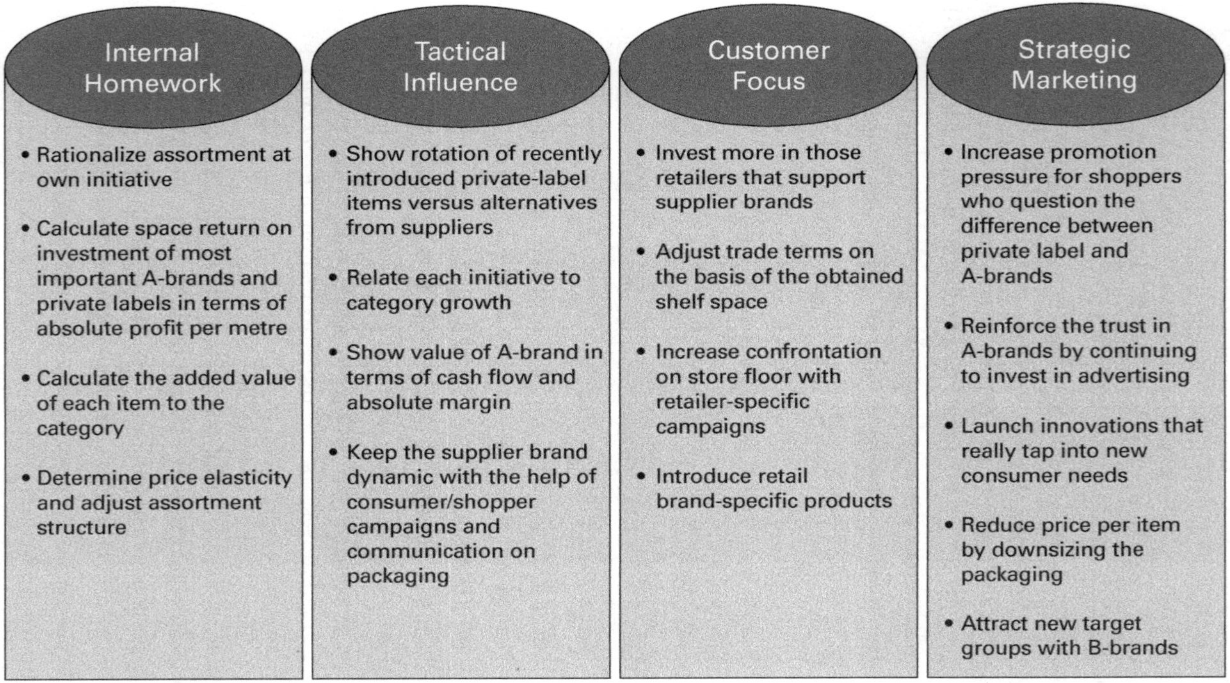

Internal Homework

- Rationalize assortment at own initiative
- Calculate space return on investment of most important A-brands and private labels in terms of absolute profit per metre
- Calculate the added value of each item to the category
- Determine price elasticity and adjust assortment structure

Tactical Influence

- Show rotation of recently introduced private-label items versus alternatives from suppliers
- Relate each initiative to category growth
- Show value of A-brand in terms of cash flow and absolute margin
- Keep the supplier brand dynamic with the help of consumer/shopper campaigns and communication on packaging

Customer Focus

- Invest more in those retailers that support supplier brands
- Adjust trade terms on the basis of the obtained shelf space
- Increase confrontation on store floor with retailer-specific campaigns
- Introduce retail brand-specific products

Strategic Marketing

- Increase promotion pressure for shoppers who question the difference between private label and A-brands
- Reinforce the trust in A-brands by continuing to invest in advertising
- Launch innovations that really tap into new consumer needs
- Reduce price per item by downsizing the packaging
- Attract new target groups with B-brands

What can you do to make your shoppers happy?

Shoppers expect the quality of the standard private label to be as good as the A-brands. All private labels should be benchmarked against their leading A-brand competitor in consumer tests on a regular basis.

Shoppers perceive private labels to be a real brand. They will understand retailers allocating more time to private labels, but do not enjoy tactics such as overspacing on the shelf after the initial launch period.

Which marketing strategies can retailers apply?

Private labels fulfil an important role, creating a positive price image for the retailer, especially when the private label carries the name of the retailer's store.

In the short term, the expansion of private labels could be an objective in itself, for example if company profitability is below standard, or if a supplier becomes too dominant in a particular category. However, it is worth keeping in mind that other tools might be available to achieve the same objectives.

Notes

1   Europanel (2014) [accessed 22 July 2015] Europanel Global FMCG Barometer [Online] http://www.europanel.com/insights.php
2   Lamey, L, Deleersnyder, B, Dekimpe, M and Steenkamp, J (2005) [accessed 22 July 2015] The Impact of Business-cycle Fluctuations on Private-label Share, ERIM Report Series, Research in Management, *Erasmus Research Institute of Management* [Online] http://papers.ssrn.com/sol3/papers.cfm?abstract_id=830286
3   Kumar, N and Steenkamp, J (2007) *Private Label Strategy: How to meet the store brand challenge*, Harvard Business School Press, Boston
4   Ailawadi, K and Harlam, B (2004) [accessed 22 July 2015] An empirical analysis of the determinants of retail margins: the role of store-brand share, *Journal of Marketing* [Online] http://www.jstor.org/stable/30161980?seq=1#page_scan_tab_contents

The unexplainable effect of music

11

The traditional marketing-mix instruments in retail, such as promotion and store layout, tap into the visual sensory system. Yet retailers realize increasingly that shoppers use their other senses as well, and therefore the retail sector has seen a burst of stores with ambient scents. The motivation is usually simple: retailers wish to improve the 'shopping experience' and hope to connect with more of the shoppers' senses in order to stimulate additional, deeper emotions. It is often believed that scents give unfiltered access to the brain: the impression retailers may have is that the sensory marketing instruments are easy to control, and have a direct and immediate impact on the shopper, and therefore sales. Considering all the popular press around the impact of music and scents, I decided to investigate their effectiveness in controlled retail experiments. In this chapter I analyse music played in-store.

The effect of music on people seems unexplainable. It evokes powerful emotions. It makes people feel relaxed or excited, and allows those who listen to it to return in their imagination to a special moment or place. Music is a form of communication, an art form that can incite deep feelings. So it is no wonder that retailers play music in their stores in order to make shoppers feel good. Academic research proves that retailers are right to use music: music played in a supermarket, for example, leads to more revenue. Retailers play music for three key reasons: 1) there is a belief in retail that if shoppers feel better, they automatically spend more; 2) in comparison with other marketing instruments it is not expensive and can be adjusted easily; 3) shoppers have become accustomed to continually having music around them. Still, the style of music that retailers play seems to be chosen in a random manner.

Effects of music

The first study on the effect of music in a retail environment comes from Smith and Curnow in 1966.[1] They concluded that loud music in a supermarket leads to shorter shopper trips. Marketing practitioners only began to pay attention to this in 1973 when Kotler defined music as a marketing instrument and referenced its emotional effects as increasing the buying intention.[2]

In the past 50 years the effect of music in a retail environment has been investigated surprisingly little. Most likely this is because the workings of music are so complex. What effect music has on shoppers is caused by the functioning of their bodies and the working of their brains. Apart from the physiological aspects the effects are related to the shopper's upbringing, generation, culture, religion and, even more difficult to get a grip on, taste. Academic studies have generated very insightful conclusions about genre, speed, complexity and volume; however, the research does not show a consistent relationship between music and the revenue of the store. Research papers often investigate three types of effects of music: revenue and buying intention, shopping behaviour and image.

Revenue and buying intention

The first study that found a correlation between music and revenue was in 1982. Milliman stated that a supermarket that chose music with a slow tempo achieved 38 per cent more revenue than a supermarket with high-tempo music.[3] Slower music resulted in a 17 per cent longer shopping trip. Four years later, Milliman found something similar with respect to restaurants.[4] In the case of music with a slow tempo, restaurant guests sat at a table longer and spent 40 per cent more on drinks than in the case of fast music. There were no differences with regards to the spend on food. After examining scientific studies back to the 1970s Garlin and Owen conclude that music does not always lead to more sales and a higher buying intention.[5]

Shopping behaviour

Shoppers stay longer in a store with music than in a store without music. Visiting time is higher if shoppers like the music, if the music has a low volume, a slow tempo and if shoppers know or recognize the music. However, it is important to realize that the actual length of stay may not be equal to the perceived length of stay. For example, music with a high tempo, at a high volume and that does not match the taste of the shopper gives the shopper the feeling that they have been in the store longer than they actually have.

Image

A retailer should realize that a shopper associates the style of the music played, either consciously or subconsciously, in their evaluation of the retail brand. To say the same thing differently, if the store remains unchanged other than that music is being played, the shopper nevertheless perceives the retail brand in a different manner because of the music. Hargreaves, McKendrick, North and Shilcock found evidence for the effects on retail image in several environments:

- In an English restaurant pop music had no effect on the revenue but classical music did. Classical music led to 10 per cent more expenditure on food when compared to pop music, and 11 per cent more when compared to a music-free restaurant. This was explained by the fact that classical music fitted the positioning of the restaurant, which had above-average pricing. Additional reasons for this conclusion were that music had a significant effect on the starter and on the coffee after the dessert (courses whereby the visitor may allow him or herself to spend more time/money) but not on the drinks and other courses of the meal. In conclusion, the effect of music on sales is highly dependent on the type of music being played and the context.[6]

- A bar also obtained the perception of luxury and richness when classical music was played. When pop music was played, visitors perceived the bar as more upbeat than without music. The association with luxury and richness stimulated the visitors to a higher purchasing intent in the case of both classical and pop music when compared to a store without music. With classical music the intended purchase amount was 21 per cent higher when compared to no music, 19 per cent higher compared to easy-listening music and 4 per cent higher than pop music.[7]

- In the reception area of a bank, visitors heard alternatingly no music, classical music and easy-listening music. When music was playing the visitors thought the bank was more dynamic. In the case of classical music the visitors perceived the bank to be more inspiring than without music or with easy-listening tunes being played.[8]

- When rock music with a slow tempo was played shoppers thought a sport retail chain was dull and tired, while the same store was perceived as cool and modern when upbeat and fast rock music was played.[9]

This research is very significant. As I said, shoppers associate the music with their perception of the retail brand. Let's say for instance that the shopper thinks music by Justin Bieber is cheap, then the shopper perceives the store in the same way. Shoppers who do not know a particular store use the music as a sign of the quality of the product assortment and of the type of shoppers the store aims to attract. On such a scenario, the music serves to draw the shoppers into the store, or otherwise.

Emotions

The researchers Donovan and Rossiter applied the pleasure–arousal–dominance (PAD) model of Mehrabian and Russell to the retail environment.[10] This provides a good starting point to understand how music works in-store. According to their model, environmental factors such as store layout and music lead to three types of fundamental, emotional responses: pleasure, arousal and dominance. These emotional responses influence the shopper's decision to avoid or enter the store. The model is applicable for all kinds of store stimuli, not just music. Many studies have found the arousal and pleasure responses useful for explaining emotions in marketing contexts; however, the degree of dominance or submissiveness of shopper emotions seems less applicable. As said above, academics still have a hard nut to crack to understand our physical and psychological responses to music. On the basis of many studies Garlin and Owen conclude that music leads to more pleasure, and the higher the tempo the greater the excitement.[11] The best-demonstrated and clearest explanations for the way music works deal with core elements such as tempo, pitch and volume. These explanations feel very intuitive:

- *Tempo*
  When music with a fast tempo is played within a store, the shopper's physical and/or emotional state moves along with it. This is not so strange, as the number of beats per minute (rhythm) relates to the beat or rhythm of a human heart. At 60–80 beats per minute a shopper's heartbeat is quiet – at that tempo the music feels calm and relaxed.

- *Pitch*

  Large instruments move more air and make deeper sounds than smaller instruments. As a result of evolution people are generally more afraid of large things than small things; similarly, we associate low-pitch sounds with threats, danger and sadness. In contrast, shoppers relate high-pitched sounds with lightness, happiness and a carefree attitude. Of course, however, there are exceptions.

- *Volume*

  Loud volume brings shoppers to a state of excitement, but could also cause a shopper to avoid an environment. Therefore, in a retail environment shoppers usually hear background music: there is music but it is not the most important point of attention. Music in the foreground requires an effort from a shopper, such as concentration.

Together, tempo, pitch and volume form a list of initial criteria that a retailer should be guided by when deciding whether a piece of music fits the store. Yet music can, of course, be categorized in many more ways: genre, style, instrumental or vocal, simplicity, complexity, harmony, melody, rhythm, etc. With the help of these typologies a retailer can identify the music that fits its store more effectively. I think it is helpful for a retailer to absorb insights from academic studies regarding which effects are most significant. In this way, the retailer has a starting point to conduct experiments within the context of its own stores. To the academic insights from retail stores (eg supermarkets, department stores) I will add examples from 'out of home' channel contexts (eg restaurants) because the effects are comparable. Six studies are discussed briefly below.

Restaurant full or empty

Caldwell and Hibbert investigated the effect of music in an Italian restaurant in a prosperous part of Glasgow.[12] They compared the tempo of music with 72 or fewer beats per minute (defined as slow music) and 94 or more beats (fast music). Under the influence of slow music the clients dined for 17 per cent longer time, spent 51 per cent more on drinks and 12 per cent more on food. The practical recommendation of Caldwell and Hibbert was that restaurant owners are better off playing slow music if there are few tables occupied. This will create a pleasurable, occupied atmosphere. However, if the restaurant is quite full and more guests will arrive shortly, faster music will result in higher turnaround and more free tables in time.

Liquor store and choice of wine

Areni and Kim discovered that shoppers select more expensive wines when hearing classical music in the background of a wine store rather than Top 40 music.[13] The genre did not have an effect on other types of shopping behaviour such as the number of purchased bottles, the number of considered products on the shelf or the number of bottles picked up. Areni and Kim explained that in the United States both wine and classical music are associated with prestige, taste and a higher socio-economic status. In the case of classical music, shoppers expect higher quality and they feel stimulated to choose a more expensive wine.

Luxury goods and classical music

Classical music also seems to fit well with luxury items. According to Grewal *et al* classical music in a US jewellery store led to a more positive evaluation of the atmosphere than a store without music.[14] Further, the atmosphere correlated positively with the buying intention. The lingerie chain Victoria's Secret also plays classical music because it strives for a prestigious atmosphere and hopes that shoppers, in light of this, judge the quality of the service and product assortment as better.

Wine in supermarkets

North, Hargreaves and McKendrick demonstrated that music that is clearly recognizable as originating from a certain country influences the behaviour of shoppers.[15] For example, an English supermarket played alternatingly traditional French and German music at the wine aisle that offered four German and four French wines. The prices and the flavours (sweet and dry) of the wines were identical. When French music was played, the supermarket sold three times more French than German wine. In the case of German music, the supermarket sold twice as much German wine as French. Even more remarkable was the fact that only 7 per cent of the wine buyers actually admitted to being influenced by the music.

Restaurant and genre

Wilson played four different types of music in a popular restaurant in Sydney: classical, jazz, pop and easy listening.[16] Each of the genres of music provoked a different perception of the restaurant by the guests:

- classical music: upmarket and sophisticated;
- popular: upbeat;

- jazz: invigorating and stimulating and least peaceful/passive;
- easy listening: tacky.

The genre also impacted purchasing intent. Without music the guests were less willing to spend money, for example, 12 per cent less in comparison to a restaurant with easy-listening music. Jazz music most inspired the guests to spend more. When classical music played, fewer drinks were ordered compared to other genres; however, this situation was still significantly different to playing no music at all. The guests indicated that classical music was, to a moderate extent, fitting for a restaurant atmosphere.

Department store

Large stores like department stores attract many different target groups. Yalch and Spangenberg wondered how retailers could adapt their music to suit such a variety.[17] In two departments (sports articles for men and coats/dresses for women) of a department store in the United States they played three types of music: 1) background/instrumental/slow tempo; 2) background/instrumental/high tempo; and 3) foreground/vocal/slow tempo. Their main finding was that the effect of music depends mainly on age and less on gender. Shoppers less than 50 years old preferred foreground music while shoppers over 50 preferred background music. This was noticeable in the revenue: The latter group spend more money (+58 per cent!) and time (+18 per cent) while background music is playing in comparison to foreground music. In contrast, the age group 25–50 spent more money (+32 per cent) and time (+8 per cent) when listening to foreground music. Shoppers under 25 years spent more time when there was background music, just like the next age group (+33 per cent), but ended up spending less money (–69 per cent).

In addition, the perception of time differed among the age groups. Young shoppers thought they were spending more time shopping when background music played, and older shoppers thought the same with foreground music.

When asked about their perceptions of music, male and female shoppers gave different opinions. In the case of background music, the female shoppers perceived the department with coats and dresses as more friendly and sophisticated; 57 per cent of the female shoppers indicated they felt like spending money when background music was playing, in comparison with 26 per cent with foreground music – and indeed, in the survey, they spent one and a half times as much. The purchasing intent of male shoppers in the men's department was higher when foreground music was playing: 76 per cent, versus 57 per cent for background music. The intent showed a real difference as the basket spend came out almost twice as high. Finally, men perceived the department to be more spacious with foreground music. Both men and women perceive the department as having the least expensive merchandise and as most down-to-earth in the case of foreground music.

Music and store employees

There is proof of the many effects of music on shoppers. For example, it is said that music decreases stress. However, retailers should be careful with such conclusions because this is based on studies with patients in a hospital – a completely different research situation. An important question for retailers is: what effect does music in-store have on staff? Most research on this relationship focuses on music used as a means to keep morale high (this was a practice deployed by the BBC, for instance, during the Second World War). Several studies show that music increases productivity in employees in comparison to no music, and that faster music leads to a higher level of productivity than slow music. However, the other side of the coin is that optimistic music puts an employee in such a good mood that they are prepared to take more risk than they would while listening to music that has a neutral or negative mood. Further, perhaps retailers should ask what music store employees want to listen to. According to a survey by the UK Noise Association, 40 per cent of people who work with continuous background music want to stop it and 28 per cent try very hard not to hear it; only 7 per cent of the employees actually liked the music.[18]

Turn down the music

There is a social movement known as Pipedown consisting of zealous advocates for more silence and for people only to hear music if they want to themselves. In Britain, Pipedown works hard for silent zones. According to this association, being forced to hear music leads to raised blood pressure and a deficient immune system. Pipedown tries to persuade supermarkets such as Tesco to turn off the music in-store and refers to chains like Waitrose and Lidl as examples that are leading the way. There are equivalents to Pipedown in other countries, such as Bescherming Akoestisch Milieu (BAM) in the Netherlands, Lautsprecheraus in Germany and The Right to Quiet Society in Canada. BAM maintains a so-called 'silence list' of stores and retail chains (supermarkets, restaurants, book stores, garden centres and pet stores) that do not play music in their stores, listed by city. What retailers can learn from these social movements is that, at the very least, store music should not irritate the employees and shoppers. This is actually very challenging because style and volume preferences are very personal. Take for example people with introverted personalities who, according to Staum and Brotons, prefer quiet music.[19]

Practice

Supermarkets compete heavily on product assortment and price but music may be a good alternative. Music has a direct impact on revenue, shopping behaviour, staff morale and brand image. It is possible to use music as a means for differentiation. The music choice by retailers at Starbucks and Abercombie & Fitch, for example, has become so appealing to shoppers that it is now available to buy online. Most retailers pay little attention to the choice of music for their stores – and often the music does not remain consistent over time. This is not too strange, because retailers often have a diverse appeal and want to attract a target group as broad as possible. However, retailers' lack of interest in a specific type of in-store music is understandable, however, because it is often difficult to select the right type of music and shape the retail context in such a way that the effects on revenue, shopper and staff are predictable. In light of this, choosing the *right* music for a store becomes an art. Therefore, below I offer a few suggestions to help make the selection easier:

- The fundamental characteristics of music such as tempo and volume directly impact our walking tempo. By choosing the right tempo the retailer will encourage the shopper to stay longer: giving the perception of a full store, further encouraging shoppers to make a choice at their own convenience and persuading them to visit more of the store.

- If shoppers convey the music associations to the brand image, the first question for the retailer is which personality fits well with the brand, and then to find suitable music. Marks & Spencer in the UK desires younger shoppers, but does not want to alienate the older shoppers. Therefore, the stores play different music on weekdays when more older shoppers visit than on the weekends when young shoppers visit.

- Music leaves an impression on the shopper that is combined with all other in-store targeting such as communication messages, lighting, space and store inventory. All these factors interrelate.

- Do not fixate on genre. The definition of genre is not only related to music but is more culturally determined. Genres are dynamic, evolve into new shapes, split into subgenres. Genres come and go very quickly. Finally, the preference of a certain genre is personal, so that in stores that attract a broad audience a divergent genre probably leads to little changes in the shopper groups.

- More could be done to empathize with the shopper group and shopping trip on a specific day. What mood is the shopper in and what will they do after shopping? Let's say, for example, the retailer could play relaxed music for stressed parents on Thursday afternoons, who soon need to pick up their children from school; on a rainy Monday the supermarket may choose exceptionally cheerful music to improve the shopper's mood.

- Consider zoning – this is the adjustment of music to different parts of the store in order to address certain shopper groups or occasions better. For example, shoppers may particularly enjoy music at the service department, which reduces their perception of waiting times.

Music shapes the personal identity of people. This can also happen for retail brands. Little is still known about the power of music, but what is known can be applied by retailers more effectively.

What can you do to make your shoppers happy?

Music evokes deep emotions, and this has an impact when people are shopping. The music may remind them of special moments and places; playing music can help to create a positive shopping atmosphere.

Shoppers may feel overwhelmed if there is too much ambient music that they cannot avoid. Music is an instrument for shopper satisfaction, and that also means knowing when to keep it mute.

Which marketing strategies can retailers apply?

When choosing the right music for their stores retailers should first consider tempo, pitch and volume, as these influence shopping behaviour directly. Next, they need to find out which associations the shopper transfers from the music to the retail brand.

The shopper integrates the image of the ambient music with the other retail instruments to a complete evaluation of the retail context. Retailers may change the perception of the store and the retail brand without any changes to the physical environment.

Notes

1 Smith, P and Curnow, R (1966) [accessed 22 July 2015] Arousal hypothesis and the effects of music on purchasing behaviour, *Journal of Applied Psychology* [Online] http://psycnet.apa.org/journals/apl/50/3/255/

2 Kotler, P (1973) Atmospherics as a marketing tool, *Journal of Marketing*, **49** (4), pp 48–64

3 Milliman, R (1982) Using background music to affect the behaviour of supermarket shoppers, *Journal of Marketing*, **46** (3), pp 86–91

4 Milliman, R (1986) The influence of background music on the behavior of restaurant patrons, *Journal of Consumer Research*, **13** (2), pp 286–89

5 Garlin, F and Owen, K (2006) Setting the tone with the tune: a meta-analytic review of the effects of background music in retail settings, *Journal of Business Research*, **59** (6), pp 755–64

6 North, A, Shilcock, A and Hargreaves, D (2003) The effect of musical style on restaurant customers' spending, *Environment and Behaviour*, **35** (5), pp 712–18

7 North, A and Hargreaves, D (1998) The effect of music on atmosphere and purchase intentions in a cafeteria, *Journal of Applied Psychology*, **28** (24), pp 2254–73

8 North, A, Hargreaves, D and Mckendrick, J (2000) The effects of music on atmosphere in a bank and a bar, *Journal of Applied Social Psychology*, **30** (7), pp 1507–22

9 North, A, Hargreaves, D and McKendrick, J (1997) The perceived importance of in-store music and its effects on store atmosphere

10 Donovan, R and Rossiter, J (1982) Store atmosphere: an environmental psychology approach, *Journal of Retailing*, **58** (1), pp 34–57

11 Garlin, F and Owen, K (2006) Setting the tone with the tune: a meta-analytic review of the effects of background music in retail settings, *Journal of Business Research*, **59** (6), pp 755–64

12 Caldwell, C and Hibbert, S (1999) [accessed 22 July 2015] Play That One Again: The Effect of Music Tempo on Consumer Behaviour in A Restaurant, *European Advances in Consumer Research* [Online] http://acrwebsite.org/volumes/11116/volumes/e04/E-04

13 Areni, C and Kim, D (1993) [accessed 22 July 2015] The Influence of Background Music on Shopping Behavior: Classical Versus Top-Forty Music in a Wine Store, *Advances in Consumer Research* [Online] http://acrwebsite.org/volumes/7467/volumes/v20/NA-20

14 Grewal, D, Baker, J, Levy, M and Voss, G (2003) The effects of wait expectations and store atmosphere evaluations on patronage intentions in service-intensive retail stores, *Journal of Retailing*, **79** (4), pp 259–68

15 North, A, Hargreaves, D and McKendrick, J (1999) The influence of in-store music on wine selections, *Journal of Applied Psychology*, **84** (2), pp 271–76

16 Wilson, S (2003) The effect of music on perceived atmosphere and purchase intentions in a restaurant, *Psychology of Music*, **31** (1), pp 93–112

17 Yalch, R and Spangenberg, E (1993) [accessed 22 July 2015] Using Store Music For Retail Zoning: A Field Experiment, *Advances in Consumer Research* [Online] http://acrwebsite.org/volumes/7531/volumes/v20/NA-20

18 Hallam, S (2012) The effects of background music on health and well-being, in *Music, Health and Wellbeing*, ed R MacDonald, G Kreutz and L Mitchell, p. 491, Oxford University Press, Oxford. (This is referring to a survey by UK Noise Association in 2007.)

19 Staum, M and Brotons, M (2000) The effect of music amplitude on the relaxation response, *Journal of MusicTherapy*, **37** (1), pp 22–39

Can scents work wonders?

12

In Chapter 11 I discussed the relevance of music as an in-store marketing instrument. When it comes to in-store instruments it is all about flawless execution. Of course, the retail marketing mix should be based on an understanding of the shopper's emotional needs, and all decisions should be underpinned by research and facts. This enables the retailer to meet shoppers' needs and operate through strategy. In the case of scents, retailers should ask themselves whether ambient scents really serve the purpose of making their shoppers happy.

Retailers love to believe that scents work for them. It sounds so logical. When the smell of freshly baked bread leaves the oven, the bread sells itself; similarly, for coffee chains such as Starbucks the scent of coffee has always been very important to get passers-by to enter. In addition to the use of aromas in specific product groups, retailers can release scents in their stores. The purpose of these scents is to create a pleasant ambience, make shoppers more willing to hang around, make them behave more impulsively and open their wallets more easily.

The market of scents explodes in many directions. For example, suppliers add aromas to products such as cleaning agents, though the scent does not make any difference to the cleaning performance. Extreme examples are toilet paper with a friendly scent; and cream that includes aromatherapy health benefits. In addition, the number of stores that experiment with scents is increasing, with stores using scent as a means through which to create a better atmosphere and to seek more sales. Scents find their way into various and diverse industries such as supermarkets, hotels and casinos.

Are scents effective?

Do scents really work in retail? There are few hard facts available about their effect on shopping behaviour and revenue. There are several reasons for this. Often retailers keep the outcomes of experiments to themselves. In addition, in practical store tests it is often very difficult to correlate the effects exclusively to a scent. Scientific studies are working with experiments in controlled retail environments. In this chapter I discuss the academic studies that are most relevant to retail. A great starting point is a meta-analysis by Bone and Ellen.[1] After studying 143 scientific studies on the use of scents in retail contexts, they come to the conclusion that most studies deduce that scents have no effect (63 per cent of cases). This disappointingly low success rate motivates retailers to critically evaluate as to when using scents in a store is useful. Marketing teams need to attempt to better understand how scents influence shopping behaviour.

Indirect effect on mood

The oldest and best-known model to understand how store atmosphere comes into being was developed by Donovan and Rossiter,[2] based on the earlier work of Mehrabian and Russell.[3] Donovan and Rossiter find that a shopper reaches a good mood at the right combination of pleasure and excitement. Shoppers perceive scents especially in terms of pleasant and unpleasant. In addition, scents can excite. Between the two dimensions there is a U-shaped relationship: shoppers experience the least pleasure from scents that generate little excitement or very intense scents. Between those peaks there is an optimum level. The model assumes that stimuli such as scents lead shoppers into a certain mood. This mood next leads to a certain type of behaviour, such as looking around longer or spending more on impulse. This perfectly fits the intuition that scents influence the shopper's emotions first, and then propel the shopper into action. Chebat and Michon provided evidence in 1998 that this order of responses is not correct: a cognitive process occurs *before* an emotion.[4] In an experiment, they circulated a lightly pleasant citrus scent in the aisles of a Canadian shopping mall. This scent was a combination of orange, lemon and grapefruit that shoppers perceived without irritation. In their mall experiment they were able to find out that a scent initially influences the physical environment. The relationships are visualized in Figure 12.1 and explained below.

First, a scent has an effect on the physical environment. This includes the manner in which the shopper perceives the store (upbeat, stimulating, interesting) and the specific products in the store (high quality, modern). A scent influences the product quality in a direct manner, but the perceived product quality is more dependent on the total store image than on a specific scent.

FIGURE 12.1   Scents work via physical environment resulting in emotion

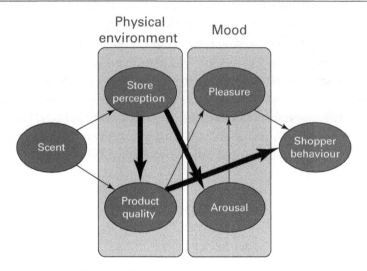

NOTE: The thicker lines indicate that the relationship is stronger between the connected terms than in those connected by the thinner lines.
SOURCE: Model adapted by Constant Berkhout, based on Chebat and Michon, 2003

Chebat and Michon discovered that product quality was the principal explanatory variable of the shopper's expenditure. The perception of the product quality makes the spend increase both directly and indirectly. An enhanced perception of the product quality results in greater pleasure in shopping, which in itself leads to a greater spend. The implications of these findings are significant. The shopper perceives a scent in the first instance without a change of mood. Shoppers use the scent as a signal that influences the context and the product evaluation. This means that a scent evokes an emotion through a cognitive process together with many other stimuli such as store layout and music. Another implication is that though product quality is an essential, it is not the complete explanation for what shoppers spend.

Primed to respond

Sometimes scents are processed more rapidly. In Chapter 3 on irrational shopping behaviours I referred to a study by Holland, Hendriks and Aarts from 2005.[5] It is worth highlighting the three experiments in their study in detail, as they clearly demonstrate the fact that scents are processed sub-consciously – and how scents are interpreted may lead to a direct change in behaviour. In the first experiment some of the participants carried out the test in a room with a citrus scent: results showed that participants working with a citrus scent responded more quickly to words that were associated with cleaning. In a second experiment the participants were asked to list five activities that they were planning to carry out during the remainder of the day: 36 per cent of those in a citrus-scented environment declared they intended to clean later in the day as compared to 11 per cent of those in the control group. This implies that the citrus scent increases associations with cleaning. In a third experiment participants filled out a questionnaire – some in a citrus-scented room and others in a neutral room. After the completion of the questionnaire they were taken to another room and given a Dutch cracker (these are impossible to eat without making crumbs). The researchers observed that participants from the citrus-scented room were more likely to clear the crumbs from the table than the control group. This means that a subconsciously activated scent can change behaviour without shoppers realizing the cause.

The human capacity to smell

Our olfactory organ, or nose, is a very special organ for a number of reasons. For other senses, a part of our brains called the thalamus first reviews the stimulus in order to decide whether it really deserves our attention. However, when we smell, the receptor cells in the back of the nostrils in the olfactory epithelium lead the stimulus directly to the section of the brain involved in long-term memory and associative learning (hippocampus), and the part of the brain that processes aggression and fear (amygdala). This explains why scents invoke such strong associations and can trigger vivid memories from the past. When people encounter a scent for the first time, they relate it to that particular occurrence, person, case or moment going forward. This helps to explain two things. Because people experience most scents for the first time when they are young, a particular scent often leads them to call on memories from their time as a child. To be even more specific, the olfactory organ matures when people are around five years old, so our most powerful scent experiences occur between the ages of five and 10 years old. The second implication is that associations to scents are often very personal: one person associates a floral scent with spring, someone else may be reminded of a funeral. The only other chemical body system that can identify, interpret and remember so fast is the immune system.

The human olfactory system is very refined in comparison to the other senses. People can differentiate some 10,000 scents and some say it is even more, 1.7 billion scents. According to research by the University of Pittsburgh the scents can be reduced to 10 primary odours that together describe all variation in the human olfactory experience:

- fragrant;

- woody/resinous;

- fruity (non-citrus);

- chemical;

- minty/peppermint;

- sweet;

- popcorn;

- lemon;

- pungent;

- decayed.[6]

In the case of colours and taste, the number of primary variations is more limited (red, blue, yellow; and sweet, salt, sour, bitter, umami). After reading all the unique characteristics of people's olfactory capabilities, it is important to remember that people absorb most information from their environment visually. Evolution has made humans so that 25 per cent of brain cells are involved in visual processing, more than in any other sensory process, and so that 70 per cent of the sensory receptor cells are in the eyes.

Congruency with all retail marketing variables

From the studies mentioned above, it is clear that the addition of a scent to a retail context requires precision. It more commonly results in no effect at all, rather than the desired positive effect. In addition, studies show that scents can influence shoppers' behaviour directly and subconsciously. The popular belief that scents can carry shoppers away on a tide of emotion needs refinement. Chebat and Michon demonstrate that a scent first influences the perception of the total retail environment, and then the resulting perception changes the mood and spending habits of shoppers. Therefore, retailers need to realize that scents are just one of many variables useful for creating the right atmosphere. To appreciate the wide variety of store variables that retailers can use, the following checklist has been developed by Turley and Milliman:[7]

- external variables, such as colour and height of the store, and use of exterior display window;
- general interior variables, such as flooring, temperature, scents and music;
- layout and design variables such as type and location of furniture and racks;
- point-of-purchase and decoration variables such as displays, certificates and pictures;
- human variables such as crowding, customer characteristic and uniforms.

To be applied effectively in-store, retailers need to regard scents as one element of the many marketing instruments. As a result, it is important to select a scent that is congruent with the specific retail environment. The necessity of congruency with the store environment and the products in the store comes up in a variety of studies.

A study by Matilla and Wirtz from 2001 shows the importance of aligning the effects of scents with the other instruments used to establish the store atmosphere.[8] In a gift shop they experimented with several combinations of an exciting grapefruit scent, a calming lavender scent, and types of music with low and high tempos. The results show that using a scent alone does not lead the shopper to consider the store environment to be significantly different, or make them spend more on impulse. The optimal effect was only reached when the intensity of the scent was in alignment with the music. In short, playing music with a high tempo has a more positive effect on shopping when combined with the exciting grapefruit scent rather than the calming lavender scent. The researchers found that this interaction influenced the shopper's intention to return to the store, the planned expenditure of money and time, impulse purchases, satisfaction with the store and pleasure in shopping.

Comparable results were found by Spangenberg, Grohmann and Sprott.[9] They experimented with several combinations of scents (Christmas scent versus no scent) and music (Christmas music versus no music). Shoppers judged a store with both a Christmas scent and Christmas music playing more positively. They liked the assortment better, and this increased their buying intent. If the scent and music were not aligned the effect was neutral, or even negative if there was no music playing. The studies reaffirm that shoppers respond more positively to the environment if all stimuli create a consistent atmosphere.

Congruency helps. The evaluation of specific products in a store happens faster when congruent scents help to retrieve information from the shopper's memory. If the scent is incongruent the shopper perceives less relevant information and the task becomes more difficult. This is explained by the fact that shoppers tend to attach more value to negative and conflicting information. In conclusion, scent congruency shortens the search time. However, total shopping time might still be lengthy, as became evident in a study by Mitchell, Kahn and Knasko.[10] They investigated the effect of chocolate and floral scents with respectively a candy and flower assortment. Congruency improved the complete retail context, allowing better holistic understanding and the researchers found that people relied more on information they already possessed rather than seeking it in-store. On the other hand, the total shopping time increased when congruent scents were used, because the shopper sought more varieties and spent more time considering various products. Their approach became more thorough. With congruent scents, shoppers spread their preferences between the products in a balanced manner, while with incongruent scents shoppers more often choose the most popular product option. Finally, a remarkable finding was that the researchers discovered a significant difference between types of scents, but did not see a difference between the presence and absence of a scent.

The level of congruency does not only depend on the sort of product, but also its appearance. For example, a shopper's ability to identify a scent also depends on the colour of a product. People can identify a citrus scent more easily if the object is yellow rather than red. The reverse also occurs. Bone and Jantrania demonstrated that adding incongruent scents to a cleaning agent and suntan lotion leads to a negative product judgement, as does the addition of, for example, a pineapple scent to advertisements for flowers.[11]

Three types of shopper responses to scents

Bone and Ellen mention three types of shopper responses to scents in a retail environment.[12] First, scents have a primitive role that can be explained by processing scents without the intervention of cognitive processes. For example, the smell of rotten meat gives a warning, while the scent of roasted chicken makes shoppers feel hungry. When a store is unsafe (for example, if there is a fire) or unpleasant, shoppers automatically feel short of breath and want to leave. Second, in addition to this autonomous response, scents can influence shoppers through their mood. Shoppers divide scents quickly into two categories: pleasant or unpleasant. A pleasant scent leads indirectly to a pleasant mood. These are seldom significant mood changes.

The third response is when shoppers have learnt to associate certain experiences with scents. This could be food (orange, chocolate), products with a natural or artificial scent (Playdoh, bubblegum), events or time periods (Christmas, birthdays, childhood). The scents help to retrieve stored information. If there is a positive scent association, it can correspondingly influence shoppers' moods positively. For example, a dairy company could dispense the scent of fresh grass in the milk aisle to remind shoppers of cows grazing outside. Johnson & Johnson even experimented by adding the scent of its baby powder to the ink of their advertisements in newspapers in order to strengthen relationships with parents.

It is pleasing for a retailer to know that scents may improve the atmosphere in their stores. However, they would rather know if their consistent usage results in desired shopping behaviours and an increase in revenue. To understand this better Spangenberg, Crowley and Henderson created their own store with non-food articles such as kitchen aids, plants, books, clothing and calendars.[13] They varied both the type of scents (neutral: lavender and ginger; and pleasant: spearmint and orange) and intensity (low, medium, high – depending on the number of seconds the scent was released in the room). The most important findings of their research are:

- Through the use of scents, shoppers perceived the store to be more attractive, stimulating, cheerful, motivating, interesting and modern. Also, the products in the store received a more positive evaluation and were considered to be of higher quality and more attractive. It is good to note that the perceptions changed without changing the physical characteristics of the product.

- A store with a scent led to a higher visiting intent. The actual number of minutes of the visit did not differ, but shoppers in a scented store thought they had stayed less time than they actually had. Apparently, shoppers divert themselves so that the ambient scent influences their perception of time.

- There is no difference in shopping behaviour between the types and intensity of scents. The researchers explain this by pointing to the fact that they did not use unpleasant scents.

Scent used as a differentiator in retail marketing

How shoppers choose and judge a supermarket has always depended a lot on factors such as location, assortment, price and staff service. The increased competition, both among supermarkets and from the new online players, makes it more difficult than ever for supermarkets to differentiate themselves on the basis of these factors. Supermarkets could attempt to make the difference through store atmosphere. Although little is known of how the five senses work, recent academic studies give retailers good pointers on how to integrate scents in the retail marketing mix:

- Align the scent with the other retail marketing instruments. Everything together (the music, staff clothing, the furniture etc) and not just the scent creates the atmosphere.

- Some scents call on associations, as a result of which the store perception shifts without changing the physical layout or products themselves. Stores with uniform categories, such as Nike sports stores or the clothing chain Abercrombie & Fitch, could even choose scents to allow them to differentiate themselves from the competition: either conspicuously in terms of shopper awareness (ie letting the shopper know that the intention is to create a positive, scented atmosphere), or more subtly (ie without telling the shopper directly).

- The most effective scents are those that are congruent with the relevant product category, such as a floral scent in a flower shop. For a supermarket or shopping mall it is difficult to identify the right scent. The least that retailers can do is to drop any scent that is incongruent with one of the offered categories.

Retail trade magazines and online blogs have countless stories about the success of scent marketing. The anecdotal evidence excels in simplicity and effectiveness. Readers may find stories about the Fanta soft drink brand that saw its sales increase by more than 60 per cent after dispersing a fruity scent in a display. Koopmans, a brand of baking products, reported a sales increase of 50 per cent after dispersing the scent of apple pie close to apples and baking products in nine C1000 supermarkets in the Netherlands. The scent marketing agency Consumatics published positive stories after a pilot in a Dutch shopping mall. A fresh scent and a mandarin scent seemingly had positive effects on the revenue of the 80 stores in the mall, but later it became clear that the sales effect could only be attributed to new decorations in the mall consisting of large pots containing plants and greenery. Each time that positive stories about scents are published, retailers smell quick and easy opportunities to increase their revenue. Intuitively it feels correct because it sounds logical to fully leverage the sensory experience of shoppers in supermarkets. Unfortunately, the anecdotal stories are in strident contrast with the evidence from academic studies. In conclusion, scents are not the most promising candidate from the retail marketing mix, for a combination of reasons:

- Scents need to fit the product group in order to be effective, but this is difficult to achieve in practice. For example, the smell of fresh coffee goes well with coffee and biscuits but not with the meat department. It is easier for a specialist retailer such as a flower shop, fashion store or cheese specialist than a supermarket with many diverse categories.

- The experience of a certain scent is very personal and may even go back to the time when the shopper first experienced the scent as a child.

- After a few minutes in a room all receptors become occupied and the shopper hardly perceives any scent.

- It is easier said than done for a retailer to regulate the type and intensity of ambient scents. There are a large number of things that can happen to scents in a store: the cooker hood at the meat department sucks up the scent; the weather influences the atmospheric humidity; the variation in outside temperature; the perfume worn by the checkout person; outside air may be entering the store; the mixture of scents resulting from, for example, baking and catering; retail density (as highlighted in the case study from Canada set out below). Finally, add to this list the amount of time it takes to research and develop a good-quality scent.

CASE STUDY   Retail density

Retail density is the measure of the number of shoppers and objects per square metre of selling space. A study by Michon, Chebat and Turley in a Canadian shopping mall showed that a pleasant citrus scent only resulted in a positive mood among shoppers if the retail density was on an average level.[14] At a low and a high retail density the relationship becomes negative, which means it is better to use no scent at all. The researchers came up with a number of answers as to why scents are ineffective at a high retail density. First, as it becomes more crowded, the temperature changes and as a result the olfactory experience evolves as well. Second, a high density leads to more general stimulation, which reduces the perception of scents. In short, there are already so many stimuli that the scent machine can be turned off. In cases of a low retail density the researchers assumed that there was an overrepresentation of older, recreational, non-task-focused shoppers who were indeed searching for stimulating activities and were open to more intense scent experiences. This study shows that the effectiveness of a scent is very dependent on the type of shopping trip and type of shopper.

When to apply scents

Of course, the scent marketing industry does not stand still. For example, it will soon be possible to regulate scents for each store individually from a distance. Still the opportunities for application in grocery retail are limited. In supermarkets, ambient scents can work well at the entrance to welcome shoppers, or at the coffee machine or cafe to give a relaxed feeling. It is unlikely that a shopper will want to walk into a new cloud of scents every few minutes. Therefore, it is more likely that the marketing departments of retailers will appoint only a selective number of categories for scent marketing, which are probably the most essential, or destination categories of the retail brand. Perhaps they could even become famous for their proprietary scent, as hotel chains and fashion stores do.

In addition to integrating scents into the retail brand, the supermarket may choose to apply scents in an ad hoc manner with displays. This could be very functional, for example when a brand of fabric softener launches a new scent variety, or in order to avoid deodorants from the shelf being used as testers. If retailers launch a new variety of cereal bar with grapefruit, working with a grapefruit-scented display could attract attention positively. In such cases the scents should not disperse too far and disrupt the shopping experience at other categories. The chosen scents need to be accepted broadly and fit the product. When considering all these conditions it is clear that supermarkets still have much to gain from other marketing instruments such as layout, hospitable staff and perhaps music, before scent marketing becomes relevant.

What can you do to make your shoppers happy?

Applying the right scents for the retail environment helps shoppers to judge whether the retail context is safe, and creates a positive mood in combination with other retail instruments that may remind the shopper of positive personal experiences. This effect is strong because scents reach the shoppers' brains directly and without filtering, as happens with the other senses. Therefore, scents evoke strong associations. In addition, science makes it clear that the effect might be fully subconscious.

Which marketing strategies can retailers apply?

Scents might create a positive atmosphere and contribute to expanding the dimensions of the retail brand. Retailers face many hurdles when implementing scents, such as not knowing which personal emotions are related to which scents, and the high number of uncontrollable, in-store variables. Retailers that benefit most operate in a single product category with a clearly defined homogeneous target group, for example florists and bakers.

When selecting a scent it is important that it is in congruence with the other instruments in the environment, because the shoppers first build a perception of the complete retail context before the scent influences decisions.

Notes

1 Bone, P and Ellen, P (1999) Scents in the marketplace: explaining a fraction of olfaction, *Journal of Retailing*, **75** (2), pp 243–62

2 Donovan, R and Rossiter, J (1982) Store atmosphere: an environmental psychology approach, *Journal of Retailing*, **58** (1), p 34

3 Mehrabian, A and Russell, J (1974) *An Approach to Environmental Psychology*, MIT Press, Boston

4 Chebat, J and Michon, R (2003) Impact of ambient odors on mall shoppers' emotions, cognition, and spending: a test of competitive causal theories, *Journal of Business Research*, **56** (7), pp 529–36

5 Holland, R, Hendriks, M and Aarts, H (2005) [accessed 22 July 2015] Smells like clean spirit nonconscious effects of scent on cognition and behavior, *Psychological Science* [Online] http://goallab.nl/publications/documents/ Holland,%20Hendriks,%20Aarts%20(2005)%20-%20noncsious%20 effects%20of%20scent%20on%20behavior.pdf

6 Roberts, M (2013) [accessed 22 July 2015] Humans Sense 10 Basic Types of Smell, scientists say, *BBC*, 19 September [Online] http://www.bbc.co.uk/news/ health-24123676

7 Turley, L and Milliman, R (2000) Atmospheric effects on shopping behavior: a review of the experimental evidence, *Journal of Business Research*, **49** (2), pp 193–211

8 Mattila, A and Wirtz, J (2001) Congruency of scent and music as a driver of in-store evaluations and behaviour, *Journal of Retailing*, **77** (2), pp 273–89

9 Spangenberg, E, Grohmann, B and Sprott, D (2005) It's beginning to smell (and sound) a lot like Christmas: the interactive effects of ambient scent and music in a retail setting, *Journal of Business Research*, **58** (11), pp 1583–89

10 Mitchell, D, Kahn, B and Knasko, S (1995) There's something in the air: effects of congruent or incongruent ambient odor on consumer decision making, *Journal of Consumer Research*, **22** (2), pp 229–38

11 Bone, P and Jantrania, S (1992) Olfaction as a cue for product quality, *Marketing Letters*, **3** (3), pp 289–96

12 Bone, P and Ellen, P (1999) Scents in the marketplace: explaining a fraction of olfaction, *Journal of Retailing*, **75** (2), pp 243–62

13 Spangenberg, E, Crowley, A and Henderson, P (1996) Improving the store environment: do olfactory cues affect evaluations and behaviours?, *Journal of Marketing*, **60** (2), pp 67–80

14 Michon, R, Chebat, J and Turley, L (2005) Mall atmospherics: the interaction effects of the mall environment on shopping behaviour, *Journal of Business Research*, **58** (5), pp 576–83

Self-scanning is more than savings

13

As in the three previous chapters (which looked at private labels, music and ambient scents) this chapter on self-scanning deals with in-store execution. With the help of these instruments, retailers have the primary objective of optimizing the current retail organization. However, whereas retailers use private labels, music and ambient scents with a focus on doing things better, decisions relating to self-scanning are often motivated by cost reductions. Yet self-scanning can do much more. It has the potential to make the shopping journey more pleasurable, and to generate data that offers a better understanding of shopping needs.

Self-scanning seems to be a no-brainer for supermarkets. The supermarket saves on labour costs where they are highest – at the checkout area – and frees up space. It has grown quickly since it was introduced in the United States in the mid 1990s. Roll-out followed quickly in Europe with Albert Heijn as one of the pioneers. Retailers in France, Belgium, Italy and Spain have followed quickly. Often the supermarket only has an eye for the financial aspect, while in fact self-scanning impacts many more areas now and in the future. Suppliers of self-scanning equipment have brought forward the idea that self-scanning influences the service experience and, ultimately, the retail brand.

According to research company RBR, the globally installed base counted some 191,000 self-scanning terminals in 2013.[1] This includes instalments in non-grocery retail. Most of them are installed in the United States. In 2013 the number of instalments grew significantly by 24 per cent thanks to a large roll-out by Walmart in the United States. Further growth to 329,000 terminals in 2019 is expected because large countries in Western Europe such as Germany have yet to adopt self-scanning. Brazil and China are seen as promising new markets with pilots running. In Europe some 35 per cent of transactions are completed through self-checkout.[2]

No effect on stock-loss

Let's look first at the financial consideration of self-scanning in supermarkets, and especially the risk of increased stock-loss. The biggest fear is that the shopper misuses the system by not scanning the products, or by scanning other, less expensive products. According to an ECR Europe report in 2011 this fear is undeserved. The study 'The impact and control of shrinkage at self-scan checkouts' produced for the first time detailed figures on the effect of self-scanning on stock-loss:[3] 66 British supermarkets with self-scanning terminals suffered a stock-loss of 0.76 per cent, which is not significantly different to 0.79 per cent at 38 similar high-risk supermarkets without self-scanning. This undisclosed British supermarket also measured stock-loss at 27 stores before and after the introduction of self-scanning. Indeed, the percentage stock-loss actually decreased, though this was not statistically significant. These studies took place in 2009.

For the same ECR report a US retailer permitted the sharing of information about the extent to which products were not scanned in 2010. To this end, the retailer connected cameras to the scanning system so that it registers at both staffed checkouts and at self-service points if products are not scanned. This registration provides clear insight into stock-loss as a result of non-scanning; however, unfortunately this does not show other deliberate types of stock-loss such as scanning without payment or scanning less expensive sorts of fruit and vegetables. Surprisingly, stock-loss at self-scanning was three times lower than stock-loss at staffed checkouts. The researchers explain this by pointing to the fear of being caught, shoppers being more honest than staff, and the fact that shoppers do not perform this task as often as cashiers. Staff have become more indifferent by the routine nature of the task, or else are deliberately acting dishonestly. Finally, it was striking that non-scanning was rarely used as a form of deceit by shoppers, if it occurred consciously at all. Only 0.002 per cent of the 23 million measured products were not scanned, and this represented a value of only US$2,500. The ECR report has an especially significant value: it marked the first time that numbers were published by more independent organizations like ECR Europe and retailers. Until then, retail professionals had to rely on numbers from the store equipment and software industry. In addition, the ECR report was based on large groups of stores that were tracked over a long period of time.

Through the eyes of offenders

The numbers cited above leave the door wide open for self-scanning. A survey among six large British retailers in the same ECR report show that staff can have some objections to self-scanning checkouts: 42 per cent of checkout staff think it is easy not to scan products without getting caught; 44 per cent think that the introduction of self-scanning has made theft by shoppers easier. The level of stock-loss also depends on the manner in which the supermarket implements self-scanning. When executing security measures it is helpful to think from the perspective of an offender:

- What is the risk of getting caught?
- How easy is it to steal?
- How will I be punished?
- What is the perceived reward?

The perceived reward can be reduced by applying special security measures to a number of highly theft-sensitive products. For example, think of tags that release ineradicable ink if the thief removes the tag. It will be difficult for a supermarket to exercise more influence over this risk, and impossible to influence the sentence or punishment. The supermarket has a better chance of making it harder for the thief to commit the offence, and of increasing the likelihood of catching the offender. A number of approaches are possible:

- Layout principles. There is less chance of theft if the self-scanning area is further removed from the exit, if the self-scanning area is in plain view of all checkouts, and if the offender's departure is delayed by a gate or zig-zag fences.
- Staff training. In addition to paying enough attention to servicing the equipment, store employees should be trained about types of stock-loss and the ways in which shoppers cheat.

- Personal supervision. Staff walk along among the checkouts as much as possible rather than standing behind a desk. The number of self-checkouts should be limited to between four and six.

- Security cameras. Make sure they are not fake with only blinking red lights, as offenders can see what is real and what is not.

- Invest in high-quality equipment, databases and EAN maintenance. If EAN codes are unreadable, staff spend too much time on solving an issue for one shopper, which leaves them less time to watch and service other shoppers. Staff should be able to operate the equipment intuitively.

Retailers should not overestimate the impact of technology to prevent stock-loss. This is one of the most important lessons I learnt when I was Product Availability Manager at Gillette, now part of Procter & Gamble. In this role I was responsible for designing and implementing programmes with retailers to prevent stock-loss in any form across the complete value chain, from Gillette warehouse to retailer store. Gillette had conducted thorough research in this area. Of course, some of the stock-loss issues, ranging from administrative mistakes to theft by employees, were Gillette's responsibility. However, most stock-loss occurred under the responsibility of the retailer. My real challenge in the role was to convey this message in a politically sensitive manner to Gillette's customers. Gillette had come up with a number of merchandising solutions, such as a shelf rail in the shape of a swan's neck. This rail had bent bars to slow down theft and to make it more difficult to steal multiple products. This merchandising helped for a while. Next came the double swan neck, plastic bars in front of the shelf, locked plastic boxes covering the shelf, and safer cases. Each time thieves managed to work around the anti-theft merchandising, however, and it took them less time for each wave of merchandising. It cost Gillette a small fortune to remain in open sale. Therefore, Gillette switched its attention to optimizing the store processes, improving communication between Gillette and stores, and training staff. This message can also be found in *S(h)elf Help Guide: The smart lifter's handbook*, which is based on interviews with active and 'retired' shoplifters, a great read for everyone in retail: 'Whatever the technology is, it can be countered. Technology will never be the answer, but attitude might be.'[4] In a note to retailers the authors Gabriel Caime and Gabriel Ghone give the following recommendations to retailers:

- Spend your money on people, not gizmos.

- Have more sales staff on the floor.

- Pay your employees better, and create a better working environment for them.

- Train your employees to be both more aware of customer needs and faster at completing sales.

- Treat your customers with courtesy. Be helpful but not pushy. Nothing will turn shoplifters away faster than the attentive, courteous service that every customer deserves.

Two examples from my time at Gillette make this even clearer. From our process mapping at a chain of drugstores, it appeared that most thefts took place between 12 noon and 2 pm when a lot of lunchtime shoppers popped into the store. This meant that shoplifters could more easily get lost in the crowd. Unfortunately, this was also the time that staff took their own breaks in the canteen. Theft was reduced considerably when staff took lunch at different times and were walking within the store. The other example demonstrates the importance of store management. Data analysis of stores over time showed that, for some reason, stock-loss decreased in one store and rose suddenly in another store. The stock-loss prevention could link this pattern to store managers who were less attentive to stock-loss programmes and changed stores as part of the regular rotation programme.

The business case for self-checkout

Ultimately, stock-loss is only one of the elements of the business case that a supermarket needs to take into consideration. Admittedly, a very important one. On the basis of the above ECR Europe study I assume that stock-loss in the case of self-scanning is equivalent to stock-loss at staffed checkouts. Stock-loss is often the focus point of the costs side of the business case. What about the benefits and possible incremental revenue as a result of the introduction of self-scanning?

Business case: effect on revenue

NCR, a supplier of scanning equipment, suggests that self-scanning is a differentiating factor as to why shoppers visit a certain store. It is said that self-scanning could lead to 20 per cent more shoppers, and correspondingly higher sales.[5] The basis for this argument is weak in my eyes. NCR refers to a study it commissioned in 2008 in which 72 per cent of the shoppers in the United States say they are *somewhat more likely or much more likely to shop with a retailer that gives them the flexibility to interact easily via online, mobile and kiosk self-service channels versus a retailer that does not*.[6] What I can imagine is that a small group of shoppers consciously chooses a super-market with self-scanning and ignores another, equal supermarket without self-scanning. This competitive advantage is of course easily copied. Finally, sales increase as a result of a higher purchasing frequency of higher basket value seems unlikely. In fact, it could be argued that self-scanning leads to a loss of sales. It is certainly easier for the retailer to calculate the loss of sales that can be attributed to self-scanning. Many retailers prefer a self-scanning area that is perceived as quiet and spacious. Therefore, they often do not offer an assortment of impulse products at the self-scanning checkouts. This is incremental revenue that a supermarket cannot generate elsewhere in-store. The increasing use of self-scanning terminals has very large consequences for suppliers of brands and categories that are sold mostly at checkouts, such as the Ferrero brand Kinder Bueno, and the chewing gum category.

Let's assume that self-scanning generates some sales growth, as certain shoppers attach high importance to checking out fast and in a self-reliant manner, and therefore start preferring one particular store above a competitor. On the other hand, the retailer will miss out on impulse sales. Therefore, for the business case the retailer can assume more or less the same revenue that is split between staffed and self-service checkouts.

Business case: options for cost savings

The retailer should then focus on the cost side, and calculating the cost savings is simpler. Two staffed checkouts can be replaced by four to six self-scanning checkouts that are under the supervision of one staff member. As staffing the checkouts absorbs the majority of the labour cost it becomes clear that self-scanning has a large financial implication. Additionally, space that was formerly devoted to checkouts can now be converted into effective sales space, which is a second source of savings. If the self-scanning checkout only offers debit and credit card facilities, then a further cost saving is made – as cash payments by shoppers carry more costs for retailers (ie counting money, secure transportation etc). Finally, after the introduction of self-scan-ning, retailers will find that fewer basket shoppers visit the staffed checkouts. This leads to improved efficiency at the staffed checkout transactions.

Types of self-scanning

Of course, the business case is very sensitive to the type of self-scanning that the retailer selects. There are roughly two shapes. The first option allows the shopper to select products themselves with a hand-held scanner during the shopping trip. Payment occurs in such instance either at a staffed checkout where the shopper hands over the scanner to the cashier, or the shopper completes the transaction alone at a terminal. A second option for self-scanning is when the shopper picks up products as usual, scans the products themselves at the end of the shopping trip, and finally pays. The latter option is popular in Germany, the United States, Britain and Belgium. An average supermarket requires some 120 hand-held scanners and five payment terminals, which equals an investment of some €125,000. Wincor Nixdorf, a supplier of products and services for payment traffic and other store infrastructure, suggests an average payback time of three years, though this is dependent on many variables in the execution. The return on investment is better if the supermarket chooses self-scanning checkouts at the end of the trip rather than hand-held scanners, if it does not use a permanent self-scanning card and if it does not permit cash payments. The equipment suppliers recommend self-scanning to supermarkets with an average weekly revenue of €350,000 and store surface of at least 1,200 square metres. Of course, this is an average. The discounter Red Market in Belgium, for example, has no permanent self-checkout card and does not allow cash payments, and has an average size of 1,200 square metres and only some €90,000 weekly sales, but still enjoys the benefits. In each country and at each retailer there are circumstances that change the business case. For example, in Belgium companies provide cheques for employees to buy lunches; however, these do not have EAN codes printed on them. So shoppers with a lunch cheque in Belgian supermarkets who use a hand-held scanner or pay terminal are still required to visit a staffed checkout to redeem the lunch cheque.

Business case: emotional benefits

In addition to hard numbers, there are a number of other benefits of self-scanning, according to the suppliers of the equipment and software. In NCR's 2009 report it argues that self-scanning leads to higher shopper satisfaction and loyalty by reducing waiting times by 40 per cent, and increasing the speed of product registration by 20 per cent. Yet it is unclear whether self-scanning leads to a shorter overall shopping trip. The time saved at the checkout might be lost at the beginning of the shopping trip.

In the case of hand-held scanners, selecting and turning on the scanner absorb some time at the start of the trip. In the case of self-scan checkouts, supermarkets discover that, as would be expected, less experienced shoppers scan significantly slower than trained cashiers. Though actual shopping trip times may be stable or even rise, the shoppers may have the perception that they shopped more quickly. The reason for this difference in perception is that shoppers have the feeling of greater control over their shopping trip. Often shoppers can see a running total of what they have spent so far on a particular store visit. Some shoppers may become fanatic in checking the running total and become more price-conscious. The effect of hand-held scanners on price consciousness may have unexpected effects on shoppers, as became evident in research conducted by Van Ittersum et al.[7] They found that the impact of real-time information during shopping depends a lot on whether the shopper sets themselves a budget before the trip. The so-called budget shoppers who receive real-time feedback, for example from their hand-held scanner, spend 35 per cent more than other budget shoppers who do not use a scanner with real-time feedback on how much they spent. Though this group spends more, they manage to remain just under the budget they set for themselves. They buy more A-brand products and keep the number of private-label items stable. In contrast, the non-budget shoppers who receive real-time feedback reduce their spending by 25 per cent in comparison with non-budget shoppers without real-time information. The total number of products in the basket remains more or less the same, but the composition changes: there are fewer A-brands and more private labels. It seems that the introduction of self-scanning may have some un-intended effects. Non-budget shoppers are typically most loyal and without real-time feedback they are often insensitive to price as buyers. The un-expected behaviour may be explained by the fact that budget shoppers use the preset budget as an anchor. Any underspend is perceived as a windfall or profit, and the shopper is inclined to reward themselves immediately for shopping so cleverly. They know they are already doing well because they like tracking themselves with other means, such as a shopping list or calculator. Therefore, budget shoppers also start buying more hedonic products such as chocolate and ice cream if they use hand-held scanners with real-time spending information. In contrast, the non-budget shoppers, who never took price into consideration very seriously, become more aware of their behaviour. They suddenly realize how the price tag is attached to their decisions in the supermarket.

Business case: service

There are unexpected consequences to self-scanning in areas other than pricing. On the other side of the value spectrum there is a delicate balance for the service argument. For some shoppers self-scanning symbolizes a lack of service, while for others it offers a fantastic opportunity to hide what they have purchased from the cashier, for example low-priced private labels and contraceptives. This brings me to the point of view that in the business case it is not sufficient to look only at the financial argument of self-scanning – and that the perception of service is a very important one. Since the 1950s personal contact has been increasingly removed from the grocery shopping floor. First this was welcomed by shoppers; they wished to spend their time more efficiently and were increasingly open to the introduction of technology on the shopping floor. Expressed differently, society was ready for it. The result has been a reduction in the amount of time spent in the store, and also more impersonal treatment. Some shoppers have the feeling that self-scanning replaces the friendly person they know at the checkout with a mistrustful security officer who wants to look into their shopping bags. This could be avoided if the supermarket informs shoppers that staff who previously worked at the checkout will now be helping to pack the shoppers' grocery bags. In this way the brand equity of the retailer is not damaged, should it position itself on service. All this pleads for both shoppers and staff to be introduced to the system carefully. At the time of the first installations Albert Heijn ensured that hostesses explained to shoppers during a six-week period how the equipment worked, the rules for checking bags and the reasons for doing so. Staff need to be trained to recognize stock-loss, to address shoppers regarding any harmful behaviour and to check bags effectively.

A less-used argument for self-scanning is that it offers the opportunity to personalize and improve the shopper experience. In the case of hand-held scanners it is smart, though not essential, to let the shopper register him- or herself with a personalized loyalty card, possibly just for self-scanning purposes. In this way the supermarket could show the shopping list from the shopper's previous trip, or offer personalized promotions. Another benefit that is not often considered is the opportunity to observe and understand the shopper better. The scanner stores all sorts of information such as the order in which products are purchased, the speed of shopping and the loyalty to the store and brands over a longer period. Using this, the supermarket can adjust its store layout or change shelf communication. The scanners have the possibility of new additional services, such as a personalized alarm for allergens or suggestions on how to prepare the food items purchased. Finally, the customer card keeps score of which shoppers run into problems when the shopping bags are checked. This allows the supermarket only to carry out the check with shoppers where this is necessary, instead of fully random checks. The application of the customer card and the data analysis could be a great way to increase the loyalty of shoppers. It may make the business case more positive. Self-scanning does not only offer opportunities to increase the efficiency of the supermarket, but applying new technology provides chances to sell more.

In Table 13.1 the benefits and disadvantages of self-scanning are summarized. In conclusion, retailers are encouraged to calculate the return on self-scanning investment for their particular context. When looking at the revenue side, retailers may only hope that self-scanning increases the revenue for as long as they are unique in this service in their catchment areas. Cost savings may follow from less labour, but investments in equipment and

TABLE 13.1 Benefits and disadvantages of self-scanning

	Benefits	Disadvantages
For supermarket	Saving on labour cost	Risk of more stock-loss
	Solution for lack of employees	Reduced quality impression: less service, higher price focus
	More tailored promotions as a result of customer card	
	Additional information on shopper behaviour	
For shopper	(Perception of) shorter waiting time and transaction time	Less personal attention
	Sense of control on spending	Technology and systems complicate shopping trip
	Personalization improves shopping experience	

training are high. Finally, retailers need to dedicate a description in the business case of what the expected effects for their shoppers are in terms of waiting time and service perception.

What can you do to make your shoppers happy?

Self-scanning gives shoppers the pleasurable feeling of being more in control and shopping more efficiently.

Retailers are encouraged not only to include financial numbers in the business case for self-scanning, but to include the shopper experience as well, because the implementation of self-service has far-reaching consequences regarding service perception and time experience.

Which marketing strategies can retailers apply?

Through a combination of store layout, equipment and store labour procedures, retailers can avoid an increased level of stock-loss while at the same time enjoying the benefits of self-scanning.

If the primary objective of self-scanning is cost reduction, self-scanning should be compared to other cost measures. If retailers see self-scanning as a strategy to increase differentiation and shopping satisfaction, self-scanning retailers can compare this with other options such as checkout staff training.

Notes

1 RBR (2014) [accessed 22 July 2015] Global EPOS and Self-Checkout 2014, 7 August [Online] http://www.rbrlondon.com/about/SCO_Press_Release_070814.pdf

2 Kalašinskas, A (2011) [accessed 22 July 2015] Managing Your Checkout Zone, NV INCO, 10 November [Online] http://www.ecr-baltic.org/f/docs/52_Managing_your_checkout_zone-New_Vision_Inco.pdf

3 ECR Europe (2011) [accessed 22 July 2015] The Impact and Control of Shrinkage at Self-scan Checkouts: An ECR Europe White Paper [Online] http://www.ecr-shrink-group.com/files/ECR-Self-Scan-Report.pdf

4 Caime, G and Ghone, G (1996) *S(h)elf Help Guide: The smart lifter's handbook*, TriX Publishing, London

5 Sanders, D (2012) [accessed 22 July 2015] Why Self-service is on the Rise, 9 April [Online] www.selfserviceworld.com

6 NCR (2009) [accessed 22 July 2015] Opportunities Emerge for Self-service in Retail and Hospitality, *Kiosk Marketplace Self-service News, Trends and Commentary* [Online] http://www.popai.com/uploads/downloads/WhitePaper-SelfService-Retail-Hospitality-2009.pdf

7 Van Ittersum, K, Wansink, B, Pennings, J and Sheehan, D (2014) [accessed 22 July 2015] Smart shopping carts: how real-time feedback influences spending, *Journal of Marketing* [Online] http://www.researchgate.net/profile/Joost_M_E_Pennings/publication/250916533_Smart_Shopping_Carts_How_Real-Time_Feedback_Influences_Spending/links/0deec52b700ccee229000000.pdf

PART SIX
Organizational development

The birth of category management

14

The effectiveness of instruments and concepts such as big data analysis and irrational shopper behaviour depends on the ways in which organizations are shaped. This is not only about the structure of the organization, but also about its culture, values and processes. At the core is the question of who the retailer wants to be. The environment will continue to change at an increasing speed, and organizations need to decide who they are when embracing – and perhaps leading – new developments in areas such as shopper preferences and technology. Part Six addresses how both suppliers and retailers can adapt their organizations in the areas of marketing, selling and buying. In this chapter I discuss category management, which is a relatively young concept that significantly changed the retail buying organization and the way retailers work together with suppliers. In Chapters 15 and 16 I look into organizational responses from suppliers.

The first category management project

Category management is often defined as a retail/supplier process of managing categories as strategic business units, producing advanced results by focusing on delivering consumer value.[1] This may seem a bit abstract and it helps to realize that the concept rests on four principles:

- Think category rather than brand or product segment level.
- Include all supply-and-demand activities in a holistic retail perspective.
- Delivering value to consumers.
- Close collaboration between retailer and supplier.

Examining the origins of category management helps to explain why business leaders in so many countries around the world think it is a valuable concept. Perhaps the third principle in the above list, 'consumer value', is not new in itself, but combined they provided an industry-changing framework. The first principle is explained by returning to the very first project.

The first-ever category management project took off under the leadership of Procter & Gamble (P&G) and Walmart in 1987. Walmart had come to realize that a high number of promotions led to distortions in the supply chain. The inefficiencies were not only costly, but the out-of-stocks were causing Walmart and P&G to fail to meet consumer demand. Until then P&G had looked at promotions on an event basis or by product division. In addition, Walmart complained about the high number of representatives from different P&G divisions it had to meet. P&G realized it needed to take an integrated approach towards this major customer. As an initial step P&G sorted out all shipments and cost drivers for Walmart promotions manually. In doing so P&G could calculate the profitability of its promotions at Walmart. After the manual proof-of-concept, P&G adapted its information systems in 1989 to enable this new customer perspective on a continuous basis. Admittedly, the first category management project had more of a supply-chain perspective than a consumer-demand vision. Nonetheless, it allowed P&G to realize that it could improve its customer relationships more effectively if it started thinking on a category level. This is over and beyond customer focus. Rather than focusing on the effects of a promotion just for one of its brands, such as Head&Shoulders shampoo, it investigated what impact the Head&Shoulders promotion might have on the complete shampoo category. For customers such as Walmart there is little to gain if a promotion only makes shoppers switch brands without an improvement in sales or the profits of the complete shampoo category. What is a given for a retailer started to make sense for a large supplier like P&G. Moving from a brand perspective to a total category perspective allowed the first category management between P&G and Walmart.

A second aspect of this new way of working is that retailers consider all activities and costs linked to the category. A good buyer at the time did what their title stated: searching vendors, selecting products and negotiating prices. In other words, this isolated buying sometimes had significant negative impacts on other retail functions. A buyer might negotiate a fantastic deal with its fresh produce supplier on cauliflower, let's say a 50 per cent discount on the regular buying price. Next the buyer passes on most of the discount to the shopper and the category sales go over the top. The buyer is pleased with the increased category sales and improved relative margin. This will positively affect the buyer's bonus at the end of the year. Their colleagues in supply-chain functions probably think they have made a big mistake. Cauliflowers require a lot of storage space in the warehouse, so other products are removed or ordered less frequently in order to create space. It is a fresh product, so you need large quantities every day. Trucks that would normally carry other vegetables are now full of cauliflowers. The effects further along in the supply chain might be even more disastrous. A large retailer like Tesco in the UK or REWE in Germany might not even be able to find sufficient quantities of the cauliflower, and farmers need to know months ahead of time how much product retailers want to buy before they start sowing the cauliflower seed. Cauliflower in this example could be easily replaced with many other fresh products, such as cheese, or other bulky products such as 12-roll packs of kitchen paper. What works well for the buyer's objectives – higher category sales and relative margin – may very well result in additional costs elsewhere in the supply chain. This makes up the second pillar of category management: costs in all retail functions need to be considered in order to achieve profits for the retailer as a company.

A third important characteristic of category management is delivering consumer value. The consumer is central to the marketing paradigm, so it might seem as though category management will not bring news to the table. However, delivering value to the consumer gets a new flavour if both the retailer and supplier work together to reach this goal, for example by sharing information on shopper behaviour.

The close collaboration between retailer and supplier is the fourth critical element of category management. The reason the impact of the category management philosophy has been so great is because it has not only changed retailers' mindsets, but also the way that retailers and suppliers work together. For a new and deeper supplier–retailer relationship, openness and trust are needed. Such a relationship is not built overnight and will require both emotional and financial investments from both sides. Suppliers had several reasons to invest in such a relationship:

- decreasing brand loyalty;
- more decisions influenced on store level;
- fragmented media behaviour;
- A-brands under attack of rising private labels;
- need to counterbalance increasing concentration and internationalization of retailers.

From the retailers' perspective they also had reasons to deepen the relationship with key suppliers:

- solve supply-chain inefficiencies;
- maintain market share and margins in response to price pressure from discounters and hypermarkets;
- increasing concentration and internationalization of suppliers;
- activate insights derived from scanning data and loyalty card programmes;
- use new technologies such as EDI to optimize value-chain processes.

Thus suppliers had good reasons to set aside their typical brand focus, and retailers downplayed the importance of buying prices, leading to the adoption of category management practices across the globe (Table 14.1).

Walmart could have chosen to solve its own promotional challenges. Still, Walmart liked the new way of working together. P&G introduced the term category management to Walmart and this concept immediately went down well. Walmart liked the fact that category management promoted ways to improve the service to the end customer. Walmart's shopper focus is symbolized by Sam Walton's words: 'Everything we've done since we started Walmart has been devoted to this idea that the customer is our boss.'[2] Walmart could have picked another supplier as P&G was a powerful supplier and would undoubtedly do its best to get the most out of the arrangement for itself. However, both companies realized that though they were giants in their own fields of retail and consumer products, they could not do without each other if they wanted to grow faster. They had the courage to leave the traditional supplier–retailer price negotiation trenches for approaches to find mutual growth. The first project was a mix of supply-and-demand management, with probably more of an emphasis on cost savings in the first area. Walmart gave P&G insight into Walmart's sales and stock figures. In this way P&G could adjust its supply of products to Walmart stores, and as a result its production. For P&G to make category management work, it completely overhauled its organizational structure. After 1989 it restructured its sales forces that were split by product divisions to category teams by customer. In addition, P&G added other functions, such as supply-chain experts, to the customer teams. The creation of multifunctional customer teams, which seem so logical nowadays, was completely new at the time. Heads of the product divisions were afraid of losing focus on their brands and tried to resist the change. Being the giant organization that P&G is, the complete restructuring of the sales and marketing departments was not finished until 1993.

TABLE 14.1   Timeline milestones – category management and ECR

1980s	Brian Harris coins the term category management and lays theoretical foundation
1985	First planogram tool (Apollo)
1987	First category management project ever, between Walmart and P&G
1989	P&G includes category management as a function into organization Sainsbury's embraces category management as first retailer in Europe
1990	Foundation of The Partnering Group, consultancy focused on category management
1991	At CIES conference concept of category management and best practices are shared
1992	Term ECR appeared when working group of retailers and suppliers met to find response to the threat of new channels
1993	Publication by Kurt Salmon Associates about supply-chain concepts under the umbrella of ECR that improve the distribution of consumer goods
1994	Foundation of ECR Europe organization
1997	ECR Europe publishes ECR blue book that integrates improvement concepts for supply chain, category management and enabling technologies

New term: category management

The term category management was used internally within P&G before 1987 when the first project took place, but it had never been practised before. Much of the theoretical groundwork for category management was laid by Brian Harris. He also coined the term itself. In a discussion in the mid 1980s when asked to describe the function that is responsible for the various merchandising functions for a set of products at US supermarket

Schnuck's, Brian Harris suggested the title 'category manager'.[3] Subsequently the term 'category management' was used to describe joint business planning between a retailer and supplier.

At the time Brian Harris was a professor of marketing in the Graduate School of Business Administration at the University of Southern California and a Director of USC's Food Industry Management Program from 1978 to 1983. Later he co-founded ABA Groups, which developed the first planogram design tool (Apollo Space Management System) in 1985. Brian Harris was consulting with P&G where his Space Management application Apollo was being implemented.[4]

Brian Harris observed that many discussions between retailer and supplier focused on pricing and that the interests of the end consumer were neglected. He designed a model of collaboration that attracted P&G's attention for its project with Walmart. The first project between Walmart and P&G had shown it could work. People at P&G wanted to take the new thinking model outside P&G to encourage collaboration in the industry. This was not necessarily in the best interest of P&G. Subsequently, six employees left P&G and in 1990 started a new consulting group together with two others who had worked together in the company Retail Directions – Mike McPartland and Brian Harris. The group of eight named their new consulting firm 'The Partnering Group' (actually they first named their company 'Partnering Group', or for short PG as a pun on P&G, but later added 'The' to avoid any legal issues).[5]

The Partnering Group developed many of the theories, tools and working practices that allowed category management to spread across the industry as a new function. This was essential to make it a sustainable movement, rather than one or more P&G projects. The most well-known model is the category management business process, better known as the eight-step model. This framework helps decide if a single product (or stockkeeping unit, SKU) should be part of a category, how to assign roles to the category, and which retail marketing strategies and tactics can be applied. The model stands as the basis of category management and it will be explored in more detail later in this chapter. However, at that stage category management had not made it big, because although the concept of category management and its benefits were shared as early as 1991 at a CIES conference in Nice, category management only became widely accepted when it was well explained in the famous blue book *Category Management Best Practices Report* published by ECR Europe in 1997 – and this brings me to the term efficient consumer response (ECR).

Category management as part of ECR

The term ECR appeared in 1992 when a group of companies including Safeway, Kroger and P&G came together as a working group. Their objective was to find an appropriate strategic response by traditional grocery supermarkets to the threat imposed by growing channels like discount mass merchants such as Walmart, and 24/7 convenience stores such as 7-Eleven. They were supported by the consultancy Kurt Salmon Associates (KSA). In 1993 KSA published a report with a range of supply-chain concepts that could improve the distribution of consumer goods.[6] It called for integrated replenishment – the merger of the replenishment from supplier to retailer warehouse, and the replenishment from retailer warehouse to stores. By using the aggregated scanning data of individual stores the supply chain should be transformed from loading inventory by suppliers (push) to responding to consumer demand (pull). The KSA report stated that more efficient replenishment led to at least 50 per cent less inventory and a reduction of supply-chain costs of 2.8 per cent. KSA was optimistic enough to add that the effort could be completed by 1996. ECR as such was not entirely new, and can be viewed as a specific type of the quick response (QR) strategy applied in the apparel industry and the just-in-time (JIT) inventory management system in the automotive industry.[7] Although the threat of disruptive channels by mass merchants was absent, the potential of saving supply costs appealed to Europe as well. This led to the foundation of the ECR Europe organization in 1994.

Transfer of ECR to Europe

After its initiation in the United States, the category management philosophy first landed in Europe and later in Latin America and Asia. In 1989 in Europe, Sainsbury's was the first retailer to embrace category management. Sainsbury's reviewed the role of each of its 75+ categories and designed a category strategy for each, often in conjunction with a large supplier of the category. The effort took more than two and a half years. As Sainsbury's offered open training courses it educated much of the industry, which was crucial for the roll-out of category management functions in the UK and perhaps even in Europe.

My first involvement with category management was when I worked as Research Manager at the Market Research and Strategic Planning department at Albert Heijn in the Netherlands. Albert Heijn is recognized as one of the forerunners of category management, and its experience gives a good idea of what happened at retailers generally across Europe. As early as the mid 1980s Albert Heijn had combined the responsibilities of buying and marketing the products in-store, rather than having separated functions. The new role was named 'Assortment Manager' and reported to the commercial director for either fresh products or non-perishables. In 1995 the assortment manager gained more decision power on the logistical process from supplier to retailer warehouse, and was renamed 'Category Manager'. The restructuring also included a new organizational layer of seven unit managers reporting to a buying and merchandising director. A separate team was created for marketing retail formats. This created the opportunity to look at the categories in a far more strategic manner. While Albert Heijn previously focused on revenue, fair share and gross buying margins, it undertook the significant effort of allocating all costs to all categories so that Albert Heijn understood for the first time what was the net profit contribution for each category. The redefinition of type categories and the type of costs that were allocated revealed that some categories had a far lower profitability than previously thought. Albert Heijn made it publicly known that it suffered a loss of tens of millions of Dutch guilders on five product groups, namely bread, soft drinks, beer, dairy and plants/flowers. In order to emphasize that immediate action was needed, Albert Heijn called these categories 'megalosers'. Restructuring the supply chain and renegotiation with suppliers was similar: Albert Heijn grouped all categories under one unit leadership. Often suppliers thought they were operating in a category with high profits for Albert Heijn, so it came as a shock to them to learn that they were co-responsible for letting Albert Heijn bleed in these categories. This was the case for soft drinks. Albert Heijn found that the collection of used bottles at their stores placed a high burden on the stores, transport and warehouses.[8] It was even more revealing when they found out that shoppers returned bottles to Albert Heijn that were purchased in discount stores and abroad. In response, the association of soft drinks industry (NFI) published a study claiming that soft drinks delivered more than one million Dutch guilders in profit to Albert Heijn. Despite this study Albert Heijn pushed for supply-chain improvements in all megaloser categories. Suppliers that collaborated well according to the perspective of Albert Heijn were rewarded with a category management project as sole supplier, or 'category captain' as it was often named.

Consultants like The Partnering Group used the interest in ECR to promote the concept of category management. In 1997 the ECR blue book successfully combined supply-chain initiatives with the category-management concept on the principle that both were consumer driven. The overall objective is to promote collaboration among companies in the complete supply chain with the objective of meeting the demands of the consumer better, faster and more cheaply. In the mid 1990s the category management concept was connected inextricably with the term ECR. The ECR concept was the overarching principle for better collaboration in any touch-point between retailer and supplier. In Eastern Europe ECR is still the strong and active movement for better collaboration in the consumer goods industry, as it was in Western Europe in the mid 1990s. Three integrated working areas were identified for the integration of ECR with category management:

- Supply management or efficient replenishment: the optimization of all supply-chain processes that occur up until the goods are delivered in-store. ECR Europe differentiated several improvement areas such as integrated suppliers, synchronized production, continuous replenishment, automated store ordering, reliable operations and cross docking.

- Demand management or category management: optimization of all processes that touch the shopper up to consumption. Typically these are split into four improvement areas: promotions, product assortment, new product introduction and demand management capabilities, such as organization structure and objective setting.

- Enabling technologies: in order to optimize the supply-and-demand processes, new and improved technologies had to be implemented. The technologies that received the most attention at the start of ECR were electronic commerce (electronic data interchange, EDI), electronic data transfer and activity-based costing (ABC).

Many of the ECR improvement areas were not new at the time. The significant change of the ECR concept was more embedded in the fact that organizations started implementing the improvement levers in an integrated, rather than isolated, manner. Indeed, ECR is directed at solving inefficiencies in the whole supply chain, from handling raw material to consumer marketing. In addition, ECR stimulates the collaboration among organizations, especially those between suppliers and retailers. Out of the three ECR working areas, the one most focused on in the 1990s was supply management and enabling technologies. Retailers that adopted ECR first wished to reduce costs before looking at the category from a consumer perspective. For example, EDI replaces paper notes for shipping and invoices (among other things), is much faster and leads to cost savings. According to the concept of continuous replenishment, the system reorders and redelivers products automatically once the cashier scans the product for the consumer. This makes stocks redundant both in-store and at the retail warehouse, resulting in cost savings.

The eight-step category management process

The 1997 ECR blue book provides a thorough and clear description of the eight-step category management process (Figure 14.1). It is still valid at the time of writing, as in essence it is a strategic planning methodology that helps to determine which business the organization operates in, and identifies the drivers of future category growth. The eight-step process guides retailers and suppliers, step by step, through the collective activities that are necessary to define, develop and evaluate a category. The eight phases are:

1 Category definition: understand the needs that products fulfil in the category; select those products that are measurable and manageable for all parties; set up a shopper decision tree that explains how shoppers make a choice from the assortment range; if necessary give a new category name that reflects the consumer needs and language.

2 Category role: design a model for allocating resources across categories; allocate roles to each category based on their value to the retailer, shopper, market trends and competitive position of the retailer.

   The 1997 ECR blue book describes four types of category roles. Destination categories are categories that differentiate the retailer from competition. They are profitable to the retailer and shoppers connect with them (for example: the wine category at Delhaize or the chilled ready-made meals category at Albert Heijn). Most categories are routine or preferred categories: they are frequently in the shopper's basket, such as coffee, and are very important to the retailer's cash flow and shoppers cannot miss them. Convenience categories meet the shopper's need for one-stop shopping. However,

FIGURE 14.1   The category management process

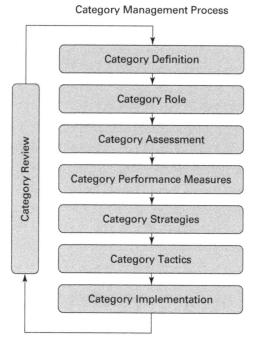

SOURCE: ECR blue book (The Partnering Group + Roland Berger & Partner)

shoppers do not see the retailer as a primary sales channel for such categories. Examples are magazines and lottery tickets in supermarkets. Finally, seasonal or occasional categories can help to reinforce the retailer's image and are important for the retailer's profits.

3 Category assessment: describe the market and consumer trends; determine the performance of the retailer and suppliers via thorough analysis; find the best opportunities for improvement and quantify these.

4 Category performance measures: describe which qualitative and quantitative objectives you would like to achieve, and tailor the category plan.

5 Category strategies: assign marketing strategies to the categories and its segments. The 1997 ECR blue book describes seven strategies. Examples include transaction building to increase the value of the shopper basket, and image enhancement to allow the category to communicate the desired retail image.

6 Category tactics: the category strategy is detailed in a range of specific marketing actions. The success of a category and the value of the basket could be increased by allocating more space. Whether or not this is a viable strategy also depends on how important the category is to the retailer. For a destination category, a retailer is prepared to create more space and wants product segments with above-average margins. The end-overview of all category tactics is called a tactogram.

7 Category implementation: design an overview of all planned actions; allocate people and timing; obtain permission from senior management; test and implement.

8 Category review: the results of the category plan are measured and evaluated as a minimum on an annual level. The original model foresees this evaluation as an opportunity to feed back into the first step – category definition.

The model became outdated

In the mid 1990s retailers and suppliers followed the category management process step by step. The eight-step model has been very instrumental in helping retailers and suppliers to begin category management. Its numerous templates clarified which precise action organizations could undertake. The model's strategic view helped to professionalize buying and supplier management in retail. Because of its holistic and strategic approach, the model is (as already mentioned) still a useful thinking model today. However, for several reasons it has been applied less and less:

- The eight-step model takes a project approach. This may be useful when category management is new to an organization, but once organizations have adopted the philosophy most seek process-driven models.

- The model is associated with a high number of very quantitative templates that require a lot of data and resources to utilize. In the beginning organizations accepted this as normal because everything was new. Later, this implication scared organizations away from the model. Automation and all sorts of three-step models arrived too late to change the perception of a heavy workload.

- Retailers have come up with their own models to accommodate their specific needs. Often I find that these models contain all or most of the original eight steps. Most of the time, though, retailers require suppliers to follow their processes instead of using the original model or developing it jointly.

- The first steps have been absorbed into the exclusive retailer domain. Some of these decisions are made once and then not often revised. Take the assignment of category roles, for example. These tend to be stable over time. A change of category role could occur when it changes strategy, if shopper trends shift significantly or if, after a couple of years, they notice that their current category strategy needs revision.

- The model misses an important phase before category definition, namely strategic alignment. Before retailers invest time and money they need to find out whether the model helps them to manage their buying and supplier processes. Before dedicating a multifunctional project team and investing in market research, suppliers need to find out whether the retailer's senior management is open to sharing information, freeing up resources and trusting research findings rather than basing decisions on gut feel. A supplier must secure a sounding board at senior level if the category manager refuses collaboration or threatens to only implement the category plan if the supplier reduces prices. Many category management projects were killed when they became part of the daily buying and negotiation routine.

As of 2015 it is rare for retailers and suppliers to work through each step of the original category management business process. They often just identify a certain part of the approach and work with it, either collaboratively or alone. Category management has transitioned from a collaborative project-based approach to a continuous process whereby the retailer decides on most of the first steps in the model and may call in support from suppliers for tactical and operational decisions. Aligned with this new reality, and in addition to its formal definition, the Category Management Association (CMA) gives a very useful and pragmatic perspective on category management:

Category Management is a collaborative continuous process between manufacturers and retailers to manage a shopper need state which we refer to as a 'category'. The purpose of this process is to optimize shopper satisfaction and fulfil the role chosen by the retailer for that category within the overall portfolio of categories in the retail format. The end state of the category management process is that combination of assortment, price, shelf presentation and promotion which optimizes the category role over time.[9]

Category management is data intensive and analytical in nature. Category management is about understanding data. In contrast, the term 'shopper marketing' is more about understanding emotions or motivations.

ECR's contribution

So what is the result of the ECR initiative? ECR set the objectives of making the shopper happier, improving relationships in the value chain and delivering more money as a result. Let's start with an assessment of the monetary value of ECR, because there has been some research in this area. Initially, estimates of ECR savings ranged between 4 per cent and 10 per cent of consumer revenue. On the low end there are countries such as the Netherlands, with highly efficient logistics where there was less to gain than in, for example, the United States. In its study 'The Case for ECR', ECR Europe concludes that 10 years after the start of the ECR movement in Europe it has achieved 3.6 per cent of the potential 6.9 per cent savings – calculated as a percentage of consumer expenditures.[10] Still there is much to be done before it reaches its end goal. At the time there was still the potential for savings of 3.3 per cent, or €28 billion. In addition, the study said that retail sales could increase an incremental 4.9 per cent by fulfilling the needs of the shopper more effectively. It is safe to say that the potential for improvement remains, without knowing exactly what is the value expressed in euros. The ECR concept remains valid – whether the ECR movement will continue to play an important role is yet to be seen. With fewer conferences, fewer studies commissioned and national ECR organizations dissolving into the GS1 network, the movement has become much less salient in many countries.[11] Exceptions can be found in emerging markets such as Russia and the Baltics where the ECR organization serves as a platform to bring retailers and suppliers together for better collaboration across the industry.

The other objectives of the category management/ECR movement were to achieve higher shopper satisfaction and better working relationships between retailer and supplier. It is difficult to prove that shopper and value-chain players have become happier over the years and to attribute this to the ECR movement. However, there are some organizational effects of category management and ECR that are worth discussing. The movement has led to structural changes within organizations. On the retail side, buying departments are transformed into category management departments with buyers, supply-chain experts and merchandising managers. This expertise is needed in order to buy at the lowest costs ('gross margin') and to manage the products in terms of logistics, warehouse, space occupation in-store and marketing pull from the shopper ('net margin'). Of course, this also means that the desired profile of the buyer/category manager changes.

When category management started, large suppliers often had a few people working in trade marketing, possibly combined with other marketing activities. When the first pilots started, these teams were upgraded in terms of the number of people and their seniority. The team then started reporting to the sales director. Sometimes they were rebranded into 'category management departments', just like their retail counterparts. Later, since the mid 1990s, suppliers might have once again split the responsibilities over several departments. For example, category management for assortment and space management, trade marketing for display execution and shelf merchandising, shopper marketing for customer promotional campaigns, and shopper insights for market research. Reporting lines often lead to the marketing or sales director, and for a minority of suppliers the position has obtained a seat on the management board. In addition to the effect on organizational structure, category management has stimulated the formation of customer teams that focus on serving one or a few customers. Such teams attempt to mirror the capabilities in the retail team such as logistics, bid-to-cash and research. The leader of the team may take responsibility for the negotiation process or focus on the overall relationship and give the selling role to a team member.

The structural changes allow better communication between retailer and supplier. Several roles from both sides talk directly to each other. Higher-quality relationships are needed. Unfortunately, it is difficult to say whether the relationships have improved or become more balanced. Today there are still retailers that copy the packaging of A-brands, send letters for special discounts and demand terms without counter-performance. On the other hand, suppliers dump leftovers in discount stores, are reluctant to adapt to local markets as a result of multi-country production, and use their field merchandising teams to correct planograms in local stores.

The rise of the new trade marketing responsibilities in supplier organizations has impacted other departments. First, until then the marketing department was the dominant factor in setting the course for the organization in regards to its brand plans and advertising. With the introduction of category management, this changed. Trade marketing has entered territories that traditionally belonged to marketing. A-brands are only successful if their growth is subject to the growth of the category. One hundred per cent distribution of each product is no longer possible and category management shows which brands fit the needs of a certain channel and retailer, how much space is available and what price is acceptable. In some organizations, category management has taken over the responsibility of packaging design from consumer brand teams as the salience from the shelf has become more crucial than knowing how to list the ingredients and product benefits on the pack. Market shares used to be calculated for small segments described in product terms, such as chocolate blocks below 100 grams. After the introduction of category management, suppliers realized that they had to define market shares from a shopper perspective (for example, the sugary snack category) and take into account the holistic operational model of retailers (total snacks rather than only the chocolate snacks). Finally, suppliers have shifted their budgets and focus from research into packaging, concepts and advertising to shopper-related research (decision trees, planograms) and retailer-related research (satisfaction surveys, store selection). In conclusion, category management has become deeply immersed in both retail and supplier operations and I expect it will continue to evolve as the understanding of what matters to the shopper becomes more central to retailers and suppliers alike.

What can you do to make your shoppers happy?

At the core of category management is will, the enthusiasm to really understand shoppers and serve them in the best way possible. For each retail marketing decision that practitioners make, they should write down how it will help the shopper. And be honest if the only purpose of the decision is to increase the company's profitability or fight competition.

Which marketing strategies can retailers apply?

Sainsbury's showed us that taking suppliers along on a new business collaboration model in an open manner can shake up the supply chain while still allowing the greatest profitability from the fruit of the investment.

Category management was founded as a response to the threat of new channels such as mass-merchant discounters. The same collaboration model could serve the industry when responding to new online players such as Amazon.com and Google.

I often find that practitioners cherry-pick in the orchard of category management, gathering tools that seem to apply to the problem at hand. However, category management is an integrated concept. Only working on a new planogram may impact the promotion tactics negatively, or else the retailer may find itself disconnected from consumer needs by failing to invest in the early category management phases.

Notes

1 Harris, B, Berger, R and The Partnering Group (1997) *Category Management Best Practices Report*, ECR Europe Publications Office, Brussels

2 Walton, S (1992) *Sam Walton: Made in America, my story*, Bantam Books, New York

3 The Partnering Group Website (2015) [accessed 22 July 2015] Dr Brian Harris: TPG Role [Online] http://www.thepartneringgroup.com/our-people/brian-harris/

4 *Ibid*.

5 Category Management Incorporation (2015) [accessed 22 July 2015] Jerry Singh, Managing Partner [Online] http://www.categorymanagement.com/about-jerry-singh.html

6 Kurt Salmon Associates (1993) Efficient Consumer Response: Enhancing Consumer Value in the Grocery Industry, Food Marketing Institute, Arlington Virginia

7 Kurnia, S, Swatman, P and Schaude, D (1993) Efficient consumer response: a preliminary comparison of US and European experiences, *Progressive Grocer* [Online] http://userpages.uni-koblenz.de/~swatmanp/pdfs/C_Kurnia+Swatman+Schauder_Bled98.pdf

8 Hansen-Love, E (1995) [accessed 22 July 2015] AH lijdt verlies op fris en bloemen, *Volkskrant*, 24 August[Online] http://www.volkskrant.nl/ dossier-archief/ah-lijdt-verlies-op-fris-en-bloemen~a397487/

9 Category Management Association (2014) Clarifying Definitions of Category Management [Online] http://www.cpgcatnet.org/page/ whatisCatMan/?cm_c=202922

10 ECR Europe (2006) The Case for ECR: A Review and Outlook of Continuous ECR Adoption in Western Europe, ECR Europe, Brussels

11 ECR [accessed 22 July 2015] ECR Australasia; The Consumer Goods Forum [Online] http://www.ecr-europe.org/about-ecr/related-organisations

True customer understanding

15

The category management principles discussed in Chapter 14 introduce a wide array of approaches, including instruments that are quite data driven and analytical in nature. These approaches need to be converted into insights, and then implemented for the shopper through conversations between retailers and suppliers. The end objective of retailers should be to make shoppers happy. To make this happen they need suppliers who understand their goals and ways of working. On the flip side, it became clear in Chapter 14 that suppliers need retailers more than ever to build a relationship with consumers. Therefore, understanding the needs of the retailers around the table is a prerequisite for suppliers. If you understand the retailer needs you can conduct the right analysis for the right challenge that the retailer faces. In addition, understanding retailer needs leads to a better, tailored way of communicating the essence of the proposal/analysis. The communication modus (short versus long; minimal versus a lot of detail etc) depends on the retailer preferences that you distilled in the understanding phase. It is not only about the quality of the message that suppliers convey to retailers, but also how they convey that message and whether they consider the retailer's interests. In this chapter I discuss the ways that suppliers can adapt their culture, structure and other organizational dimensions in order to truly understand the needs of retailers.

Wasting the time of retailers

Many customer managers and trade marketing managers have fallen into the trap of wasting the category managers' time with irrelevant or badly focused presentations, featuring irrelevant data that is not linked to their customers' priorities and needs. Category managers are not interested in all the jobs that the customer manager has performed, a detailed description of the production process or the company history since its foundation. Badly focused presentations will be met with disdain. In a similar manner many meaningless questions are raised by customer managers, who tend to request details about the buying behaviour of category managers for the categories they deal with. So, category managers for cleaning products, for example, are asked about hygiene in their own homes, and category managers for pet food are asked how many pets they have. When I worked with retail consultant Al Forbes, he gave me a list of 10 things to avoid when dealing with category managers:[1]

1 meaningless questions (for example 'How's business?');

2 irrelevant data such as market statistics with no insight;

3 criticisms without solutions;

4 meetings with no real purpose;

5 presentations without good incremental analysis;

6 supplier jargon;

7 branded presentations not in a category context;

8 presentations not linked to priorities/needs;

9 proposals that lead to fragmentation and duplication of product assortment;

10 not telling the buyer of issues that are likely to impact them – until after the event.

Trade marketer as a transactional partner

It has become common practice for trade marketers to accompany customer managers on visits to category managers, or even visit the customer on their own. Category managers do in fact appreciate their participation, because trade marketing is perceived to be more objective and they tend to focus less on selling. It does also mean, however, that many of the skills that are expected from account managers are now also required from trade marketers, as they also make the visits. Category managers need several things from trade marketers. In essence, category managers need fast and accurate information on how the retailer's category is performing. A trade marketer needs to know the facts about the category, such as: the latest period's growth, rotation of at least the top and bottom 10 products, and the latest product launches by competitive retailers. Knowing these basics will make a trade marketing team a great **transactional partner**.

Dealing with the issues

A category manager needs more from trade marketing than the points mentioned above. After identifying the strengths and gaps relative to the competition, the category manager expects proposals to address short-term 'issues'. For example, if competitor retailers are attracting shoppers with heavy promotions, they expect trade marketers to show which shoppers are leaving and which promotions or price changes will make people return to specific, price-elastic products. Category managers appreciate competitive intelligence without compromising the supplier. When you are capable of offering this, they will then recognize you as an advisor and a **trusted partner.** If you look deep into the hearts of category managers, there is still much more that they would like to see from trade marketers, such as fresh ideas from other categories and innovation based on shopper insights. Category managers want to be one step ahead of the competition. Trade marketers can help them achieve this. They may support the retailer by presenting them with a vision of what the category will look like in the future, and offer them enablers that will allow the retailers to reach their category objectives more quickly and efficiently. These suppliers are **strategic partners.**

Taking up the challenge

Transitions often go smoothly and parties may not even notice that they are entering a 'new' phase. It is best to start with relatively simple category performance information in order to build up trust with the customer. There is no reason why challengers in the category should not take this approach as well. I discovered this personally when Kraft Foods (now Mondelēz) managed to become the preferred category management partner of Albert Heijn, although Mars and Nestlé were much larger suppliers at the time. I won the confidence of the category manager first by delivering simple rotation lists and Pareto graphs every four weeks. These gave insight into short- and long-term performance and were supplemented with suggestions for action. The category manager had little time and came to like the continuous flow of information presented in an objective manner. At the same time I carried out several kinds of shopper research and worked hard on building a category vision. We began to win the customer's heart not only through the promise of a complete new category story but also by offering a helicopter flight to our meeting place and a tour of Kraft Foods chocolate factory near Brussels in Belgium. As a result of these efforts, Kraft Foods won the lead in a category management project, much to the surprise of other suppliers. One of the big changes I presented was a new planogram in which groups of products that were likely to be purchased together were presented vertically (Figure 15.1). This planogram was quickly picked up by other retailers and is still the standard presentation modus in the Netherlands today.

FIGURE 15.1   Chocolate planogram change

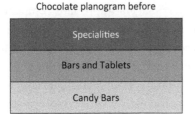

Chocolate planogram before

... and now

| Specialities |
| Bars and Tablets |
| Candy Bars |

Specialities in Box	Large Tablets	Candy Bars Multipacks
Specialities in Bag	Small Bars	Candy Bars Minis in Bag

Required service

Figure 15.2 summarizes the three services that a category manager needs from trade marketing: category performance, category solutions and category future. It works like a Maslow pyramid. Unless you satisfy the basic service level, a category manager will not let a trade marketing team progress to the next level:

- At the bottom: how is the category performing?
- In the middle: what are the solutions to problems that the category faces?
- On top: what is the future of the category?

In addition, working on the first layer is not inferior to operating on the two other layers. The real question to be asked is: what is most relevant to the retailer? Different retailers need different types of information depending on their position in the market. Retailers in industries such as electronics, toys and DIY, for example, started up professional category management later than those in food groceries. Retailers in these industries have often been able to grow comfortably by expanding the number of stores or through diversification. When like-for-like sales start to crumble and competition becomes fiercer, they realize the need for a more strategic and fact-based approach to category management. Competition becomes more intense and retailers see the need for additional support from trade marketing departments at suppliers.

FIGURE 15.2 Support that a category manager expects

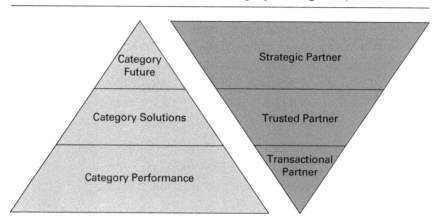

The impetus for change usually comes when top management at the retailer sees the potential of category management. Sometimes leading suppliers set in the change. I have seen this in emerging markets such as Russia and Ukraine where top fast-moving consumer goods (FMCG) companies train their category managers on the category management concept in order to develop a more in-depth relationship with customers. However, the consequence of late adoption of category management in industries such as electronics has been that suppliers focus on delivering basic, supplier-specific information on product assortment and promotions. When allocating resources to customers, suppliers naturally try to match the experience and capabilities of the customer. I experienced this first hand at Gillette before Procter & Gamble acquired this company. The portfolio of Gillette products was very broad and included, among other items, razor blades, coffee machines, batteries and pens. These products found their way to highly diverse customers such as wholesalers who specialized in prisons, hotels, pharmacies, the military and online retailers. This diversity was reflected in the capabilities and size of the customer and trade marketing teams.

Trade marketing evolution

To identify the level and type of support that the category manager needs, it is helpful to identify the objectives and capabilities of the retailer and the competitive situation that the retailer is facing. This in turn determines the potential extent of the support that a supplier can provide. It is still up to the supplier to decide whether trade marketing is an effective instrument for them to use. An important question that should be asked is whether the supplier has the capability and ambition to meet the retailer's needs. I differentiate four phases of trade marketing: transaction, support, advice and shopper marketing. Figure 15.3 shows the objectives and main focus of the four phases. Indeed, if you drill deeper you find that each phase brings with it its own data requirements, organizational structure, staff capabilities, functions, processes etc:

1 *Transaction phase*: in the first phase filling the plant production and hitting volume targets seems more important than anything else. Like phase 2 it is short-term driven and internally focused.

2 *Support phase*: in the second phase suppliers become more sensitive to the needs of customers as they want to find the right arguments to expand the number of supplier promotions and product assortment.

3 *Advice phase*: in the third phase of trade marketing suppliers become externally focused. Marketing campaigns are adapted to suit customer needs as long as they do not breach goals and standards set by the marketing team.

4 *Shopper marketing phase*: in the last phase suppliers truly work on the growth of the total category in the belief that all stakeholders reap the fruits of this way of working. When category growth is not possible, for example because almost every shopper buys the product (such as milk or toilet paper), the supplier works with the retailer to improve the financial health of the category. At this stage the supplier finds the right balance between consumer-focused and customer-focused activities.

At any point in time, a category manager may deal with suppliers in different phases. They may work in very different categories and/or deal with suppliers with different levels of professionalism. When thinking back to the three service needs of a category manager, you can see that a category manager will develop a vision of the future state of the category from suppliers that are in one of the last two phases of the trade marketing model. Many FMCG suppliers in Eastern Europe are in the first phase and most companies in continental Western Europe operate in the second or third phase of trade marketing. The UK market is the most advanced with the majority of the suppliers operating in the third, advisory phase of trade marketing, and some even in the fourth phase, shopper marketing. Shopper marketing is the strategic approach used by suppliers that promotes the brand equities of

FIGURE 15.3 Trade marketing evolution

	Transaction	Support	Advice	Shopper Marketing
Goals	• Support sales of supplier	• Help realize objectives of Key Account Manager (KAM) • Convince customer to buy through promotions and new products	• Implement marketing campaigns on customer level, in a timely and effective manner	• Achieve sustainable category growth and/or health • Innovation based on shopper behaviour
Focus	• Internal • Short term • Supplier • Volume supplier • Annual negotiation	• Internal • Short term • Customer • Volume supplier and customer	• External • Medium term • Consumer and product • Promo and new product • Volume and revenue	• Balance internal and external • Shopper and category • Category drivers • Volume, revenue, profit

both retailer and supplier brands and satisfies the needs of shoppers. It is the most impactful way that a supplier can organize its trade marketing resources around a retailer, and I will return to this in Chapter 16 after suggesting some skills to make an organization more customer focused.

In response to the context of the organization the trade marketing department adjusts its objectives and responsibilities. When evolving to the fourth phase, shopper marketing, the organization becomes both more strategic, and externally oriented, as shown in Figure 15.4.

FIGURE 15.4   Growth path – trade marketing organization

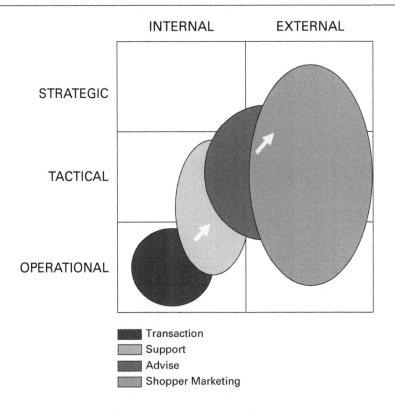

INTERNAL   EXTERNAL

STRATEGIC

TACTICAL

OPERATIONAL

- Transaction
- Support
- Advise
- Shopper Marketing

Overcoming the barriers at each phase

Transitioning from one phase to another requires extra effort. Each transition has its own specific points that require additional attention. For example, the lack of talented trade marketers with both strategic marketing and consumer insight skills is often considered to be a bottleneck to progressing to shopper marketing. In the first phases, the trade marketing manager will often struggle to obtain budget from management for the new function. The trade marketing manager plays a crucial role in overcoming the barriers at each phase. Some of the skills required from trade marketing managers relate to change management, and so are no different to what would be required from other positions that involve professional organizational management. And when moving from the first transactional phase, focused purely on supplier interests, to a shopper marketing phase with a balanced view on stakeholder interests, the function of trade marketing becomes more strategic and externally oriented. What makes this evolution more specific is that the trade marketing manager should understand and interact well with those at all levels and functions in the organization. To achieve this, the trade marketing organization needs to possess deep insights into the needs of the customer.

An understanding of the customer as a condition for professionalizing trade marketing

For the organization to make the transition to the next phase, a base level of understanding of three aspects is required. These can act as a springboard for acquiring customer insights:

1 Understand the category manager's daily life.

2 Know the category manager's KPIs.

3 Understand how other retail functions influence category management.

Daily life of the category manager

Knowing the operational pressures and ever-present deadlines helps you to empathize more with a category manager. Figure 15.5 shows what a typical day for a category manager looks like. The day starts with checking the numbers and making sure that sufficient stock is available. The promotional calendar is still missing two promotional events and needs to be sent to the action marketing team by the end of the day. Calls from store managers come through from the store service desk as information on price changes of crucial products is missing. Short-term issues frequently absorb most of the category manager's day.

FIGURE 15.5   Daily life of a category manager

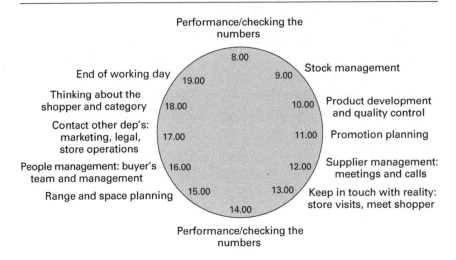

The real revelation is that category managers spend less than 5 per cent of their time on gaining a better understanding of the shopper's needs and ensuring that the category matches their future needs. These are the exact areas the trade marketing managers on the supplier side want to focus their visit on. Of course, not each day is the same, and category managers take different roles depending on the type of category, state of the economy, organizational goals and personality (Figure 15.6).

Category manager's KPIs

Knowing the category manager's KPIs can help trade marketers to develop a better understanding of the category manager's needs. These needs relate to the category, such as percentage trade margins or out-of-stock levels, and also personal needs such as career ambitions or goals to achieve annual incentives and corporate requirements. As an example of the latter, when Walmart in the United States had put strategic sustainability objectives in place, it required each supplier to hold meetings with the category manager to offer an update on what the supplier had contributed to Walmart's environment and sustainability efforts. Understanding the category manager's KPIs is fundamental to establishing common ground between the retailer and supplier, and in turn gives the supplier the capability to provide solutions.

Knowing and understanding customer KPIs does not mean that they are the same for both parties. An example of a mismatch that I experienced was

FIGURE 15.6   Factors influencing the activities of the category manager

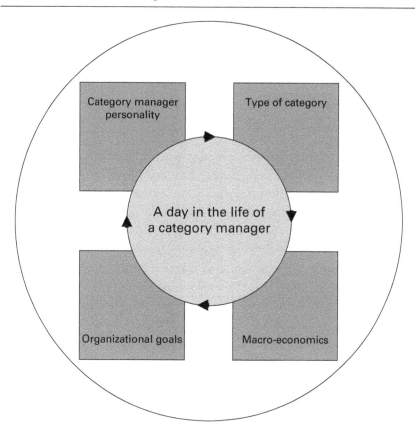

when the category manager at Albert Heijn aimed to increase the percentage category margin while PepsiCo's goal was much more focused on driving volume. PepsiCo did not even realize the discrepancy of KPIs until the shelf was flooded with private labels and competitive niche brands. This opened their eyes and PepsiCo quickly put product innovations in place to increase category margin and initiatives to regain the trust of the customer. It had to reset its objectives. As a matter of fact, Albert Heijn changed its strategy as well, as many of the private labels failed to rotate well. KPI discrepancies may also occur when retailers and suppliers measure them differently. Tobacco companies, for example, often think that their category is very profitable. However, most retailers include overhead costs from the check-out or service staff into the calculation. Tobacco suppliers often ignore this. As a result of the retailer's way of measuring, the tobacco category is a far less profitable and attractive category than suppliers think it is.

Understand retail roles

I once found out the hard way that functions other than category management can influence decisions regarding a category. When I started at PepsiCo I was asked to make a newly developed display for their Dutch business one of my top priorities. PepsiCo had the great idea to facilitate the purchases across related categories, and hoped to improve basket spend through a permanent display that could hold multiple categories such as potato chips, soft drinks, nuts and wine. PepsiCo knew from the category manager that the initiative would meet his needs of incremental sales and margin. The trade marketing team conducted pilots in several stores but, unfortunately, the test was never rolled out nationally and died silently after a year or so. After all the effort and enthusiasm my team had put into the display, I was determined to find out why we had failed. Only a year after the project closure I found out that one person in the retailer's merchandising department had objected to the look and feel of the display. In a regular marketing meeting that evaluated and approved all store merchandising, the display project was killed in five minutes. Had I known of this role and this meeting, I could have matched the display to the customer's requirements in relation to material, size and brand equity. It makes sense for trade marketing not just to visit the category manager but also to call on those who fulfil roles with other functions in the retailer, such as store operations, promotion planning and space management. In advanced markets such as the UK, trade marketers are in contact with some 30 people inside the retail organization. This is in sharp contrast with the supplier–retailer engagement model, where only the category manager and customer manager interact. Category managers work according to guidelines set by other departments, such as store operations and format marketing. By meeting these functions the supplier obtains a holistic understanding of the retail process, knows where to adapt early on, and may discover areas where it can offer help. Learning about their needs first-hand stimulates collaboration. In some organizations this principle has evolved to such a level that the customer manager only visits the category manager, and trade marketing only calls on the other functions in the retailer.

Five things a category manager wants in a category management proposal

An improved understanding and skill set are required to make the content of a category proposal work. Of course, the proposal needs to be attractive in itself as well. A category manager would like category management proposals to fulfil these criteria:

1 best terms;

2 exclusivity;

3 insights to gain first-mover competitive advantage;

4 solutions that are wholly aligned to his/her needs;

5 forewarning of significant changes (market, competitors, consumers, category, channel etc).

Before presenting their plan to the customer, trade marketers can check to see how customer focused its category management proposal is by comparing it against these five criteria. If one or more is missing, the trade marketer will be able to predict the types of questions that the category manager is likely to ask during the conversation and prepare accordingly.

There always seem to be good reasons for organizations to delay starting work on better customer understanding. The category manager is only interested in today's promotion proposal, or in their incentive based on supplier volume. Some trade marketing managers mention their category itself as a reason for keeping things the same. Agreed, a category such as toilet paper, for example, offers less excitement than soft drinks. Still, there are possible methods to include fun in the shopper's journey or make the category more customer-centric, perhaps through the use of seasonal activities or tailored promotion campaigns. The category may seem boring, but when trade marketers visit a different store every week they may gain inspiration from new places. Get started today! The box overleaf shows some ideas to get you started.

Getting started with customer focus

1 Visit a different store each week. Share what you have learned with the category manager on a quarterly basis.

2 Be clear on priorities – personal, category and corporate.

3 Identify low-hanging fruit.

4 Identify the true category wins that are open to the retailer.

5 Offer real, relevant insights into the shopper and the category.

6 Identify competitive actions that are likely to impact the customer.

7 Identify relevant category best practices (competitors, other markets, other channels).

8 Identify potentially relevant non-category best practices.

9 Identify bigger-picture perspectives: consumer and shopper trends, macro-economic factors.

10 Hold meetings without rigid agendas.

If these suggestions are followed, I hope that category managers will no longer be approached with irrelevant data that does not offer real insight. Category managers only have limited time available for category strategy as they have many daily pressures. A supplier should know the short- and long-term goals of both the category manager and those who fulfil other functions in the retailer. Trade marketing teams face the challenge of communicating their story in a concise way, and adjusting it to the preferences of the category manager. Understanding the customer forms the basis for collaboration, which is essential for implementing trade marketing plans.

What can you do to make your shoppers happy?

Train suppliers on the retail operating model and share what the retail brand is about. This allows trade marketing teams at the supplier to obtain a better understanding of what shoppers expect to find in the store.

Which marketing strategies can retailers apply?

Building a relationship directly with trade marketing managers at key suppliers allows deeper insights into both the category and the shopper. These insights are the basis for innovation.

In a supplier management system, retailers can know which phase of the trade marketing evolution model each supplier is in. As a result, the needs of the categories can be aligned with the capabilities of the category manager and the score of the supplier trade marketing team.

Note

1 Al Forbes, owner of Solvinus retail consultancy (www.solvinus.com), personal communication

16

Shopper marketing
New phase of trade marketing

Category management is primarily perceived as the way that a retailer professionalizes their organization. Ever since its introduction, the concept has influenced the interaction between suppliers and their selling models; trade marketing is the suppliers' response to the increasing power of retailers. In Chapter 15 the terms 'trade marketing' and 'shopper marketing' were introduced. In Figure 15.3 I described shopper marketing as an evolutionary phase within the trade marketing discipline. Rather than creating new hype and suggesting that shopper marketing is brand new, I recommend thinking of shopper marketing as the advanced phase of the trade marketing discipline. In this chapter I explore shopper marketing in more depth. In this phase the organization resolutely decides to focus on satisfying the needs of the shopper, which constitutes a more meaningful step than merely creating larger, healthier categories. It is an even bigger step away from just representing supplier interest. By spending more time on definitions and discussing best practices, I hope that shopper marketing can come to represent a strategic approach that drives innovations based on careful shopping analysis to make shoppers really enjoy the experience, and also improve the financial health of the retail organizations.

Definition of shopper marketing

Sometimes the term shopper marketing is used for simple, customer-specific promotions or events. I would argue that this is not much different from what happened in the retail marketing area in the mid 1990s. So before launching a new term, I want to make sure it is helpful in conversations between retailers and suppliers, and that it allows the partners to take the next step. Trade marketing is a young profession. Trade marketers may find – just like I do – that at birthday parties it takes some time to explain to other guests what your job is and why it is necessary. Even large suppliers struggle to define and understand the role. As a result, all too often trade marketing is shifted into the sales or marketing departments where it performs important – but purely tactical – tasks. In order to have a sustainable impact on the organization, earn a place in the management team and, in my view, to survive as a role, trade marketing should help to create shopper insights based on innovations that create incremental value for the category. These innovations could be product-based but could also be built in pricing, merchandising or any other retail marketing areas. The Grocery Manufacturers Association (GMA) and Deloitte proposed a very useful definition of shopper marketing in 2007:[1]

> All marketing stimuli, developed based on a deep understanding of shopper behaviour, designed to build brand equity, engage the shopper (ie, consumer in 'shopping mode'), and lead him/her to make a purchase.

This definition reaches to the core of what it is all about. This definition clearly emphasizes the strategic component of shopper marketing and the importance of gaining insights into the shopper rather than only into consumer behaviour. By using the words 'marketing stimuli' GMA/Deloitte include all marketing instruments, ie not just a display but also packaging and pricing. For a shopper it makes no difference if the signal is sent by the marketing department of a supplier or by the sales team. Through this holistic approach, organizations can reach shoppers better and more con-sistently. Still, for me the end goal is not so much a single transaction but incremental growth of the category through innovation. I also would like to emphasize that the brand equity of the retailer and supplier benefit from shopper marketing. When incorporating these elements I think a sharper definition for shopper marketing is:

> Marketing activities that use insights into shopper segments in order to create tailor-made innovations, whereby brand equities of the retailer's banner and manufacturer's brand strengthen each other.

The most important objective of shopper marketing is creating incremental value for organizations through innovations. Indeed, the consumer marketing team on the supplier side also works on innovation, but as they focus on insights that arise from consumption moments, the shopper marketing team can add insights from the shopping process. Shopper marketing works with insights about anyone who is in a shopping mode. This mode is switched on in-store but also when travelling to the store and searching online. The above definition of shopper marketing emphasizes a strong focus on results because only certain target shopping groups take the brand activities of both retailer and supplier personally. Within each target group there is the possibility of further differentiation by shopping trip.

Best-in-class shopper marketing

When applying this definition it is hard to find examples of campaigns that truly meet all requirements. My personal favourite is the 'Seasons' shopper marketing campaign by ConAgra Foods, a US company that produces packaged foods. Through qualitative interviews and focus groups with mothers, ConAgra Foods identified the five characteristic mood periods that occur during each year. Specific times of the year, or seasons, were driven by a set of emotions that influence purchasing behaviour. For example, November and December focus on the festive holiday period, which is fun and family-oriented, and a time when tradition is important. I imagine families prefer suppliers that offer recipes which have worked since the time of their grandmothers, rather than 20 recipes that allow experimentation with the turkey. ConAgra Foods worked out the 'Seasons' theme differently for each retailer so that they can strengthen the particular brand elements that they want to bolster.

Another great example comes from PepsiCo in the United States. Sam's Club, Walmart's outlet designed for wholesalers, looked for supplier initiatives to achieve its strategic objectives of sustainability and being a centre of the community. PepsiCo made sustainability a high priority in its 'Performance with Purpose' policy. In a collaborative setting, Walmart and PepsiCo developed a shopper marketing campaign where shoppers could return empty bottles to Sam's Club. These were then processed into fleece jackets. The schools that collected the most bottles were rewarded with $1,000 and fleece jackets for their community. The fit to the strategic objectives of both the retailer and supplier is clear. But what about the shopper insight? Young people do not usually purchase their soft drinks at Sam's club – it is not a primary channel for them. Recycling the bottles at Sam's Club therefore generated additional traffic from this relatively new shopper group.

Two main drivers of shopper marketing

The rise of shopper marketing does not mean that everything learnt and built in trade marketing can go by the board. And not every in-store activity should be called shopper marketing. It could be, but it does not have to be that way. Shopper marketing is not a completely new profession but a new phase within trade marketing. By implementing shopper marketing, organizations allow trade marketing to become more strategic and externally focused. In the evolution model of trade marketing presented in Chapter 15, each supplier can select a suitable phase and operate accordingly with their own objectives. Suppliers may also choose a different trade marketing phase by retailer. For instance, the supplier could use shopper marketing for a select number of supermarkets with high selling potential, and other retail customers receive advice as defined in the third phase. Shopper marketing is a strategic trade marketing response to the growing importance of the shopper as well as the growing power of retailers. Let me explain both factors in more detail.

Growing importance of the shopper

Don't forget that 'shopper thinking' is relatively new. Only in 2004 did Procter & Gamble (P&G) CEO Alan George Lafley introduce the term 'First Moment of Truth' (or FMOT for short). P&G recognized that a lot of its advertising failed. The media had undergone drastic changes in regards to their forms and reach, and the number of retail channels had exploded. According to Malcolm Gladwell in his book *The Tipping Point*, people are confronted with some 254 commercial messages per day.[2] All of this makes it more difficult to reach people and promotes a lack of loyalty to retail and supplier brands. People often get acquainted with supplier products for the first time at the supermarket shelf. Retailers have come to understand that factors influencing the consumption of a product could be different from the ones that make shoppers buy the product. In addition, there could be a difference between who it is that consumes the product and the people who purchase it – consumers and shoppers. This is not just true for obvious products such as baby food and pet food but also, for example, for male fragrances that are often bought by women. As a result of this insight, P&G started investing in order to learn more about how people make a decision in front of a shelf. This effort resulted in decision trees and more attention on planograms and in-store promotions. Since the 'discovery' of the shopper, retailers found that people could be in shopping mood outside the store as well. The journey to the store has an impact on the final decision in the store. Think of the way that the shopping list is written, and the way in which one retail channel is chosen over another to suit different shopping trips. In 2011 Google's Kim Lecinski introduced the 'Zero Moment of Truth' (ZMOT). Further, Google believes that shoppers discover the product first online before seeing it in reality. This could occur through direct internet sales or product reviews. Whether or not it is true that online research precedes other shopping phases, it does point to new technologies that change the way people shop. Finally, some organizations have started to integrate all marketing and sales instruments in order to influence the shopper's decision. Finding the best return on brand investment for in-store, online and traditional above-the-line communication is the big challenge for the coming years. In Figure 16.1 the four phases of the evolution of the shopper thinking are illustrated.

FIGURE 16.1   The four steps in the thinking on shopper marketing

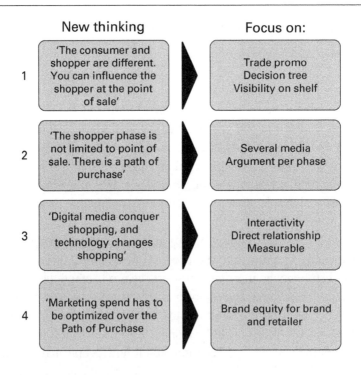

Growing power of retailers

Shopper marketing is also a response to the growing power of retailers. In Western Europe the top three retailers typically dominate some 70–80 per cent of the market. Though the modern retail segment in emerging countries such as Russia is still small, the large players try to grow aggressively by expanding the store network and acquisitions. It is not just size. Starting in the UK, retailers hired experienced marketing professionals from suppliers. Their thinking, tools and processes have increased the levels of marketing professionalism. Private labels are a good example of this, and shoppers can now enjoy better quality, multilayered brand architecture and attractive packaging. Through a refined format strategy, retailers unlock the needs of shoppers at different locations and moments of the day. A factor fuelling the power of retailers is that they have started to go beyond collecting vast amounts of data, and are now obtaining insights from these data. The scanning and loyalty card data is often more accurate and efficient than other data sources. From a power-play position, the retailers can choose whether or not to share with suppliers. Suppliers that do not want to hand over too much power need to listen more carefully to the customer and invest selectively in their retailers, then apply shopper marketing as a tool to find mutual benefits and return. With each phase of the trade marketing evolution the supplier becomes more customer-oriented until it gives trade marketing a strategic role in the final phase.

A new role for consumer marketing

A shopper marketer in the final phase will take over the activities that the consumer marketer used to perform. Take packaging – packaging used to be the sole responsibility of consumer marketing. Now there are organizations where the shopper marketer is responsible for making the packaging so attractive and appealing that it will stand out from the shelf while still communicating all the brand information. Both the emergence of new media and the importance of the purchase drivers shift the responsibility of consumer marketing more towards:

- definition of brand identity and personality;
- national online and television campaigns;
- market research into image and competition;
- market scoping and profit expectations;

- setting brand guidelines and objectives;
- innovation.

In contrast with the consumption moment focused on by consumer marketers, shopper marketers deal with many moments of truth. The latter are more concerned about the future and health of the total category rather than just those of the supplier brand. The relationship with retailers is key in order to reach the shopper. Typical activities are:

- activation programmes that meet the needs of brands of both the supplier and the retailer;
- search for shopper insights;
- analyse the category and build category vision;
- select optimal channels and develop retailer partnerships;
- use all instruments from the typical retailer marketing mix: for example, price, staff, store layout, packaging.

There is a lot of confusion about what shopper marketing really is. If the team designs and implements displays, it could be a very effective instrument and well chosen for the trade marketing phase you operate in. But I would not call it shopper marketing if there is no category-specific shopper insight, if it is not part of a larger, strategic campaign, or if the type of programme could easily be targeted at any other retailer.

A great example of the role of shopper marketing comes from P&G. In their continuous quest for a better understanding of the shopper, P&G hung cameras above the hair-colouring shelf. They noticed that some shoppers bought one bottle and others two bottles. In consumer panel tables this would come up as something like 'average category purchase is 1.4' and little further thought would be given to it. However, the cameras on the shopping floor enabled P&G to understand the real shopping driver – women with long hair bought more bottles than women with short hair, which makes perfect sense, of course. A deeper dive showed that the long-haired women threw away half of the contents of one of the bottles. As a result, the shopper marketing team developed a bottle that was 1.5 times as big. This instance shows how shopper marketing can develop innovations based on shopper insights. In addition, it demonstrates why it makes sense for shopper marketers to take over at least some of the packaging responsibility, such as optimizing the size of the packaging. In other areas that are crucial for the brand image, like packaging design, the brand management and shopper marketing teams could assume shared responsibilities.

The instruments that shopper marketing depends on are the same that the marketing team on the retail side applies. This is not to say that suppliers take over the retailer role or have the same kind of control when it comes to, for example, consumer pricing and promotions. Some shopper marketing teams have started to advise retailers on store layout. Unilever leads a successful programme called 'Partners for Growth' that helps convenience stores in the UK to optimize their merchandising. This programme is rooted in the trial in 2005 when Unilever rebuilt the 'co-operative food store' in Stoke-on-Trent in a virtual manner. Shoppers were asked about their current shopping trips and to shop in a new, virtually designed store. This led to a whole range of recommendations such as wider aisles, better visibility of fresh products through the windows from outside, and a different category layout. The results were an increase of 9 per cent in sales for the Stoke-on-Trent store and 8 per cent for other redeveloped stores. P&G has similar techniques whereby it rebuilds stores in a virtual way in order to give retailers advice on the total store layout, and not just the location of the categories they operate in. PepsiCo has the same objective but uses a different approach. Based on the retailer scanning data, and with the help of proprietary software, PepsiCo helped to make the store layout more shopper-driven. By doing so they found that the total store revenue increased by some 8 per cent when compared to control stores, even in saturated food markets. When I used the software for clients such as Carrefour I found that the store layout method is a great way to better understand the strategic goals of retailers. It is also a great accelerator for working in other areas, such as the design of new retail concepts.

Obstacles for shopper marketing

The strategic approach of shopper marketing will not take place overnight. A supplier needs to decide whether shopper marketing is indeed the right approach for the development phase they are in. It will be an evolving process of adjustment. Shopper marketing is a drastic change for the organization if taken seriously and not merely paid lip service. Apart from the usual suspects – CEO support and sufficient, controllable budget – I see three specific obstacles that organizations need to overcome to allow shopper marketing to fully bloom:

- *Lack of communication between the marketing departments of the retailer and supplier*
  The marketing departments of both sides are responsible for the brand equities of their brands. Because shopper marketing tries to

fortify both, the brand owners need to decide which dimension of the brand they will work on, and how. For a number of reasons, communication between the two brand marketing teams often fails to happen. Marketing on the supplier side sees its role as being on a national level rather than a channel or even customer level. The complexity of their analysis and plans grows exponentially if supplier marketing teams start analysing data per customer, or even per store. Marketing teams on the supplier side are hesitant to support one retailer over another, as ideally they have 100 per cent distribution across all channels and at all retailers. Retailer marketing teams are hesitant to let in self-confident suppliers that seem to have more time for conceptual ideas than pragmatic store solutions. They are quick to let the supplier know that working together too closely with a competitor will close the door.

- *Effects of in-store activation are unknown*
  Shopper marketing is the new kid on the block. The way it often works in large companies is that a department first needs to prove the return on investment before it receives budget. It is up to the shopper marketer to experiment with various shopper marketing campaigns and to demonstrate which types of media, execution and instruments work better. Next, the shopper marketer needs to collaborate with consumer marketers to determine the ideal mix of above-the-line campaigns, online campaigns and in-store activation. Accountability is required – it is tough, but essential.

- *Lack of organizational talent and structure*
  Advertising to fill the role of shopper marketer is like looking for a sheep with five legs. They should be creative with campaign development, capable of dealing with large amounts of data, able to quickly turn data into pragmatic solutions, develop superior customer relationships and build strategic marketing concepts. Excelling in just a few of these areas is already fantastic. It will take time to find the right talent and to support them into fully flourishing in the organization. Hiring consumer marketers who are familiar with long-term brand thinking can offer inspiration and stimulation for both retailer marketing departments and shopper marketing teams. My suggestion is for organizations to assemble a team that has a balance of the required skills, and to seek partnership from agencies where necessary.

Getting started

Shopper marketing is a difficult job, but worth trying. When done successfully, it will let suppliers understand shopper motivations much more effectively, and develop more intimate customer relationships than before. The first step is not that difficult, and only needs the supplier to listen to the retailer's comments about their brands and marketing programmes. Next, shopper marketing checks which of its brand propositions fits best. If there is a match, then the retailer and supplier can build ideas for the short and long term. The benefits of shopper marketing correspond largely with the other phases of trade marketing. However, because they are based on shopper insights and secured in a strategic framework, the effect on the category is larger and more long-lasting. The retail brand gains an instrument that delivers more differentiation from the competition. Because the retail brand taps into the needs of the shopper, the latter becomes more loyal and the retail revenue grows. The supplier gains more alternatives to influence the shopper, more access to data, and a greater knowledge of the retailer. It can apply its new expertise to drive sales for its brands, promote innovation in the category, and achieve many tactical goals, such as decreasing the dependency of promotions.

What can you do to make your shoppers happy?

Retailers should fine-tune their shopper marketing message for each shopper (segment), make sure it arrives in the right shopper phase, and tailor it to the channel (shopping context).

The growing attention on shopper marketing leads to more research and more experimental marketing programmes that seek to serve shoppers better.

Which marketing strategies can retailers apply?

Too often retailers only look at competitors in order to obtain new ideas ('best practices'). Retailers may find more valuable insights into new products, services and operating processes by looking at the shopping behaviour of their own customers.

To make shopper marketing proposals from suppliers work for all partners, retailers should define their retail brand, specify their core target group and identify the shopping missions they want to work on. If the retailer fails to understand how the shopper marketing programme contributes to their brand, the programme will be a nice sales boost at best.

Brand thinking is more ingrained in supplier organizations, and retailers may benefit from hiring marketing talent from the FMCG industry to foster a culture of consumer focus and innovation.

Notes

1 GMA Deloitte (2007) [accessed 22 July 2015] Shopper Marketing: Capturing a Shopper's Mind, Heart and Wallet, *GMA Online* [Online] http://www.gmaonline.org/downloads/research-and-reports/shoppermarketing.pdf

2 Gladwell, M (2012) *The Tipping Point: How little things can make a big difference*, Abacus, London

PART SEVEN
Embracing
the shopper

Retailers in action to increase shopper happiness

17

All humans seek happiness. We maximize our positive experiences and seek to avoid pain and discomfort. Retail is one of many places in this modern world where shoppers seek happiness. Making them happy can be a source of great satisfaction as well as revenue.

Retail practice is evolving from being a purely managerial and logistical task to being the business of serving people. The initial approaches led to a separatist view of the different categories in-store, an efficiency-driven need to manage large product assortments, and retail marketing aimed at revenue growth. Operating with this focus leads to poor shopper experiences. Shoppers experience retail, whether in-store or online, as one journey, not as individual categories. There is an opportunity to create happy shoppers through experiences that are inspiring, well-orchestrated and service-driven. This may lead to better, smarter and more relevant retail experiences to ensure that shoppers stay happy.

Achieving shopper happiness is, therefore, the ultimate goal of great retailing. However, because retail operations are so complex, this element does not receive enough attention. In mass-market retail especially, there is a great emphasis on the different aspects of the operation and little overview of the whole. It takes a lot of energy and time to run retail operations well. But without the focus on the shopper, that energy may dissipate all too quickly and seep away if there is no understanding of what makes shoppers tick. To streamline those efforts, it is time to put the shopper at the centre – to align everything retailers do towards making shoppers happy, from rational modelling to delivering shopper happiness. Shoppers are human beings, after all. No matter what big data, loyalty cards, market studies and digital footprints tell us in quantitative terms, at the basis of our behaviour we are sentient, irrational human beings. Trade marketing, category management and retail marketing practices have tried to uncover models to help understand and project shopper behaviour. These have contributed hugely to the professionalization of retail practices.

With no disrespect for what has been achieved so far, it is now time for retail marketers to take a step forward. In this book I covered the different aspects of retail marketing, from its initial phases of modelling into the newer approaches that will be instrumental to delivering better shopper experiences. The objective is to make the shopper feel happy in the store. The mindset that works towards shopper happiness and attempts to unravel the deeper emotional needs of the shopper will lead to more human, sustainable and fairer retail practice.

INDEX

Note: the Index is filed in alphabetical, word-by-word order. Headings in *italics* denote a document or publication title; numbers within main headings are filed as spelt out; acronyms are filed as presented. Page locators in *italics* denote information contained within a Figure or Table; locators as roman numerals denote material contained within the preliminary pages.